CROSSBILL GUIDES

Tenerife and La Gomera

Canary Islands – Spain

Crossbill Guides: Tenerife and La Gomera, Spain
First print: 2015
Second, revised reprint: 2024

Initiative, text and research: Dirk Hilbers, Kees Woutersen, Constant Swinkels, Peter Laan
Additional research, text and information: John Cantelo, Kim Lotterman, Albert Vliegenthart, Gino Smeulders
Editing: John Cantelo, Brian Clews, Cees Hilbers, Riet Hilbers, Kim Lotterman
Illustrations: Horst Wolter
Maps: Dirk Hilbers, Alex Tabak
Type and image setting: Oscar Lourens
Print: ORO grafic projectmanagement / PNB Letland

ISBN 978-94-91648-32-8

This book is made with FSC-certified paper. The printing process is CO_2-neutral through carbon-offsetting. To compensate for the CO_2-emissions of the printing processes, we've invested in a reafforestation project plus nature conservation in Europe. For more information, scan the qr-code. You can find the certificate of the carbon-offset on our website under 'downloads' on the Tenerife and La Gomera guidebook page.

Print product
climate contribution
ClimatePartner.com/20752-2402-1001

Published by Crossbill Guides in association with KNNV Publishing.

KNNV Publishing   SAXIFRAGA foundation

www.crossbillguides.org
www.knnvpublishing.nl
www.saxifraga.nl

CROSSBILL
GUIDES
FOUNDATION

This guidebook is a product of the non-profit foundation Crossbill Guides. By publishing these books we want to introduce more people to the joys of Europe's beautiful natural heritage and to increase the understanding of the ecological values that underlie conservation efforts. Most of this heritage is protected for ecological reasons and we want to provide insight into these reasons to the public at large. By doing so we hope that more people support the ideas behind nature conservation.

For more information about us and our guides you can visit our website at:

WWW.CROSSBILLGUIDES.ORG

4

Highlights of Tenerife and La Gomera

1 Marvel at the amazing flora of Tenerife and La Gomera and learn why the Canary Islands are named the Galapagos of Botany.

Canary Bellflower

El Teide seen from the Roques de García

2 Explore the surreal volcanic world of the Teide volcano.

3 Pull on your boots and walk the narrow paths through the mystical laurel cloud forests of Anaga or the Garajonay, ancient relicts of the tertiary era.

Walking in the Anaga mountains

4 Track down endemic birds like the Bolle's Pigeon, Blue Chaffinch or Berthelot's Pipit.

Bolle's Pigeon

5 Go stargazing on mount Teide and see the universe from one of the clearest skies on the planet.

Stargazing 5

6 Take the ferry to La Gomera and enjoy the seabirds, dolphins and pilot whales.

Bottlenose Dolphin

7 Walk down the spectacular ravines of Ruiz, Masca, or Valle Gran Rey with their extreme diversity of flora and fauna.

Garganta de los Infiernos

8 Put on your goggles and be amazed at the colourful sea life just beneath the water surface.

Subtropical sealife

About this guide

 boat trip or ferry crossing

 car route

 bicycle route

 walking route

 beautiful scenery

 interesting history

interesting geology

This guide is meant for all those who enjoy being in and learning about nature, whether you already know all about it or not. It is set up a little differently from most guides. We focus on explaining the natural and ecological features of an area rather than merely describing the site. We choose this approach because the nature of an area is more interesting, enjoyable and valuable when seen in the context of its complex relationships. The interplay of different species with each other and with their environment is astonishing. The clever tricks and gimmicks that are put to use to beat life's challenges are as fascinating as they are countless.

Take our namesake the Crossbill: at first glance it is just a big finch with an awkward bill. But there is more to the Crossbill than meets the eye. This bill is beautifully adapted for life in coniferous forests. It is used like scissors to cut open pinecones and eat the seeds that are unobtainable for other birds. In the Scandinavian countries where Pine and Spruce take up the greater part of the forests, several Crossbill species have each managed to answer two of life's most pressing questions: how to get food and avoid direct competition. By evolving crossed bills, each differing subtly, they have secured a monopoly of the seeds produced by cones of varying sizes. So complex is this relationship that scientists are still debating exactly how many different species of Crossbill actually exist. Now this should heighten the appreciation of what at first glance was merely a plumb red bird with a beak that doesn't close properly. Once its interrelationships are seen, nature comes alive, wherever you are.

To some, impressed by the 'virtual' familiarity that television has granted to the wilderness of the Amazon, the vastness of the Serengeti or the sublimity of Yellowstone, European nature may seem a puny surrogate, good merely for the casual stroll. In short, the argument seems to be that if you haven't seen a Jaguar, Lion or Grizzly Bear, then you haven't seen the 'real thing'. Nonsense, of course.

But where to go? And how? What is there to see? That is where this guide comes in. We describe the how, the why, the when, the where and the how come of Europe's most beautiful areas. In clear and accessible language, we explain the nature of Tenerife and La Gomera and refer extensively to routes where the area's features can be observed best. We try to make Tenerife and La Gomera come alive. We hope that we succeed.

How to use this guide

This guidebook contains a descriptive and a practical section. The descriptive part comes first and gives you insight into the most striking and interesting natural features of the area. It provides an understanding of what you will see when you go out exploring. The descriptive part consists of a landscape section (marked with a red bar), describing the habitats, the history and the landscape in general, and a flora and fauna section (marked with a green bar), which discusses the plants and animals that occur in the region.

The second part offers the practical information (marked with a purple bar). A series of routes (walks and car drives) are carefully selected to give you a good flavour of all the habitats, flora and fauna that Tenerife and La Gomera have to offer. At the start of each route description, a number of icons give a quick overview of the characteristics of each route. These icons are explained in the margin of this page. The final part of the book (marked with blue squares) provides some basic tourist information and some tips on finding plants, birds and other animals.

There is no need to read the book from cover to cover. Instead, each small chapter stands on its own and refers to the routes most suitable for viewing the particular features described in it. Conversely, descriptions of each route refer to the chapters that explain more in depth the most typical features that can be seen along the way.

In the back of the guide we have included a list of all the mentioned plant and animal species, with their scientific names and translations into German and Dutch. Some species names have an asterix (*) following them. This indicates that there is no official English name for this species and that we have taken the liberty of coining one. We realise this will meet with some reservations by those who are familiar with scientific names. For the sake of readability however, we have decided to translate the scientific name, or, when this made no sense, we gave a name that best describes the species' appearance or distribution. Please note that we do not want to claim these as the official names. We merely want to make the text easier to follow for those not familiar with scientific names. An overview of the area described in this book is given on the map on page 13. For your convenience we have also turned the inner side of the back flap into a map of the area indicating all the described routes. Descriptions in the explanatory text refer to these routes.

 interesting flora

 interesting invertebrate life

 interesting reptile and amphibian life

 interesting wildlife

 interesting birdlife

 site for snorkelling

 interesting for whales and dolphins

 visualising the ecological contexts described in this guide

8

Table of contents

Landscape   11
Geographical overview   12
Geology   16
Climate   23
Evolution   24
Habitats   30
Coast and submarine zone   32
The succulent scrub   36
Thermophile forest and terraced cultivations   38
Laurel cloud forest   41
Canary pine forest   46
The Cañadas and el Teide   50
Barrancos   54
History   57
Nature conservation   65

Flora and fauna   69
Flora   72
Mammals   89
Birds   91
Reptiles   102
Insects and other invertebrates   105

Practical Part   111
Routes and sites on central Tenerife – El Teide   112
Route 1: The Cañadas del Teide National Park   113
Route 2: La Fortaleza   125
Route 3: The Teide Eggs   128
Route 4: The pine forests of Los Organos   131
Additional sites on Cañadas del Teide   134
Northwest Tenerife   137
Route 5: Teno Alto to Punta Teno   138
Route 6: Cumbre de Baracán   141
Route 7: From Los Silos to Erjos   144
Route 8: Monte del Agua laurel cloud forest   147
Additional sites and routes in north-west Tenerife   150
North-east Tenerife   155
Route 9: Anaga mountains – a first exploration   156

Route 10: Baranco de Afur   162
Route 11: Through the laurel forest to Chinamada   165
Additional sites and routes in north-east Tenerife   169
South Tenerife   174
Route 12: Punta la Rasca   175
Additional sites in south Tenerife   178
Routes on La Gomera   181
Route 13: La Gomera by car   183
Route 14: Laurel forests of Garajonay   189
Route 15: Woods and lunar landscape of Agulo   192
Route 16: The thermophile woodlands of Vallehermoso   196
Route 17: The plateau and the cliffs of Valle Gran Rey   199
Additional sites and routes on La Gomera   203

Tourist information & observation tips   211
Travel and accommodation   211
Safety issues   213
Planning your trip   215
Additional information   218
Observation tips   219
Birdlist Tenerife and La Gomera   223
Picture and illustration credits   228
Species list and translation   229

LANDSCAPE

Breaking out of the dreary winter weather for some sunshine. Sun, sea and sand with a cocktail in your hand. A cool beer on a terrace by a seaside boulevard. Holiday life. This is the usual image of Tenerife.

Now for something different. Imagine an 18th or 19th century schooner arriving on the shores of a pristine island. The rush of excitement as the explorer-naturalist first sets foot in the new world. It is full of life. There are wondrous plants and animals he never knew existed. Like a boy in a sweet shop, he starts collecting...

This is the weird dual character of the Canary Islands, to which Tenerife and La Gomera belong. On the one hand, they are a favoured destination for sunseekers, predominantly northern European pensionados. The islands breathe the air of semi-permanent retreat for the elderly, tethering on the edge of dullness. Yet on the other hand, much less known, these islands are a strange and wonderful world for naturalists. Scenically superb, rough and diverse, they are terra incognita, in which every nook and cranny is filled with species never seen before. This is as close as one can get to the excitement of the 18th and 19th century naturalist explorers like Darwin, von Humboldt and Wallace, who travelled new parts of the world and discovered countless new species. In fact, as recently as 1999, a new species of Giant Lizard was discovered on a remote cliff on La Gomera!

Where the pavement of the tourist resort ends, the strange vegetation of succulent bushes begins. Literally right at its edge, as you can see on route 12. As you are drawn further afield, you'll come across alien-looking bushes with thick, sausage-like trunks and small, stiff leaves growing out of the black lava. Grey, bone-like stems grow up from between the rocks like the skeleton of a hand. Going further inland, moving up through palm-clad gorges you soon find yourself rambling through thick, moss-draped cloud forests. And you haven't even seen the desert-like environment of the central crater yet, with its white pumice fields, laced by black lava streams.

Tenerife and La Gomera, indeed all the Canary Islands, are in a different league from the Mediterranean Islands. Whereas the latter show clear resemblances to the mainland, the Canary Islands form a world of their own. The flora and fauna only show similarities with a few other Atlantic islands, particularly Madeira.

Fog in Garajonay National Park (route 14).

The secret of these beautiful islands lies in the fact that they are volcanic. They rose up from the ocean floor and so were never attached to any mainland. Only few species arrived on them by chance, and from this material, a whole set of ecosystems established, fully equipped with a flora and fauna that is unique to those islands.

No less than 40% of the plant species of Tenerife are endemics, meaning that they are are only found in a specific place. Add to this the fact that the climate of Tenerife and La Gomera is indeed very agreeable, the landscape stunning, and the options to explore, both on foot and by car, are plentiful, and you'll understand why these islands are so attractive to visit. So put on boots and sunblock (you'll need them both), pack your bins and this book and start exploring. This book will help in finding the most remarkable species of birds, plants and insects of Tenerife and La Gomera. As you get acquainted with the natural side of these islands, you'll soon discover the true mystery of Tenerife: why do so many people stick to the beach?!

Geographical overview

Tenerife and La Gomera form the central islands of the Canaries, an archipelago of seven main islands and several islets that lie some 100 km off the African coast at the latitude of southern Morocco.

West of La Gomera lie the islands of La Palma and El Hierro, while east of Tenerife lies Gran Canaria and a bit further on, Lanzarote and Fuerteventura.

With 2,034 square kilometres Tenerife is the biggest of the Canary Islands and with just over 987,000 permanent inhabitants (2022 figures) the most densely populated. The capital of Tenerife is Santa Cruz and has 207,000 inhabitants. La Gomera, barely a fifth of Tenerife´s size, is after El Hierro the smallest of the Canary islands (not counting the small islets just off the coast of Lanzarote and Fuerteventura). La Gomera counts only 22,700 souls (2022), 9,000 of which live in the capital San Sebastian. Unlike Tenerife, the population of La Gomera has been in steady decline since the 1950s.

Tenerife is not only the largest island, it is also the highest. The huge Teide volcano dominates the landscape. At 3,718 m, it is much higher than any of the other islands, and even higher than any mountain on the Spanish mainland. As a result, Tenerife has the greatest variety in landscape, vegetation types and flora and fauna of any of the Canary Islands.

On Tenerife, you can find all the Canary island landscapes, except the deserts, which are largely restricted to Lanzarote and Fuerteventura. La Gomera is much smaller and less diverse, but its ecosystems are much less disturbed. The main attraction of this island, which lies very close to Tenerife and can easily be visited by ferry, is its tranquil atmosphere, relative lack of tourists, stunning, palm-clad barrancos and the swathe of the laurel cloud forest, which is much larger and more intact than on Tenerife.

Brief overview of Tenerife

Tenerife's centre is entirely dominated by the Teide. In the north-west and the north-east lie the craggy remains of two older volcanic massifs, the Teno mountains and the Anaga mountains. Both are extremely rocky and cracked.

All inhabitants of Tenerife live in the lower zone, in a ring around the Teide. Historically, the north side of the island with its benign climate, is the most densely populated. All major cities lie here: Santa Cruz, La Laguna, Puerto and Icod de los Vinos. They are as modern and busy as any European city. The bone-dry southern coast harboured little more than a few fishing villages, until tourism started to develop. Today, there are beach resorts dotted all along the southern coasts, although

Overview of Tenerife and La Gomera.

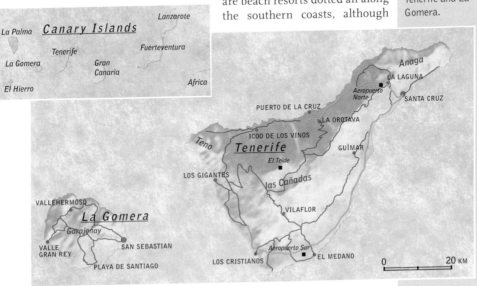

El Teide in the morning sun

only the area of Los Cristianos – Las Américas is truly built up. This is where the island's major beach resorts are.

Tenerife has two international airports. Tenerife Norte lies close to Santa Cruz, while Tenerife Sur is not far from Los Cristianos. The latter is where most international tourist flights arrive. The boat to La Gomera departs from Los Cristianos.

Los Cristianos is connected to Santa Cruz and the other northeastern towns by an excellent motorway. It takes you little over half an hour to drive to Santa Cruz from Los Cristianos. The motorway is being extended to make a complete circuit around the island, but until it is finished, it takes quite some time to drive the winding roads that currently connect the resorts in the southwest with the north coast.

Brief overview of La Gomera

La Gomera is much less developed than Tenerife and will show itself immediately as a laid-back, relaxed and genuine sort of place. The capital is San Sebastian, which is connected by ferry with Los Cristianos in Tenerife. You can also fly to La Gomera, but the small airport only connects with Tenerife Norte and lies an hour's drive from San Sebastian, making the ferry usually the faster and more attractive option.

Apart from San Sebastian, there are three great draws for tourists: the small resort of Playa de Santiago in the south, Valle Gran Rey in the south-west and the laurel cloud forests in Garajonay NP in the centre of the island. The coastal resorts are in no way comparable to those on Tenerife – not

Macaronesia and the Canary Islands – another world

Biologically the Canary Islands are not a part of Europe, but of Macaronesia – an obscure name for the well-known archipelagos of the Azores, Madeira, the Selvages, the Cape Verde and Canary Islands. All these are volcanic islands situated in the Atlantic, off the coasts of Europe and Africa. They are biologi-

cally different from the nearby continents because of their isolation. The Canary Islands and Madeira are at the heart of this Macaronesian Ecoregion. The Western Canary Islands of El Hierro, La Palma, La Gomera, Tenerife and Gran Canaria all share an extremely rugged terrain, with lushly vegetated northern slopes and dry southern slopes. Lanzarote and Fuerteventura lie much further east, closer to Africa. They are flatter and desert-like and their flora and fauna, influenced by the Sahara desert, is rather different from the 'western islands'.

The Canary islands

	Surface (km²)	Perimeter (km)	Max. Altitude (m)	Population (2010)
El Hierro	269	110	1,501	10,960
La Palma	708	166	2,423	86,324
La Gomera	370	100	1,487	22,776
Tenerife	2,034	342	3,718	906,854
Gran Canaria	1,560	256	1,949	845,676
Fuerteventura	1,660	304	807	103,492
Lanzarote	846	191	671	141,437

nearly as built up, relaxed and attractive. Valle Gran Rey, set in a superb, grand canyon-like gorge (see page 191), is also a little hippyish. In the north, Vallehermoso and Hermigua are the only villages of any size.

La Gomera is nearly circular in shape and only about 22 km in diameter. Its highest peak, the Alto de Garajonay, rises to only 1,487 m – peanuts in comparison to the Teide. But don't let this trick you into thinking La Gomera is less rugged or spectacular than Tenerife. Quite the contrary, the radial system of ravines make this island far more mountainous than most parts of Tenerife and this ruggedness makes travel very slow (even though its network of minor roads is in good condition). Driving to Valle Gran Rey from San Sebastian takes longer than driving between Los Cristianos and Santa Cruz – almost the entire length of Tenerife! The central area of La Gomera is an elevated volcanic platform between 800 and 1,300 metres above sea level. The highest crests are shaped in a U, providing the perfect catchment for moist air, which collects in the central valley of El Cedro – the heart of the laurel forest.

Geology

> Locations of specific geological features are given in the box on page 22.

Opposite page:
The geological birth of the oldest islands, Lanzarote and Fuerteventura, took place 20 million years ago from volcanic eruptions from a mantle plume – a thin spot in the earth's crust. As the tectonic movements caused the islands to move further east, new islands arose from subsequent eruptions from the mantle plume. The oldest parts of Tenerife emerged 11.5 million years ago. La Gomera is younger, but has lost the direct connection to the mantle plume. Currently, the island of El Hierro lies right above the hotspot.

Sheer crater walls, deep canyons, dazzling cliffs, barren lava fields and tall, isolated monoliths that rise high above the landscape: there is no shortage in geological drama on Tenerife and La Gomera. The landscape is more than rugged, with extremely steep slopes and few areas of level land. All of this begs the question how this land was formed. The Canary Islands are, geologically speaking, young islands, entirely born from volcanic eruptions. It is amazing to see the enormous diversity of land forms volcanic action can produce. In particular Tenerife, where the most recent eruption took place only a little over 100 years ago, has a fascinating array of volcanic land forms.

Birth of the Canary Islands

Twenty million years ago, submarine eruptions gave birth to the oldest of the Canary Islands – Fuerteventura. It rose above the ocean's surface roughly where the island of El Hierro is located today. Here lies a thin spot in the earth's crust where magma comes relatively close to the surface – a mantle plume in geological jargon. Minor tectonic unrest is sufficient to break the crust here and allow magma to flow out.

Because the Atlantic tectonic plate moves towards the African mainland and is subducted under the thicker continental land mass, the mantle crust has frequently (in geological terms) cracked open, especially on and near the mantle plume. Tectonic pressures force the sea floor to move from west to east like a piece of paper in an old-fashioned type writer. The mantle plume is stationary and periodically 'stamps out' a dot of lava on the sea floor, like the typewriter stamping letters on paper. In the course of millions of years, countless eruptions took place in this way. The water cooled the lava and contained it on the sea floor, producing submarine banks of various heights. Repeated sub-oceanic eruptions pushed the subterranean surface upwards until the lava broke the surface of the ocean and gave rise to an island. As time passed and the ocean sea floor slowly moved in a north-eastern direction, the hotspot embossed the ocean with a line of islands: the Canaries.

The oldest Canary Islands are those furthest east from the hotspot – Fuerteventura and Lanzarote. El Hierro is the youngest island and the westernmost, lying just north of the mantle plume. It is only 2 million years old. As central islands, Tenerife and La Gomera take a middle position in the age line of the Canaries. La Gomera is with an age of about 9.4 million years one of the younger islands, while the oldest parts of Tenerife are, at 11.9 million years, intermediate in age.

Although the islands follow a neat age succession from east (oldest) to west (youngest), this doesn't mean eruptions only take place on the youngest islands. Magma will always seek the easiest way to the surface. Old magma tunnels may be such an easy way out, even though the journey to the surface is not the shortest. This is why recent eruptions (within the last 500 years) not only took place on the very young islands like El Hierro, but also, via old lava tunnels, on Tenerife and even on very old islands like Lanzarote. The most recent eruption was in 2021 on La Palma.

In contrast, the magma vents that gave rise to La Gomera were cut off at a fairly early stage. Even though La Gomera is a young island, its volcanoes all became dormant over 2 million years ago. So paradoxically, an old island furthest from the mantle plume (Lanzarote and Fuerteventura) have seen recent

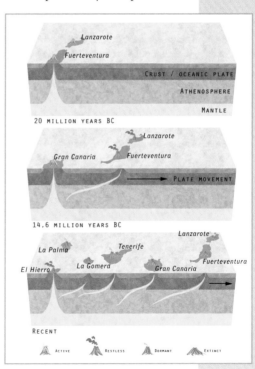

eruptions, whereas volcanic activity has ceased in a young one close to the mantle plume (La Gomera).

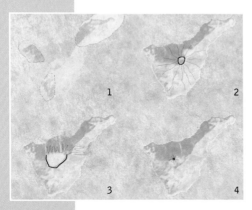

Geological history of Tenerife

Tenerife actually consists of three fairly old islands (5 – 11.5 million years) that merged together relatively recently as a result of massive eruptions in the middle of these three. Two of these old islands are easily recognised today: the old shield volcanoes of Anaga (5 million years old) and Teno (6 million years old) which are heavily eroded. They have steep cliffs and are dissected with enormous gorges. The third and oldest (11.5 million years) island lies in the south and was largely engulfed by the younger lava streams from the Cañadas del Teide crater. One of the few areas where the old island remains exposed is the table mountain of Roque del Conde near Arona.

The geological history of Tenerife in four steps. Bwtween 11.5 and 5 million years ago, three separate islands emerged (1). Then a giant central strato-volcano arose, known as the first Cañadas. It connected the separate islands (2). In a gigantic catastrophe, the first Cañadas collapsed creating an enormous crater wall and scarring of the slope. This volcano building and collapse happened three times (3). Finally, a new volcano arose, the Teide, which towers over the old Cañadas, for now (4).

Roughly 2-3 million years after the formation of the last shield volcano, new and violent eruptions took place that created the enormous strato-volcano of Las Cañadas. It rose to enormous heights – as high as today's Teide, perhaps even higher. But then, in what must have been a gigantic geological catastrophe, the summit of the Cañadas volcano collapsed. To the west, south and east, the line where the peak of the volcano broke off is still visible as the giant, 17 km long crater rim of the Cañadas (route 1). Landslides here are thought to be the result of new volcanic activity, as a new volcano rose in the scarred top of the old one. Subsequent eruptions made it grow until it collapsed too. A third volcano emerged, which peak later also collapsed down into the ocean.

These three massive landslides have scarred the landscape by creating the depressions of the Icod valley, the Orotava valley and the depression of Güímar. These places are inaccessible and form important refuges for flora and wildlife.

Where the Cañadas volcanoes broke off, a new one rose: mount Teide. The mountain is at 3,718 m., Spain's highest mountain, but that is as measured only from sea level. It is even more impressive if measured from the sea floor from which it rises to over 7,000 m – the third highest volcanic mountain on earth, after the Hawaiian volcanoes of Mauna Loa and Mauna Kea.

Geological history of La Gomera

Geologists recognise four distinct phases of volcanic activity: the formation of the shield volcano (this is happening at El Hierro), a several million year period of dormancy, the emergence of stratovolcanos, like the Cañadas and the Teide on Tenerife, and finally the erosion stage as can be seen on Lanzarote and Fuerteventura.

La Gomera is in the second phase – that of dormancy. In almost 2 million years, no new eruptions have taken place on the island. Over this long

The crater walls of the Cañadas are the remains of the old Cañadas volcano, which collapsed and crashed down into the ocean, leaving these walls behind.

Recent eruptions on Tenerife

Four recent eruptions have been described from Tenerife and their youthful volcanic structures can still be seen. The 1704 - 1705 eruption in the south-eastern part of Tenerife was a typical fissure eruption with emission centres, near Siete Fuentes, Fasnia and Montaña de Las Arenas. Thanks to the 1706 Garachico eruption in the North-west, Montaña Negra came to life during an outburst that lasted for nine days. Of all the historical eruptions in Tenerife, this is the only one that caused considerable material damage.

The Chahorra eruption is the only historical eruption that has occurred within the boundaries of what is now the Teide National Park. The activity did not come from the summit crater but from Pico Viejo. The last eruption in Tenerife was the Chinyero eruption in 1909, only 2 km east of Erjos (see route 8).

time, the soft lavas have been attacked by erosion. Water streams carved out deep barrancos, while the sea ate away the edges of the island, leaving tall cliffs on the coast. Of the original volcanoes only the hardest parts remain: the monoliths of the Roques de Agando, Cjila and Blanco.

Eruption landscapes

Volcanic eruptions can create a wide variety of land forms, depending on the type of magma that is ejected, the way it is ejected and how it cools down. Very fluid forms of lava create block lava or *Aa*-lava with a very rough and sharp surface. It is also very brittle and erodes easily, which means that only the fairly young block lava fields have this fascinating, rough appearance. The Spanish call them *Malpaíses* – bad lands, because they are hopelessly useless to farmers. There are two beautiful examples on the coast of Tenerife, as well as in the Cañadas crater (route 1).

Thicker, more viscous lava emerges as a slow flow that solidifies as a thick, wrinkly smear. It is called ropey lava or by its Hawaiian name *Pahoehoe*, which means that it can be crossed barefoot.

As block lava cools down, the rock contracts and cracks in a typical, angular shape, producing long pillars of basalt. The bedrock of both islands must consist of masses of these basalt pillars, but only at Los Organos on Tenerife (route 4) and Los Organos on the coast of La Gomera, has erosion revealed basalt cliffs. *Organos* is Spanish for organ

Lava flows in the Cañadas of central Tenerife, with ropey or pahoehoe lava (top), the light tuff and brown Aa or black lava (bottom).

pipes and with columns several hundred metres high, the 'pipes' of La Gomera's *Organos* are a particularly impressive sight (site A on page 203). During eruptions, a lot of magma does not reach the surface but slowly fills the cracks within the bedrock, where it forms veins of hard rock in the much softer surrounding matrix. Such veins are called dykes and only become visible when rocks are eroded. The surrounding rock weathers away and the dykes stand out like walls in the landscape. At Anaga, in particular, the bedrock is laced with dykes (see route 10).

Eruptions do not only produce liquid flows of lava. Sometimes they are so violent that pieces of lava are catapulted into the air and drop down as lava bombs. Cooled by spinning in the air, these lava bombs become rounded stones that are clearly different from the surrounding rock. A geological oddity are the lava bombs known as the *Huevos del Teide* – the Teide Eggs (route 3). These large boulders probably broke off the main lava flow, taking on the rounded boulder shape as they rolled along downslope.

Another product of violent eruptions is pumice. Like lava bombs they are usually roundish, but pumice gets transformed as it is ejected. Pumice is formed from highly pressurised magma that quickly decompresses as it is launched. Like the bubbles in cola, gasses that were dissolved under pressure, suddenly take on gaseous form and subsequently get trapped in the stone as it solidifies rapidly in the cool air. Due to all the bubbles, pumice is so light it floats on water. Violent eruptions also produce a lot of volcanic ash or tephra. When buried in thick layers, it is compressed to tuff stone – a highly erosive, soft rock which is easily sculpted by water and wind. Lava bombs, pumice and tuff can all be seen on Tenerife (see box on page 22).

Erosion landscapes

For many of today's monumental geological sculptures, volcanism merely provided the raw materials. The real artist is erosion. With its collection of crude tools – water, wind and gravity – erosion went to work and sculpted the drama into the massive chunks of lava. Lava is brittle and easily erodes. Over the years, streams have cut out steep barrancos down towards the coast. On La Gomera, the barrancos, which fan out from the centre of the island like spokes in a wheel, are particularly prominent. On Tenerife, the most impressive barrancos are found in the older shield volcanoes of Teno and Anaga.

The monolith of Roque de Agando on La Gomera is a lava plug – the hard solidified core of an eruption vent of a volcano that has eroded away.

In the heavily eroded mountains, it becomes clear that some rocks are harder than others. Lava that didn't surface during the eruption, but solidified under pressure, is much harder than the soft lavas, tuff and pumice ejected by volcanoes. This hard, pressurised lava remained in the eruption vents of old volcanoes (lava plugs) and in cracks in rock (dykes).

The lava plugs on La Gomera and Anaga are the only remains of the ancient volcano that now is completely eroded. The plugs are conspicuous monoliths *(roques)* in the landscape. Dykes are most visible in the cliffs of northern Anaga, where they add to the jagged appearance of the mountains. The erosive actions of the waves and tidal movement of the ocean have eaten away much of the original coastline, leaving steep cliffs all along the La Gomera coast and on the Anaga and Teno peninsulas.

A dyke in the Anaga mountains. This is hard, solidified lava that has filled the cracks and crevices of older formations.

Short geological guide

Malpaíses Areas covered in young block lava. Examples on route 1, 12 and site D on page 180.

Block or *Aa* lava Sharp, rough and brittle lava that originated from thin lava *(malpaíses)*.

Ropey or *Pahoehoe* lava Thick lava that cooled slowly, resulting in a wrinkly, smooth surface. Examples on route 1 and 3, and site D on page 180.

Obsidian or volcanic glass Dark, shiny, glass-like rock, resulting from the rapid cooling of lava. Examples on route 1 and 3.

Basalt Rock of solidified block lava. The cooling down of the lava results in contraction, causing the bedrock to crack in a typical pattern of hexagonal pillars. Examples on route 4, 10 and site A on page 203.

Dykes: Intrusions of hard lava in the bedrock. Examples on route 9 and 10.

Volcanic caves Channels in solidified lava, through which hot lava flowed. As the flow emptied, it left behind empty tunnels – the caves. Example on site E on page 152.

Pumice Very porous and light volcanic rock. Example on route 3.

Tuff Soft and smooth rock of compressed volcanic ash. Example on site D on page 136.

Monoliths or *roques* Hard lava plugs that solidified inside eruption vents of old volcanoes. The original volcano eroded away and the *roque* remained. Examples are on route 13 and site D on La Gomera and Roque de Tai and Roques de Anaga (routes 9 and 10) on Tenerife.

Cliff coasts Result of coastal erosion. Most spectacular are Los Gigantes on Tenerife and the cliffs of Valle Gran Rey and Los Organos on La Gomera (sites A and I).

Barrancos Ravines cut out by millions of years of water flow. Examples are route 7, site A on page 150, site E on page 180 and I and L on page 207-208.

Climate

Tenerife is known as the 'Island of Eternal Spring' because of the stable, benign year-round climate. The situation on La Gomera is similar.

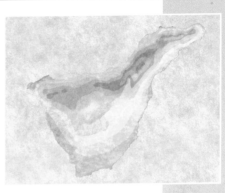

Tenerife enjoys a warm climate with an average maximum temperature at sea level of 22 °C in winter and 29 °C in summer. At night, the temperature never drops much, ranging from an average minimum of 15 °C in winter and 19 °C in summer. This even character is the result of the constant temperature of the ocean, which cools the atmosphere during summer and during the day, and keeps it warm in winter and during the night. The effect of the ocean is enormous – just consider that if you were to go straight east from Tenerife ro Africa, you eventually arrive in the deepest, driest and most forbidding part of the Sahara desert!

Paradoxically for such an even climate, the weather conditions are extremely variable between the different parts on the islands. The oh-so-familiar question of when the weather is going to be nice, is not a question at all on the Canary Islands. The question is not *when*, but *where* the weather is good. Fortunately, though, these variations in the weather are very predictable: sunny and warm in the south, cloudy at middle latitudes in the north, and sunny and cool on top.

Precipitation map
(mm/year)

< 100 mm

100 - 200 mm

200 - 300 mm

300 - 400 mm

400 - 500 mm

500 - 600 mm

600 - 700 mm

700 - 800 mm

700 - 1000 mm

View on La Gomera with the typical cloud cover over the northern part of the island.

This variety is due to the dominating north-easterly tradewinds which bring in humidity. As the mountains force the air upward, it cools and vapour condenses to form clouds. This happens at an altitude between 600 and 1,800 metres. As the clouds pass over the mountain ridge and drop down on the southern side, the air warms and they quickly evaporate – a phenomenon that is superbly witnessed at Garajonay (route 13 and 14) and Anaga (route 9). Obviously, the area with the thickest cloud layer receives the highest precipitation, but this does not mean that it always rains there. The fog is more important in sustaining the thick woodlands at this altitude. The fog droplets condense on the leaves, where they collect, merge and drop down to the ground. This phenomenon of 'horizontal rain' (*lluvia horizontal*) is a major driver of the cloud forest ecosystem (see page 43). The fog is thicker and more frequent in winter than in summer.

Evolution

In the introduction of this book, we've painted an image of Tenerife and La Gomera as exciting new worlds where visitors tread in the footsteps of the great naturalist explorers of previous centuries. A romantic image, but not that far from the truth. Tenerife and La Gomera, indeed the entire archipelago, form an entirely different world from mainland Europe or Africa. Over 40% of the plants and animals are endemic (exclusively occuring here). But that's not all. Things also became topsy-turvy and bizarre. Plants that are herbs back home, are bushes, or even trees, here. Some plant groups are completely absent, while others come in an unfamiliarly dazzling variety. The well-known birds of the continent all look that do occur on the Canaries, sound and often act a little differently.

Unlike the Mediterranean islands, the Canary Islands were never connected to the mainland. They emerged from the ocean empty and lifeless – far away from places with terrestrial life. They were new worlds that had to be colonised by living things which then, in isolation, followed their own evolutionary path. And with amazing results. That's why you can today imagine yourself to be in the shoes of those 18th and 19th century discoverers – life on the Canary Islands still feels exotic compared to that of mainland Europe.

Oddly enough, wherever evolution has acted in isolation, the results show clear similarities. Isolation always tends towards similar results: some species grow a lot taller than mainland species, whereas others become

A plethora of house-leeks evolved on the Canary Islands, with many impressive endemic species that occur only in very specific locations. This is the Pyramidal Houseleek* (Aeonium cuneatum), unique to Tenerife.

dwarfs. On Tenerife and La Gomera, there are 3 meter tall viper's-buglosses and 5 metre tall sea-lavenders. There are giant lizards (although the largest species is now extinct) and there once were giant rats, whereas the local Ravens are much smaller than their relatives on the mainland. A large number of species lost their ability to fly. There are lots of flightless beetles on the Canary Islands and there even was a flightless bird, which sadly went extinct. Of some groups of plants and animals there is a wide variety of species, whereas others are completely absent. For example, there are many species of sow-thistles, houseleeks, viper's-buglosses and marguerites on the Canaries, while there are very few orchids and lilies, and no oaks. Nor are there snakes or native amphibians or grazing animals. And finally, there is a lot of extinction – skeletal remains or historical accounts of species now long gone: the flightless bird, the giant rat, the giant lizard – all part of history.

Why does island life have these strange characteristics? Why are there on the one hand so many endemic species, while on the other hand, many species and even entire species groups are absent on the island, even though they are common on the mainland? Why has such a high number of species become extinct? Key to all of it is the isolation.

Somehow, an ancestor of all that is currently alive on the Canary Islands, must have crossed the several hundred kilometre wide ocean between the mainland and the islands – an ocean that due to its salinity, is killing to all but the hardiest terrestrial life.

Colonising the islands

The colonisation of remote islands presents various puzzles to biologists. A few larger organisms may have arrived by rafts of plant material, like a log with some branches. Much more numerous are the species that travelled through the air. Very light seeds and spores of lichens, mosses and ferns are able to travel through the air. Experiments with large nets carried out on the isolated islands of Hawaii showed that strong winds are able to transport lots of small insects and spiders (clinging on to a part of a spider web that functions as a sail) over thousands of kilometres. There is a constant, light 'rain' of invertebrates that reaches even the remotest of islands. Many plant seeds have travelled in the stomachs of birds. In particular pigeons are both seed-eaters and strong flyers that are able to reach the islands.

After colonising the Canary Islands, the reptiles evolved into distinct species. The *Eisentrauti* race of Tenerife Lizard (top) is unique to the north of Tenerife. Like all Canary Island Lizards, it belongs to the genus *Gallotia*, which is unique to the Canary Islands. The Tenerife Gecko (bottom) differs subtly from the species on La Gomera.

Evolution in overdrive

So this is how species arrive at the islands from the mainland. But that only heralds the start of the colonisation. What follows (if the castaway is able to survive) is a fast process of evolution into an entirely new species. How is that possible?

If you take all the genes of a single species (the so-called gene pool) and count how often each gene occurs in the entire population, you'll see great differences. Some genes are very common – almost every individual has them. Others are extremely rare and occur only in very few individuals. These genes get reshuffled over and over again in each new generation, but the total gene pool stays more or less the same.

However, the picture radically changes if you look at the genes of a single individual. It will typically have most of the common genes, but not all. Whilst it will lack the majority of the unusual ones, it is likely to have at least a few oddities.

Now imagine that only two or three individuals get trapped on the island and become the ancestors of an entirely new population. This population will lack some genes that are common in the main population, but some unusual ones will be common in the pioneer population. This process, called genetic drift, will cause radical changes in an isolated population within just a few generations.

That's the basis from which selection starts to work. The ecological conditions are very different in the new world. Large predators and herbivores are absent. They are either too bulky to arrive on rafts of vegetation, or require a larger area to sustain a viable population. As a result of the lack of predators, many species lose their defence mechanisms and become tame or flightless. On the mainland, predators prefer the biggest lizards and rats – they are sluggish and an easy prey. The bigger specimens are in disadvantage over the smaller ones, hence the species stays, on average, small. On the islands, the lack of predators will give the larger specimens the advantage, as they will out-compete their smaller cousins. This gives rise to the phenomenon of island gigantism – the process that makes island animals to develop into larger animals. The opposite process occurs as well – very large animals that get trapped on an island will have a disadvantage over smaller relatives as they require more energy to sustain their large bodies. The island simply isn't big enough to sustain a viable population of large animals, so many species eventually grow smaller – island dwarfism.

Had Darwin first set foot on these islands, rather than exploring the Galapagos (and he came tantalisingly close – see history section) he might have taken Canarian houseleeks, lizards or marguerites as an example of this radiation of new species rather than the famous Darwin finches of the Galapagos.

The process of speciation (the formation of new species) has been closely studied in the marguerites *(Argyranthemum)*. DNA-research has revealed where the original species arrived (Fuerteventura) and how marguerites then island-hopped to occupy the entire archipelago, each time going through a new bottleneck of genetic drift. Some marguerites became extinct (including those on ancient Canary Islands that were later swallowed by the ocean). On Tenerife, the marguerites radiated into various different species, one for each habitat – *A. frutescens* in the coastal region, *A. gracile* in the succulent scrub, *A. brousonettii* in the laurel forest, *A. adauctum* in the pine forests and *A. teneriffae* in the subalpine zone. All neatly occupy their own habitat, just like Darwin's finches. But that's not the whole story. There are 10 species of marguerites on Tenerife. Some are extremely local and occur only in the Teno mountains, Anaga or the southwest of the island. Bearing the geology in mind: for a long time, Teno and Anaga were separate islands. It was only fairly recently (geologically speaking), they became connected through the eruptions of the Cañadas volcano. Isolation and adaptation to specific habitats are the engines behind the amazing endemic biodiversity of the islands.

The group of marguerites form, like Darwin's Finches, a text book example of a group in which each species evolved to adapt to its own specific niche. These are Teide Marguarite* (top) and Broussonet's Marguerite* (bottom), respectively occupying the subalpine Cañadas and the laurel forests.

Islands as gardens of Eden

According to the Bible, the Garden of Eden was a sort of utopia where all animals lived in harmony and death was a stranger. Whilst such an Eden could never be a reality, the lack of larger predators and herbivores creates, on isolated islands the closest approximation to this ideal. The biologist, a bit more cynical, speaks of evolutionary naiveté – the in-bred anxiety and defense mechanisms have disappeared from the population.

This paradise collapses as soon as species that are tutored in harshness by the outside world arrive. These are either our domestic animals and pets or illicit stowaways. The Guanches (and perhaps their cats) caused the extinction of the Giant Rats and Lizards. A whole score of invasive weeds were also introduced which are a great threat to the ecosystem and its endemic species (see nature conservation on page 65).

Bird evolution

Apart from the endemic birds (the pigeons, the Blue Chaffinch, the Berthelot's Pipit, etc.) there are several birds whose taxonomic status isn't entirely clear. Genetic studies have revealed some very interesting facts about these species.

Chaffinch the Chaffinch can be divided into three groups: the *coelebs* group of Europe and Asia, the *spondiogenys* group of North Africa and the *canariensis* group of the Canary Islands. Genetic studies indicate that members of the

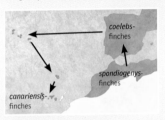

European and African groups are more closely related to one another than they are to members of the *canariensis* group, even though the Canarian birds resemble the European birds more closely than the African birds do. The study concluded that probably there was only a single wave of colonization on the Atlantic Islands, which evolved as follows: first,

Martin Collinson, *Evolution of the Atlantic-island Chaffinches.*, 2001, British Birds 94: page 121-124

remnants of an ancestral lineage of chaffinch from Tunisia gave rise to the ancestor of present day population on the European continent. Then, in rapid succession the European birds colonised the Azores, followed by Madeira and the Canary Islands. Strong north-westerly winds blow from the Azores to the Canaries in winter when chaffinches are in flocks, which should explain the north - south migration wave.

The story of the Blue Chaffinch is different. This bird is believed to have evolved from an earlier invasion by another ancestral Chaffinch.

African Blue Tit In contrast to the Chaffinch, genetic studies indicate great similarities between Canarian and African populations of blue tits (and more distantly their European cousin). The first African Blue Tit populations were located in one of the Central Islands, either Gran Canaria or Tenerife. From here it has colonised the other islands. It is believed that North African populations derived from the Canary Islands through colonization from the islands to the mainland. However, the populations of Lanzarote and Fuerteventura are now thought to be genetically closer to the north African birds than to the birds of Tenerife.

Tenerife Goldcrest It seems that the Goldcrests colonised the Canary Islands from the north in two waves. The first was the occupation of Tenerife and La Gomera some 1.9–2.3 million years ago, followed by a separate invasion of El Hierro and La Palma, about 1.3–1.8 million years ago. A 2006 study of the vocalisations of the Tenerife Goldcrest indicates that they comprise two subspecies separable on voice; *Regulus regulus teneriffae* is the one occurring on Tenerife and La Gomera.

Young Tenerife Goldcrest. Note the distinct black forehead.

Habitats

There are few places where natural habitats are as neatly divided in an area as they are on Tenerife and La Gomera. Whereas elsewhere in Europe, the soil, hydrology and above all, land use, resulted in a complicated and often diffuse patchwork of habitats, the situation here is refreshingly clear. Altitude and the amount of moisture (the latter creating a big difference in the northern and southern slopes) are almost the only factors that determine which habitat occurs where.

From sea level to the summit of the Teide, one passes through seven distinct habitats on Tenerife, starting with dry, coastal lowland, an open shrubby area of succulent plants, followed by a species-rich, dense scrubland known as thermophile forest. On southern slopes, this dense scrub gives way to open pine woods. On the north-facing slopes, the laurel cloud forest covers the slopes between 600 and 1300 metres, driving a wedge between the thermophile forest and the pine forest. The pine forest peters out between 2000 and 2200 metres on northern and southern slopes respectively. This is roughly around the main caldera of the Cañadas del Teide, the large lower crater of the Teide. The next altitude zone is dominated by the hemispherical bushes of the Teide Broom. The highest slopes of the Teide are nearly devoid of vegetation – a steep alpine desert named after one of the very few plants that is able to root here: the Teide Pansy.

La Gomera lacks the two highest altitudinal zones and the pine forest is restricted to just a few localities. But what it lacks in the number of vegetation zones, it makes up in quality. The coastal scrublands are fairly similar to those of Tenerife and stretch from sea level to 200 metres on the north side and 700 metres on the south side. The thermophile forest and scrub covers large parts of the island and is in places dominated by Canary Palm trees and Canary Junipers, two vegetations that are not present on Tenerife. The laurel forest zone covers the higher parts of the north slope of La Gomera. It is splendidly intact and covers large areas.

The one natural habitat that runs straight through these altitudinally arranged vegetation zones is that of the ravines *(barrancos)*. Both on Tenerife and La Gomera, the steep barranco cliffs, sometimes hundreds of metres tall, have, deep in their secluded depths, damp

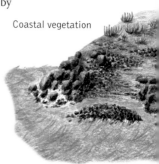

Succulent scrub

Coastal vegetation

< South

rocks or small streams that are biological treasure troves. They harbour a large number of endemic species.

The clarity in habitats is not monotonous – quite the contrary. From the coast to the highest peak, one passes from perennially warm semi-desert via damp cloud forests back to semi-desert again at the highest peaks. This is a journey over a distance of merely 20 kms as the crow flies – an exceptional landscape diversity you won't find easily elsewhere on our planet! These habitats are worlds of their own, reigned over by a different set of environmental rules, with different species that have found their own unique adaptations to survive in these places. Moreover, all of these habitats are unique to the Canary Islands.

On both islands, large areas are still intact, giving the islands roughly the appearance they had when people first arrived. Only on Tenerife have large areas been transformed into agricultural land, infrastructural works and resorts.

Overview of the habitats of Tenerife and La Gomera.

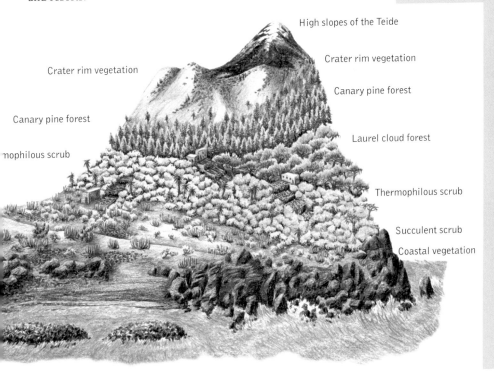

High slopes of the Teide

Crater rim vegetation

Crater rim vegetation

Canary pine forest

Canary pine forest

Laurel cloud forest

mophilous scrub

Thermophilous scrub

Succulent scrub

Coastal vegetation

North >

LANDSCAPE

Coast and submarine zone

The best routes to explore the dry, level coastal areas are routes 5 and 12, plus site B on page 150, sites A, B, C and D on pages 178-180 and site M on page 209. Tidal pools are present on route 12 and on site C on page 151, site E on page 172 and site C on page 179. For the steep coastal cliffs, try routes 5, 9 and site B on page 203. *Malpaíses* are covered in route 12 and site D on page 180.

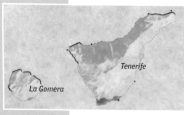

Position of the main areas of coastal cliffs (dark grey) and semi-desert plains (light grey).

For an island that sells itself as a sea-sand-and-sun destination, Tenerife's coastline is remarkably rocky, rough and unsuitable for swimming. There are only few large beaches – most notable that of Los Cristianos – Las Américas in the south-west, and San Andrés, east of Santa Cruz. Even these are not natural. The white sand was shipped in and storm break-waters were constructed to stop the carefully designed sand strips from being washed away.

The lack of beaches is quite understandable – Tenerife and La Gomera are volcanic rock islands. The heavy erosion of the ocean has created steep cliffs in some places, while elsewhere tidal movements have formed a rocky shore with tidal pools.

The small resorts on Tenerife and La Gomera make do with small beaches, consisting of sand or pebbles, their black colour revealing a volcanic origin. You'll find these beaches in sheltered coves, often at the mouth of barrancos.

The roughest coastlines fringe the oldest land masses: Teno and Anaga on Tenerife, and the entire coastline of La Gomera. La Gomera has only a few pebble beaches suitable for bathing (most notably at Coto del Rey and San Sebastian).

Tidal pools and sea life

Along much of the coast, a narrow strip of bare rock separates land from the sea. It is largely submerged when the tide is high, but when it drops, the rough, rocky fringe re-emerges, filled with countless tidal pools.

The rocky substrate is excellent for all sorts of sea life – crabs, sea anemones, small fish, shellfish, starfish and Portuguese Man o'-War (a type of jellyfish), etc. Some of them have found optimal living conditions in the constant interplay between land and sea, while others are trapped here involuntarily and will have to wait until the tide rises before they can leave again. That is if they live to see another high tide, because waders and herons readily take advantage of the low tide to fill their stomachs with the local *fruit-de-mer*.

The African west coast is a major flyway of migratory birds and although Tenerife lies quite far from the main flow, plenty of waders visit these shores, especially during migration and in winter. Whimbrel, Turnstone and Grey Plover are quite common and it is a wonderful sight to see them here – completely at ease – in an entirely different habitat than the preferred mudflats back home in Europe.

The most elaborate tidal pool systems are found where a recent lava stream flowed into the ocean, such as at Punta de Hidalgo (site E on page 172) and la Rasca (route 12). Since La Gomera hasn't had any recent eruptions, the tidal pool habitat is largely restricted to Tenerife.

Note that as you stand on the coast, you are geologically already half way up the slope. The lava hulk of Tenerife drops another 3 km to the bottom of the ocean. This is the place to put on your goggles,

Tidal pools at Punta de Hidalgo (top; site E on page 172). The pools attract lots of migratory birds and only very well-camouflaged fish are able to survive (bottom).

bite down on your snorkel and dive in. It is beyond the scope of this book to elaborate on what can be found here. We suffice to say that the coastal waters of the Canary Islands have an extraordinary rich sea life – one that isn't matched with any other area in Europe. Snorkelling will offer you no more than a glimpse of it since you are only exploring shallow places with a strong tidal influence – one of the harshest submarine environments where relatively little life occurs. Though even here you'll see many colourful fish, which are testimony to the richness of the sea. On page 222 we give tips on how to explore the submarine environment.

34

Abandoned fields in the dry coastal zone turn red due to the Small-leaved* Iceplant (top). Berthelot's Pipits (bottom) are very abundant in this habitat.

Coastal semi-desert plains

There is another coastal habitat you won't find on La Gomera: sandy and stony desert plains. This is actually a habitat of the eastern islands: Lanzarote and Fuerteventura. Gran Canaria has a fairly extensive area of dunes too at Maspalomas. On Tenerife, this type of habitat is only present around the Montaña Roja near the Aeropuerto Sur (site B on page 178). This site is very small and very much under pressure from tourists from nearby resorts of El Medano and Los Abrigos, but nevertheless it gives you a little taste of the eastern islands. Tenerife's only coastal lagunas and natural white beaches are found here. This is also the site for several desert wildflowers, which occur alongside the typical coastal flora, consisting of Canary Sea Fennel* *(Astydamia latifolia)*, Common and Small-leaved Iceplant* *(Mesembryanthemum nodiflorum)* and Canary Aizoon.

West and north of El Medano, there are more flat, coastal areas. They lie furthest away from the influence of the clouds and receive the least rainfall on the island. These plains are clearly not sandy, but their flatness and aridity make them somewhat resemble the stony desert plains of the eastern islands. Sadly the tacky, plastic-covered banana plantations have taken over much of these dry lands. You require a very positive attitude and a seriously selective vision to recognise the formidable desert plains of Lanzarote and Fuerteventura in the garbage-strewn wastelands between the plantations. There is no habitat on Tenerife that has received such heavy blows as the coastal semi-desert plains.

Even if you think these areas are all lost, there is a distinct set of desert birds that think otherwise and still find the means to survive. The scrubby deserts and abandoned dry fields scattered between Palm-mar and El Medano are home to Great Grey Shrike (the Canary subspecies), Hoopoe, Spectacled Warbler and perhaps the highest density of Berthelot's Pipits on the island. There might still be a handful of Lesser Short-toed Larks and Trumpeter Finches around, but they are on the brink of extinction.

At the southern tip of La Gomera, around the airstrip, there is a small area of level dry fields and barrancos, where some of these birds also occur.

Rocks, cliffs and the north coast

The massive cliffs of Los Gigantes, the Teno and Anaga mountains on Tenerife, and those of Los Organos and Valle Gran Rey on La Gomera, are among the most impressive landscapes of the Canary Islands. It is not just the scenic beauty that attracts. The cliffs, in particular the north-facing coastal cliffs, boast an exceptional flora. It is one of the hotspots that harbour a large number of *narrow endemics* – species that are confined to a very small area (see page 72). The north cliffs have a superb birdlife as well, with several seabird colonies hosting rare species like Barolo and Cory's Shearwaters, Madeiran Storm-petrel, Bulwer's Petrel and, rarely, the spectacular Red-billed Tropicbird, a newcomer here yet to be confirmed as breeding.

Typical of this terrain is the difficult access. There are few trails along the north coast cliffs, and none of them takes you to the seabird cliffs, which are mostly on off-shore islets. This is a little frustrating, but perhaps for the best, as these birds are easily disturbed.

If you visit the islands in winter, the coast has another delight – it is here that the reptiles are active throughout the year. In places like Punta Teno and Punta la Rasca, there are plenty of Tenerife Lizards, even in the middle of January.

The *Malpaís*

Malpaís literally means 'bad land' and is used for the very young lava fields, which have barely any soil and are therefore unsuitable for agriculture. There are two of such areas on the coast of Tenerife – the Malpaís de Guïmar (site D on page 180) and Malpaís de la Rasca (route 12). They form an exceptional landscape of gently rolling hills entirely consisting of black, brittle lava rocks, covered in the greyish bushes of Canary and Balsam Spurges and the 'skeletal fingers' of the curious Brown Ceropegia* *(Ceropegia fusca)*. The creviced ground is perfect for reptiles, which are plentiful here. Otherwise, the wildlife of these places is limited although the atmosphere is amazing.

The coastal cliffs at Teno are home to a wealth of rare wildflowers and breeding Barbary Falcons.

Succulent scrub

Beautiful examples of succulent scrub can be seen on routes 5, 6, 9, 12 and 13, and sites E and F on page 172-173, site D on page 180 and L on page 208.

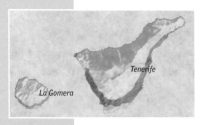

Position of the succulent scrub zone.

When you land on Tenerife south airport, the succulent scrub is the first thing you'll see. After picking up your hire car and driving up the slope of the Teide, you are greeted by a desert garden.

The dominant plants in this habitat are succulents – plants that store moisture in thick, leathery leaves and stems. They look somewhat like cacti, but these are native only to the Americas. However, the cactus growth form (thickly swollen stems and leaves – extreme succulence in other words), is widespread on the Canary Islands. It is an adaptation to the prolonged periods of drought.

This particular type of succulent scrub is unique to the Canary Islands, although a similar vegetation type is found on the Cape Verde Islands. Some of the dominant plants, such as Balsam and Canary Spurge, also occur on African and Middle-eastern coasts.

The succulent scrub, with the cactus-like Canary Spurge. This is Punta de Teno (route 5 / site B on page 150).

Originally, the succulent scrub covered the entire low-lying, south-facing slopes up to roughly 700 metres. On the northern side, only a thin strip is found, up to about 100 metres. There are sizeable areas of succulent scrub in the south-eastern and western part of Tenerife, the southern slopes of the Anaga mountains and on the entire southern coast of La Gomera. Sadly, many areas are unprotected and seen as 'mere wasteland' – incredible when you realise that this ecosystem and many of its inhabitants are unique to the islands.

The succulent scrub is a heaven for plant lovers. The key players in this warmest and sunniest vegetation zone are the oddly-shaped bushes of the Balsam *(Euphorbia balsamifera)*, Blunt-leaved Spurge* *(E. obtusiolia)* and Canary Spurge (*E. canariensis*; the latter looking like a true cactus) and the fist-thick stems of the Verode (*Kleinia neriifolia*; member of the Aster family). In some places, the Prickly Pear, a true cactus that was introduced from Mexico, has invaded the scrubland. In addition, there are many other, non-succulent bushes like the Canary Silk-vine* *(Periploca laevigata)*, Plocama* *(Plocama pendula)*, Schizogyne* *(Schizogyne sericea)* and the spiny Shrubby Launaea* *(Launaea arborescens)*. Not being succulents, their strategy against the drought, is to have hairy and waxy leaves to protect themselves against the fierce sun. The Plocama bushes invest in extremely long and elaborate root systems to reach the deep ground water. These are the only bushes that remain green during the dry summer months.

The succulent scrub is an important habitat for reptiles, in particular lizards and geckos (with each island its own species). They profit from the creviced lava rock, which offers plenty of hiding places. In summer, praying mantises (several species; see page 109) are frequently seen.

The birdlife in this zone is rather poor. Only Berthelot's Pipit is common, especially in level areas with few shrubs. A few Spectacled and Sardinian Warblers are found in suitable bushes, the odd Canary sits on an overhead wire and a Great Grey Shrike or Kestrel may be perched on a Canary Spurge.

Common succulent plants: Verode (top), Balsam Spurge (centre) and Canary Spurge (bottom).

38

Thermophile forest and terraced cultivations

Thermophilous forest and terraces are often present alongside one another. You can explore them on route 8, 9, 11, 12 and 16. Sites E on page 136, F on page 150, A and H on pages 162-166, and C, D and N on pages 187-192 are also good for exploring this habitat. Dry pastures and cereal fields are present on sites B on page 147 and D and O on pages 192.

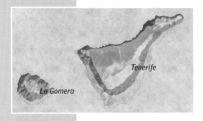

Position of the original thermophile forest. The light grey band in northern Tenerife is the zone with terraced cultivations.

Towards the upper end of the succulent scrub zone, the effects of the higher altitude start to have a marked influence on the vegetation. We are now at around 700 m on the southern side and 100 m on the northern slopes. The vegetation is denser, greener and taller, more flowery, and with a higher diversity of species. There are more butterflies and birds become more evident, with chatty flocks of Canaries, colourful African Blue Tits, a skulking Robin, some Chiffchaffs, Blackcaps and Sardinian Warblers. This is all the result of more moisture and less unforgiving temperatures. The increase in moisture is because this altitude zone is closer to, though not quite yet in, the zone where clouds usually develop due to the trade winds (see page 23). The weather is usually sunny and warm, but there is more cloud cover than in the coastal zone, and the altitude makes it a little cooler than at the coast.

The thermophile forest zone lies like a ring around the central highlands and is best developed on the northern slopes. It is not a true forest such as the laurel cloud forest, but more like a tall scrubland, not unlike the Mediterranean macchia. In this zone, the climate is not so harsh that it limits the vegetation to a few drought-adapted species, nor is it so perfect for plant growth that the battle for sunlight becomes an overriding struggle for survival. Instead it is somewhere in between, and this favours the growth of small trees and tall shrubs, which alternate with herbs and succulent plants on steep slopes and rocky terrain. Many of the key species of the succulent scrub persist in the thermophile forest, but are joined by a variety of other species, such as various sow-thistles, Giant and Broad-leaved Viper's-buglosses* *(Echium giganteum* and *E. strictum)*, Dark-red Spurge *(Euphorbia atropurpurea)* and Tree Bindweed *(Convolvulus floridus)* – all related to familiar plants in Europe, but here they've taken the stature of shrubs and small trees. The transition from succulent scrub into

thermophile forest and later laurel cloud forest is particularly visible on route 9 where you
climb up in the Anaga mountains. With every
bend in the road you climb a couple of metres
and a new plant species appears in the road
side. The walk into the Garganta del Infierno
(site E on page 180) offers a similar sensation.
The most typical species of the thermophile
forest are the Canary Palm, a classic postcard-
type palm tree, and the odd-looking Dragon
Tree (see box on page 82), a peculiar tree
which has a very wide, succulent trunk and
a small dense, single layer canopy of aloë-
type leaves that stands over the plant like an
umbrella. On La Gomera, the Dragon Tree is
very rare, but palm trees are very common.
On its northern slopes, juniper and broom
bushes play a dominant role in the vegetation,
creating three subtypes of thermophilous
forest on La Gomera that you won't find on
Tenerife: *sabinares* (juniper scrub), *palmares* (palm woods) and *retamales*
(broom scrub).

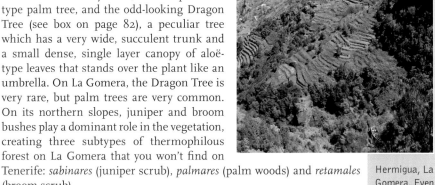

Hermigua, La
Gomera. Even the
steepest slopes within
the thermophile forest
zone are terraced
and used to cultivate
crops.

The abundant presence of wildflowers throughout the year favours insects, especially grasshoppers, bees and butterflies. Canary Islands Large
White, Canary Cleopatra, Canary Blue, Canary Speckled Wood and
Canary Red Admirals are all frequent. As their name suggests they are –
again – endemics.

Terraced cultivations

The climatic conditions in the thermophile forest zone are, together
with the laurel forest zone, the best suited for the cultivation of crops.
On Tenerife in particular, much of the original thermophile forest has
been cleared. The steep slopes are terraced to create small, level plots
where fruits, vegetables and chestnuts are cultivated – the *huertas*. Each
allotment, each house and each terrace, in fact each of the few roads that
wind along the steep slope, is a balcony with stunning views over the
ocean – views that increase in magnificence the higher you go.

The terraced allotments are not devoid of interest either. Built on steep
slopes, the allotments are small, separated by walls and rocky slopes,
patches of scrub and a scattering of colourful Canarian houses.

Many terraces are now abandoned and show a vigorous growth of brambles, giant sow-thistles, rockroses or annual herbs, which attract plenty of birds. Terraces with many flowers attract butterflies.

The rock walls are home to an enormous number of Tenerife Lizards which, on the northern slopes of Tenerife, are represented by the stout, black variant *Eisentrauti* with its beautiful blue, yellow and green spots. Geckos and skinks are common here too, although much harder to find. The many small basins, built to water the crops, are alive with Stripeless Treefrogs – again they are hard to find but all the more audible on balmy nights.

Rocky barrancos running down the slopes break the pattern of the allotments with ribbons of original or secondary laurel forest and thermophile forest, which locally harbour such delights as Barbary Falcon and Laurel Pigeon.

On higher slopes on the southern side, there are also terraces, where both dry arable farming and goat herding is practised. Today, with huge quantities of cheap food shipped in from the mainland, this small-scale form of agriculture is hardly viable economically, so it has largely disappeared. This is a shame because the birdlife, in particular, profits from these fields. Both on Tenerife and La Gomera, this is where the bulk of the Buzzards, Corn Buntings, Barbary Partridges and Rock Sparrows breed. Dry fields are still found on Tenerife at Teno Alto (route 5) and near Vallehermosa and Alajeró on La Gomera (route 16 and site M on page 209).

The Canary (top) is a common bird in allotments and villages. Canary Blue (middle) can be found in flowery spots all over the islands. The endemic Three-fingered Orchid is locally common on moist rocks and walls on north slopes.

Laurel cloud forest

41

Routes 8, 9, 10, 11, 13 and 14 cross laurel cloud forests. More walks can be done from Cruz del Carmen in Anaga. On La Gomera, the walks described under E, F and G also lead through laurel forests.

Coffee in the sun, or coffee in the mist? If you drive up the Anaga mountains on Tenerife (route 9) you have this choice. There is a bar in San Andrés at the junction before you wind up the mountains. There is another bar on the ridge, at 850 metres altitude and 5 km further on (as the crow flies) from San Andrés. Under the prevailing weather conditions, the first will be in the

sun, while the latter continuously sees shrouds of mist flying along in the wind. It is here that you enter the glorious laurel cloud forests – the leafy emerald of the Canaries.

Position of the laurel cloud forest.

The laurel cloud forests owe their existence to the fog. Trade winds from the north-east are forced upwards as they hit the mountains of the Canary islands. Roughly between 600 m and 1,000 m the moist air cools off sufficiently to form a belt of clouds. Almost like clockwork, this cloud bank forms in the course of the morning, producing fog and sometimes rain, thereby sustaining Europe's only piece of genuine subtropical cloud forest.

The mysterious laurel forests offer superb hiking opportunities.

The laurel cloud forests are a magical place – a green jungle of tall trees with thick rags of moss hanging from the branches. Ferns, wildflowers and tall, antler-like mushrooms grow from the tree trunks. The dim light, the mystical fog, the narrow and often slippery paths along steep slopes, the heavy, sweet smell of rotting leaves and wood – it all contributes to the mysterious and somewhat haunted atmosphere of the laurel cloud forest.

The tall Canary
Bellflower (top) –
unlike the European
bellflowers a winter-
flowering, climbing
plant – is a frequent
companion on your
walks.
The frequent fog cre-
ates a permanently
moist and quite cool
climate in which the
laurel forests thrive
(bottom).

The Guanches (original inhabitants of the islands) thought they were the realm of demons. Many places in the forests of La Gomera are riddled with lore and myth.

A unique, relict ecosystem

The ancient, mysterious ambience of the laurel forest fits the science. Ecologists label the laurel cloud forests as ancient relicts. In the tertiary era (the period before the cycles of ice ages and warm interglacials), the laurel cloud forests stretched out over the entire Mediterranean basin all the way into Asia. Tall and shady trees of the laurel family formed vast forests over this entire region. They thrived in the stable, moist and warm climate of that period. With the climatic fluctuations in the quarternary era, the laurel forests disappeared. Only on the edges of their vast range, they persisted and today, they are only present on the Macaronesian islands (Madeira, Azores and western Canary Islands) where the stable moist climate they need remained. On the Canary Islands, the main laurel forests are found on La Palma, Tenerife, and above all, La Gomera. On El Hierro and Gran Canaria only small patches are present.

Needless to say, the laurel cloud forests of Tenerife and La Gomera are of extreme value. As an eco-system, they are a showcase of a primeval vegetation that has disappeared throughout its original range. Hence, upon closer inspection, the trees, bushes and herbs here are nearly all unique to the Canary Islands. All dominant tree species for example, occur exclusively on the Canaries.

The entire surface cover of mature laurel cloud forest today is only about 6,000 ha (see also page 65). The most important forest is that of Garajonay in the centre of La Gomera. Of Tenerife's once large area of laurel forest, only three sizable patches remain:

the Monte del Agua in the west (route 8), the Esperanza forest in the Orotava valley in the centre and the Anaga mountains in the east (route 9).

Horizontal rain

The first thing to notice in the laurel forest is the large number of climbing and epiphytic plants. Various mosses and ferns grow on the branches of the trees. Hare's-foot Fern *(Davallia canariensis)*, readily recognisable by the brown-felty appearance of the rhizomes, is a frequent climber of trunks and rocks. The large orange bells of the Canary Bellflower* *(Canarina canariensis)* climb towards the light using branches of overhanging trees. All of these heavily depend on the presence of a permanent high humidity and frequent fogs. Even without actual rain, the vegetation will produce that of its own. In the foggy air, tiny water droplets form on the surface of the leaf. As the water accumulates, gravity, aided by the smooth surface of the leaves, causes it to run down along the edge of the leaf until it reaches the tip, where a drop is formed which swells until it is heavy enough to drop to the ground. Multiply this by the thousands and thousands of leaves in the forest and you have a very prolonged and very gentle rain, created by the vegetation itself. The trees and forest floor are soaking wet, even though it doesn't actually rain. The locals refer to these horizontal fog banks as *llúvia horizontal* or horizontal rain.

Mosses play an important role in the forest ecosystem by filtering out the water from the mist, which runs down the green rags and drops down to the ground. This is the famous 'horizontal rain' on which the forest depends.

Types of laurel forests

There are various types of laurel forests, each with its own position on the slopes. Deep in the valleys in the middle of the laurel forest zone, the tallest forests can be found. This is the shadiest part of the forest with the deepest soils. The Stink Laurel *(Octea foetens)* and the Indian Laurel* or Viñatigo *(Persea indica)*, often heavily decorated with ferns and other epiphytical plants, are the most frequent trees here. Along streams, such as the El Cedro on La Gomera (route 14), there are Canary Willows and Canary Elders* *(Sambucus n. palmensis)*, rare bushes of the laurel forest.

Climbing uphill from the valley, you enter the realm of the *Laurisilva de ribera* – the slope forest. Here Canary Laurel *(Laurus novocanariensis)* is the dominant tree. As the wind blows the fog through these slopes, this is where you usually find the most pronounced moss cover.

The lowest parts of the forest, as well as the parts that are more open due to the rocky soil, are the realm of the fourth species of laurel tree, the Barbusano Laurel* *(Apollonias barbujano)*.

The laurel forests harbours two of the most sought-after endemic birds of the Canary Islands – Bolle's Pigeon and Laurel Pigeon. Both of them only live inside these forests.

The fog does not always develop at the same altitude. Depending on wind and temperature and the time of year, the mist may be at its thickest at 600 at 700 or even at 900 metres.

The Laurel Pigeon – one of the two pigeons species that occur solely in the laurel forests of the Canary Islands.

As you climb higher up the slopes, you arrive at a zone where the fog tends to be thinner or even absent. Here the trees grow less tall and a lower but thick vegetation of Tree Heath and Tree Gale *(Myrica faya)* takes over, locally known as *Fayal-Brezal (Faya* is gale and *Brezo* is heath in Spanish). The first is a familiar plant for those who have travelled in the Mediterranean region, only on the Canary Islands and Madeira, this relative of the heather grows much taller and forms true trees. The second is a tall bush, endemic to the Canary Islands but a relative to the Sweet Gale of western Europe.

The gale-heath woods grow naturally on mountain peaks and at higher altitudes, but also grows as a secondary vegetation in old clearcuts in the middle of the laurel forest. The small Tenerife Goldcrest is a bird that is very much tied to stands of Tree Heath and is very common in the *Fayal-Brezal* forest.

The laurel forests are very rich in wildflowers. Paradoxically though, the majority of them don't grow on the shady forest floor, but in woodland clearings. Naturally, rocky outcrops (of which there are many on these slopes) receive more light and so offer better growing conditions, hence it is here you should explore the often spectacular flora of the laurel forests. One look at the topography of the forest though, will tell you that this is more easily said than done. Fortunately for you, these plants accept artificial clearings just as easily. Not infrequently, a leisurely walk along a forest track is like passing through a linear botanical garden of laurel forest flowers, with numerous species in a neat display (e.g. route 7). Butterflies also follow these tracks, feeding off the nectar provided by these plants.

Epiphytes and nectarivores – two tropical features of the laurel forest

Although it would go too far to say the laurel cloud forests are tropical, they do share two elements of tropical forests: the presence of epiphytes and nectarivores. Epiphytes are plants that grow on the trunks and branches of trees. In the tropics, there are thousands of plant species that grow exclusively in tree canopies. On Tenerife and La Gomera, frequent epiphytes are ferns like Hare's-foot Fern, Macaronesian Polypody and Ivy-leaved Spleenwort *(Asplenium hemionitis)*. Impressive are the houseleeks that hang down from tree branches. In particular Hairy Aichryson* *(Aichryson laxum)* has a habit of growing on tree trunks. None of these epiphytes grow exclusively on branches, though. They occur just as easily on shady rocks.

The majority of the epiphytes are mosses and lichens. Strictly speaking, this is not a tropical feature – in Europe there are many mosses and lichens growing on trees. However, the long rags of green mosses, ferns and rosettes of houseleeks do give the laurel forest a tropical appearance.

In the tropics, flowers are present year-round. Some bird species have specialised on a diet of energy-rich nectar. The hummingbirds of the Americas are famous for this, while in the old world tropics, the sunbirds fill the same niche. None of these specialists occur on Tenerife and La Gomera, but here, perhaps even more remarkably, 'European' species have developed a liking for flowers. The Canary Islands Chiffchaff makes the most out of feeding on nectar, but it is not unusual to see African Blue Tits, Sardinian Warblers and Chaffinches which habitually do the same. This behaviour is remarkable because their close relatives on the mainland hardly ever visit flowers.

Is this a passing fashion among the birds here or an old adaptation? It must be the latter, as several native wildflowers have completely specialised in being pollinated by birds. Eleven species have so far been counted as at least partly depending on nectarivorous birds. Canary Bellflower and Canary Foxglove are the main species in the laurel forest. Several species of viper's-buglosses are frequently pollinated by birds as well.

Hairy Aychryson (top) grows frequently on tree trunks and branches.
Nectar is a major component of the Canary Islands Chiffchaff (bottom).

Canary Pine forest

Routes 1 and 4 and site D on page 135 leads through Canary Pine forest.

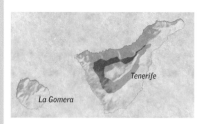

Position of the Canary pine forest.

At roughly 1200 metres above sea level, the climate is no longer subtropical and the difference between winter and summer is pronounced. On winter nights, especially, temperatures drop considerably, sometimes close to freezing point. The cloud layer on the northern slope reaches these altitudes only occasionally. Consequently, conditions are colder, drier and sunnier than further down. This is the zone of the Canary Pine Forest.

The Canary Pine forest ranges from 1,200 to 2,200 metres above sea level. This means that on La Gomera this vegetation zone has hardly developed. Only the highest peaks just reach this altitude, but they are too rocky and wind-exposed to support true forests. Canary Pine forest is also found on Gran Canaria and La Palma, but the largest and most impressive stands are on Tenerife. Here they form a large ring around the central *caldera* – a crown of forest, the *Corona Forestal*.

The cloud cover only rarely reaches as high as the Canary Pine forest zone.

As suggested the Corona Forestal is dominated by a single species of tree, the Canary Pine (*Pinus canariensis*). Like the laurel trees, it is a relict of the tertiary flora, whose closest relative is found at the far eastern edge of the tertiary forests' former range – the Himalayas. When you are walking through the Canary Pine forests, you may be forgiven for thinking you are somewhere in

the Alps. The steep cliffs are covered in dense coniferous forest, and although the sun is powerful, the air is cool and fresh.

The entire habitat revolves around this one species of tree. The Canary Pine has very long needles (in bundles of three) which have the same adaptation as many of the laurel forest plants: they filter the moisture from the air, which adheres to the needle surface, runs down the tip and drops down to the ground. Although the fog is much less frequent at these altitudes, it is still present at times, especially on the lower north-facing part of the forests. It is an important source of water in an otherwise arid environment. Next to the pine needles, the long beard lichens that grow in the branches of the pine trees are important collectors of moisture. You'll see them too on the north facing mountains.

Although the pine forests appear rather uniform at first glance, there are clear differences as you move up to higher altitudes, or circle around the mountain. Majestic tall trees, underneath which there is a well-developed growth of rockroses and other shrubs, characterise the forest in its lower reaches. Trees become smaller and more stunted as you gain altitude and the climate becomes drier and colder and the sun stronger. Close to the treeline, the trees form a strange parkland of small trees in barren volcanic grit, the yellowish needles (result of the drought) contrasting sharply with the slate-grey volcanic soil.

The forest at Los Organos (route 4). This part of Tenerife has an almost Alpine feel.
Sadly, large parts of this forest burnt down in 2023.

Life in the Canary Pine forests

As shaper of an ecosystem, the Canary Pine is both a blessing and a curse. On the one hand, it is a generous provider. The pine kernels are food for birds and the crowns offer plenty of nesting sites. This is the sole habitat of the beautiful Blue Chaffinch, unmistakable in its appearance and almost entirely restricted to the *Corona Forestal* of Tenerife. The only other places it is found (but where it is very rare)

are in the pine forests of Gran Canaria. The Blue Chaffinch shares its habitat with the Canarian subspecies of the Great Spotted Woodpecker (confined to the pine forests as well) and more widespread birds like Chiffchaff, Robin and Canary.

On the other hand, the pine is a dominant and smothering species. Its long needles form a thick layer on the ground where herbs and shrubs have a hard time establishing themselves. On northern slopes, where the forest is denser and less sunlight reaches the ground, the lack of light is another inhibiting factor. On south-facing slopes, trees are farther apart, the cover of needles is less thick and as the slopes angle towards the sun, the woodlands are much more full of light. Now drought is the problem. Without the fog the moisturising capacity of the pine is futile and the trees only subtract water. As a result of these difficulties, entire stretches of Canary Pine forest appear rather dull and uniform.

The local race of Great Spotted Woodpecker (top) and the Canary Cistus (bottom) are two typical inhabitants of the pine forest.

Birdwatchers in search of Blue Chaffinches came to this conclusion at an early stage. They discovered that whilst two life requirements for birds – food and nesting facilities – are present throughout the forest, the third one – water – is hard to come by. The few spots with water are therefore a magnet to birds. And these are... the picnic sites! Small taps for the picnickers are particularly favoured by birds which fly in from the surrounding forest to drink. Therefore you can walk through the woodlands without hearing or seeing a single bird until you arrive at the picnic sites of, for example, Las Lajas or El Chío (both route 1) to have all the birds handed to you on a platter.

Nevertheless, it would be a shame not to explore the pine forest more thoroughly. In spite of the fact that large areas of forest are rather dull, the Canary pine forest as a whole is home to a distinct set of wonderful wildflowers. Granted, it may not be able to compete with the grandeur of the thermophile forest, the laurel forest or the caldera broom desert, but the thickets of Canary Cistus *(Cistus symphytifolius)*, the bushes of Large-flowered White Broom* *(Chamaecytisus proliferus)*, Greenish Viper's-bugloss* *(Echium virescens)*, Smith Houseleek *(Aeonium smithii)* and Spade-leaved Houseleek* *(A. spathulatum)* various mountain-tea species and marguerites are a feast for the eye.

Like the birds, the flora has its particular hotspots of diversity: rocky outcrops and gullies. The outcrops are less shady and plants are less troubled by pine needles. On northern slopes, especially, the outcrops are the places to enjoy a wonderful flora. On southern slopes the gullies and barrancos are the flora hotspots, as they are less dry.

So if you plan to hike through the *Corona Forestal* (something we warmly recommend), choose your routes to cover precipitous terrain with gullies and rocky spots. Such routes are more demanding, but well worth it, both in terms of flora and birdlife, as well as for the scenery. Naturally, the routes described in this book, seek out these places.

Collecting pine needles

As you drive up to the Teide through the pine forest, you may very well see a small truck coming your way, stacked with an unusual freight: pine needles. These have been collected since time immemorial for the fertilization of the terraced allotments and as a bed for cattle.

The dry, flammable pine needles pose a serious forest fire threat to the fragile Canary pine forests, which makes this habit a win-win situation for nature and people alike. However, the pine needles are also an important source of nutrients for the ecosystem and it is unclear whether there is a damaging side to the pine needle collection as well.

Collecting pine needles.

50

The Cañadas and el Teide

Routes 1, 2, 3 and sites A, B and C on pages 134-135 lead through the subalpine habitat of the Cañadas crater.

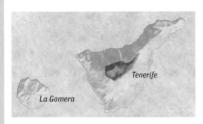

The Cañadas del Teide (dark grey).

For the dramatic effect you'd best approach from the south. Pass through the village of Vilaflora, wind up through the pine forest, conquer the last climb to the crater rim and there it is: surreal and otherworldly – the barren volcanic crater plain of the Cañadas del Teide. The crater floor is 14 km in diameter from which the crater walls rise up 300 metres from the central plain. In the middle of the rocky lava desert, more or less in front of you, rises another volcano – the actual Teide. At 3,718 metres it is the highest mountain in Spain.

The Cañadas del Teide, with the El Teide volcano in the back and Teide Broom in the foreground.

The arid plains of the Cañadas del Teide are in nothing like the pine-clad slopes you passed through on your ascent. This is a cold semi-desert, where the majority of plants and animals are endemic to just this area or are only shared with the Canary island of La Palma, which is just high enough to sport a small area of subalpine volcanic desert.

Botanists recognise two main vegetation zones in the Cañadas: the Teide Broom zone, which extends from the crater rim to the base of the Teide, and the Teide Pansy zone found above 2,700 metres on the Teide Volcano peak. The latter zone has such a harsh, dry and cold climate that hardly anything survives. One of the few exceptions is the pretty pink Teide Pansy* *(Viola cheiranthifolia)* and sky-blue Auber's Viper's-bugloss* *(Echium auberianum)* – both unique to the Teide.

51

The nectar of the Teide Scrub-scabious* *(Pterocephalus lasiospermus)* is a highly prized nectar source for butterflies, such as this Cardinal.

A journey across the base of the caldera offers breath-taking views of giant, solidified flows of lava, weird *roques*, sculpted over millennia by the wind, and large plains of volcanic sand (see geology chapter). But there is quite a lot of life here too. The two most common plants here are brooms – Sticky Broom *(Adenocarpus viscosus)* and the conspicuous rounded bushes of the Teide Broom after which the Caldera ecosystem is named. The plant's scientific name *Spartocytisus supranubius* means the broom-above-the-clouds and reveals what this ecosystem is all about. On most days of the year, the caldera lies high above the clouds. If fact, a walk or drive on the crater's edge is wonderful precisely because you look down on the clouds, almost giving you the sensation of flying.

Above-the-clouds is what defines the natural world of the caldera. As a result of the altitude, the atmosphere is much thinner and contains a lot less dust and water vapour to shield against the sun. Hence the sun's power is intense and the drought extreme. Meanwhile, that same lack of a proper atmospheric blanket makes for very cold nights. The temperatures measured on the ground oscillate during the year between -16 °C to +58 °C! The clarity of the air makes a night visit to the caldera worthwhile. The stars are simply amazing! In fact, Tenerife has been awarded the title of 'Starlight Tourist Destination' because of its exceptional clear skies (see site F on page 136).

In this extreme environment, the Teide Broom (and to lesser extent other bushes) play a hugely important role as a refuge. The thick bushes function as a vegetal version of the clouds that are lacking in this environment: they provide shade and coolness during the day and maintain the warmth at night. Research has shown that thick broom bushes can reduce the temperature by 10 °C.

Whereas on most of the island, the mild climate allows insects and reptiles to be active year round, nature takes a winter break in the Cañadas. There are no butterflies nor wildflowers in winter – it is too cold at night. The active season, in which the wildflowers bloom and butterflies are on the wing, is from March onwards. This is not to say that a winter visit to the caldera isn't worthwhile (it remains the most impressive excursion you can make on Tenerife), but it isn't until spring that the beauty of the caldera is truly appreciated.

In mid May, the wildflower feast reaches its peak: the Teide Brooms are in bloom, growing alongside Leafy Greenweed* *(Adenocarpus foliolosa)*, and the bushy Teide Flixweed *(Descurainia bourgeauana)*, which both produce seas of yellow flowers.

The most spectacular plant of the Cañadas and perhaps of the whole of Tenerife, is the Teide Viper's-bugloss *(Echium wildpretti)*, which forms a massive spike of red flowers that reaches 3 metres in height. It takes a plant about 5 years to gather enough energy to produce this proliferation of flowers – the plant spends its first years as a rosette. After it blooms and sets seed, it dies, leaving a silvery skeleton behind that is a typical feature of the Cañadas in winter.

The caldera is also a great place for butterflies. In spring, you'll see plenty of them flying around nectar-rich plants – mostly thistles and Teide Scrub-scabious* *(Pterocephalus lasiospermus)*. For butterfly enthusiasts, the Caldera Green-striped White is the big prize as it is endemic to the crater.

The massive, three metre high Teide Viper's-bugloss with Teide Scrub-scabious* on the foreground.

The spherical broom bushes play a key role in the Cañada ecosystem as they form an important shelter for fauna from the sun and the nightly cold.

It is a common butterfly, joined by good numbers of Canary Blue and, towards the summer, Tenerife Heath.

The most impressive landscapes are perhaps right in the centre of the caldera – the desolate plains with their fanciful lava sculptures and wind-sculpted *roques*. Much of this, you find right along the roads (see route 1). The highest diversity of plants and insects however, is found close to the crater rim (see route 2 and site C on page 135). Here, the diversity of habitats (shady-sunny, exposed or sheltered from the wind, a variety of altitudes) gives rise to the highest numbers of species, including of course several endemics of the crater ridge.

There are no roads along the crater rim, but there are some excellent and rather quiet trails, ranging from short and easy ones to strenuous, full day undertakings (see page 134). These are the best for exploring this beautiful habitat. Keep in mind, though, that drought and UV-radiation reigns this habitat. Don't economise on the sun screen or you'll soon match the colour of the Teide Viper's-bugloss.

Julia's Rockrose – an extreme endemic

Tenerife has its share of so-called narrow endemics – species that only occur on very small areas. There are numerous plants that are only found in a small area of the island, but none of them is as localised as Julia's Rockrose (*Helianthemum juliae*). It is restricted to less than a handful of spots in a small fraction of the crater rim.

Because of its extreme rareness, Julia's Rockrose has been the subject of intensive biological research, which showed that it is gradually disappearing due to dessication. The sites where it grows are simply too dry for the plant to survive in the long run. The deterioration of the environmental conditions are thought to be a result of climate change. Hence, the plants were moved to less exposed sites in order to preserve the species from a likely extinction.

The case of Julia's Rockrose begs the question how far we ought to go to preserve particular species. In this case, this question is not easy to answer, since it wasn't recognised as a separate species until 1986, it is just one of several yellow rockroses of a genus that is notorious for its complex taxonomy. Its species are often very hard to tell apart. Some may argue there are more pressing and more rewarding nature conservation goals (especially on Tenerife!), whereas others make the case that conservation is about an effort to preserve the species, not about keeping what appeals to us humans.

Julia's Rockrose
(*Helianthemum juliae*)

Barrancos

> The most beautiful barrancos are those on routes 7, 10, 11, 14, 15 and 16, plus site A on page 150, site A, E and F on pages 169-173, site E on page 180 and site I and L on pages 191-192.

The steep ravines that run down radially from Tenerife's and La Gomera's peaks to the ocean, are called *barrancos*. Most of them carry water only after periods of rain. Only a few have a permanent flow of water (e.g. Barranco del Infierno and Barranco de Afur on Tenerife and the Barranco El Cedro on La Gomera).

Barrancos are true biodiversity hotspots. They serve as the principal breeding grounds for many butterflies and birds. Many species of plants and dragonflies are restricted to the ravines.

The barrancos also offer some of the most spectacular hiking. Paths are often strenuous, especially when you are climbing up. Therefore, it pays to start at the top and arrange to be picked up at the bottom.

Barrancos as natural biodiversity hotspots

There are several factors that make barrancos such veins of biodiversity, and most of them boil down to the sheltered environment they provide. There is, on average, more moisture in the ground, since the rains collect in the gullies. The water also brings down nutritious soil, which

The barranco of Valle Gran Rey

accumulates in the valley. And because of the higher humidity and because during part of the day there is a cliff blocking the sun, the temperature is more constant. All this favours plant growth which, in turn, evens out the temperature.

Hence, in barrancos, the vegetation zones shift. The relatively benign conditions allows the thermophile forest vegetation to penetrate well down towards the ocean and deep into the succulent scrub vegetation. Once you have climbed the barranco up to the altitude where, according to the contour lines, the thermophile forest ought to be, you find the first species of the laurel forest.

At higher altitudes, the mild barranco climate allows for a

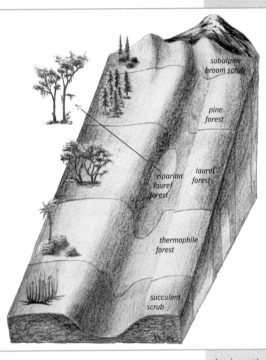

reversed pattern: Canary Pines, sequestered in the barrancos, reach well into the normally treeless alpine slopes. This stretching out of the vegetation zones into the higher and lower reaches, creates a wide area suitable for the development of laurel forests. Right in the heartland of the laurel forest zone – where the altitude brings the thickest cloud layer, and where the barranco creates the deepest shade – a special type of laurel forest grows which is characterised by the tallest trees, the greatest cover of epiphytic ferns and mosses (see page 45).

Typical of gorges is that the environmental conditions vary greatly from place to place. Some spots are always shady whilst others are very exposed. There are permanently damp places whilst elsewhere, the thin soil cannot hold any moisture. There are places where herbivores can blissfully munch through the day, and others where not even the most acrobatic goats are able to reach. The slope ranges from vertical and even overhanging to very gentle. There are both very nutrient-rich areas, and very poor ones.

A schematic illustration of a barranco from mountain top to sea. In barrancos, the usual vegetation zones are shifted. The sheltered environment not only allows laurel forest trees and pines to reach higher altitudes, but also thermophile and laurel forests to reach to lower levels too. In effect, the laurel forest zone is stretched and gives rise, in the wettest zone, to a unique riparian forest.

This variety of environmental conditions is reflected by a tremendous diversity of plant species. Many of them are restricted to barrancos, and some are even endemic to a few or even a single barranco. The Masca Houseleek* *(Aeonium mascaense)* for example only grows in the Masca gorge. The houseleeks and their relatives are well represented anyway. Most species of houseleeks belonging to the *Aeoniums, Monantheses* and *Greenovias* are restricted to barrancos, and all the others grow on all sorts of cliffs, including those in barrancos. Most botanical rarities of the thermophile forest, such as Canary Palm, Giant Viper's-bugloss and Dragon Tree find their most important refuges here, while most orchids and many fern species have important populations inside barrancos.

The barrancos house the same songbirds as the allotment zone and thermophile forest: Canaries, African Blue Tits, Canary Islands Chiffchaffs, Blackcaps and Sardinian Warblers. In addition, the cliff walls harbour the bulk of the breeding Plain Swifts, shearwaters, Kestrels and Barbary Falcons. Of special interest are the ravines with a permanent stream of water. Freshwater sites are naturally scarce on these islands. Apart from man-made reservoirs and channels, freshwater is restricted to a handful of barrancos. Such valleys are home to birds like Grey Wagtail and even Moorhen. All the dragonfly species occur in these streams and some are even restricted to such sites, like Red-veined Dropwing, Ringed Cascader and Epaulet Skimmer.

Yellow Ceropegia, one of the many wonderful wildflowers of the barrancos.

Barrancos as refuge

Today, barrancos are even more important biodiversity hotspots than they were originally. Since terracing and goat herding has destroyed the original thermophilous and laurel woods in many places, the barrancos became refuges for the flora and fauna of these habitats as well. Because barrancos are so hard to reach and even harder to transform into agricultural land, a natural vegetation persists here that has disappeared elsewhere. A glance on the satellite image of northern Tenerife clearly shows the barrancos as green veins in the allotment zone. On the ground, you'll discover that in these valleys, the most beautiful old trails lead down to the coast. They are now used by hikers and naturalists, who can marvel at the sight of numerous butterflies, dragonflies and birds, or set their teeth in identifying the confusing variety of wildflowers.

History

The history of the Tenerife and La Gomera consists of two distinct periods – the time before the Spanish conquest of 1402 and the colonial and modern times that followed.

The early inhabitants

The early, pre-colonial history of the Canary Islands is still shrouded in controversy. When the Spanish arrived, they did not find the islands unpopulated. All islands were inhabited by aboriginal people, who later became known as the Guanches. This name originally pertained to the inhabitants of Tenerife (Guan meaning man and Che coming from Chenit, an old name for Tenerife), but was later used for all native Canarian peoples.

Native is a problematic word to use for inhabitants of a volcanic archipelago like the Canary Islands. Like all life on these oceanic islands, the natives were once settlers. There is still some amount of disagreement as to where they originally came from and when they arrived.

The oldest written record of the Canary Islands comes from Pliny the Elder (23 BC– 79 AD). His source was king Juba II of Mauretania, who sent an expedition to the islands around 50 BC. The report spoke of few natives but impressive 'great buildings' suggesting that settlement was already of some antiquity. It is likely that the Phoenicians, whose galleys explored the Atlantic coast of Africa, and their Carthaginian successors visited the islands, but if so, they left no trace. By Roman times they were known as Insulae Fotunatae (Fortunate Isles) and Roman remains suggest some sort of trade with the islands. It's even suggested the original inhabitants were exiled to the islands by the Romans from inland areas of North Africa (explaining their lack of prowess as seafarers). The Moors, who occupied much of Spain and Portugal, as well as North Africa, may have visited the islands too, given the accounts of Arabic speaking locals.

The dominant – though still contested – theory concerning the Guanches is that they were Berber people who fled mainland Africa around 1000 BC (according to some sources 2500 BC and even 5000 BC). As the Northafrican climate became increasingly arid and the Sahara desert gradually encroached further and further on their arable land, they packed up and headed for the Canary Islands. Apparently, if conditions are right, the snowy peaks of the Teide can just be made out from the mainland, so they may have known the islands were there.

Guanche DNA

In 2003 and 2009, genetic research amongst the *Canarios* was conducted to shed some light on the background of the Guanches. The modern people of the Canary Islands showed a mixture of European and Berber DNA, but in a striking difference between types of DNA – whereas the male lineage Y-chromosome was predominantly European, the mitochondrial DNA (passed on only by females) was Berber. This would seem to support the theory that the Guanches were of Berber stock, but that with the arrival of the Spanish, the male Guanche DNA largely disappeared (presumably due to death in battle or enslavement). The women, though, survived as wives or concubines of the Spanish.

Evidence against this theory focusses on the poor navigation skills of the Berbers, in combination with the sea currents, which would diverge boats towards the south, making landing on the islands a difficult task. Add to this the early presence of livestock (there are early records of goats and sheep) which indicate a well-planned, purposeful colonisation of the Canaries, something that appears to be more fitting to the seafaring European peoples. However, doubts concerning the Berbers lack of seafaring skills and the difficult and unfavourable currents seem to have been washed away by recent DNA research, which favours the theory of the Berber background of the Guanches.

The Guanche society

When the Spanish arrived in 1402 they found all islands inhabited. An estimated population of 30-35,000 people lived on the Canary Islands, with Tenerife being the most densely populated. Only 2,000 people lived on La Gomera. The Guanches had divided Tenerife into nine kingdoms and La Gomera into four.

In spite of the 'great structures' reported by Juba's expedition, the Guanche culture encountered by the Spanish was fairly primitive. In a literal sense, the Guanches lived in the stone age, having no iron tools or weapons and people living in natural caves or simple stone shelters. The livelihood was centred around animal husbandry. They herded goats, cattle and pigs, which they moved up and down the mountain according to the availability of seasonal grazing. They also grew crops, but this was a secondary activity, as was fishing, harvesting shellfish and collecting fruit. It is fascinating to consider that the Guanches were poor sea navigators. Sea fishing was of minor economic importance even though the ocean around the islands would have offered a rich bounty. Apparently, there was little movement between the islands and the different tribes lived in relative isolation. Some sources suggest that the sea was a religious taboo. Except under specific conditions, sea travel was not allowed.

The Canary Islands in pre-Guanche times

In terms of the natural world, it is difficult to assess what the islands looked like before the first Guanche boat arrived on the islands. New arrivals, both human and non-human, on formerly isolated islands frequently lead to swift extinctions of the native fauna. The Dodo and the Tasmanian Tiger are just two of many examples. It was no different when the Guanches landed: the larger, native species went extinct swiftly. There are no written records, so it remains a guess what was there before, but from skeletal remains from volcanic caves (e.g. Cueva del Viento, site E on page 152), the prehistoric occurrence of a Giant Lizard and a Giant Rat are certain. Both were vegetarian and, given the lack of natural predators, both likely rather tame. They must have made a hearty meal and were probably hunted to extinction.

The Guanches also introduced new species. Livestock and cats filled two vacant niches on the islands: that of the large predator and of the large herbivore. On the semi-desert islands of Lanzarote and Fuerteventura, goats have wreaked havoc on the original vegetation. To what extent this changed the vegetation cover on Tenerife and La Gomera is unclear.

The colonisation by the Spanish

In 1341, an expedition set out from Lisbon to explore the Canary Islands. It mapped thirteen islands (seven major, six minor) and surveyed the aboriginal inhabitants, bringing back four Guanches to Lisbon. European interest in the Canaries grew quickly and it was Spain, or more correctly the Kingdom of Castille, that fully conquered the islands. This took place between 1402 and 1496. Lanzarote was the first island under Spanish rule. The small, native population faced daunting challenges just to survive on such a dry island with infertile soils, so they did not put up a fight. It was different on the western islands. La Gomera 'fell' already in 1404, but stiff opposition on Tenerife meant it remained independent until 1496. In April 1494, Spain started its conquest of Tenerife, but met such fierce opposition that they had to withdraw sustaining dramatic losses near what is today the town of La Matanza ('The slaughter'). The Guanche victory was short-lived. The Spanish returned in 1496 and overthrew the Guanche kings. Many of the natives were enslaved or succumbed to diseases such as influenza.

Old terraces at
El Cedro, La Gomera.

In the century that followed large groups of people moved from Spain to the Canary islands, repopulating the islands. The islands' economies – in particular that of Tenerife – received a great boost from this immigration. The northern slopes had suitable soils for agriculture. The steep terrain was terraced – a technique learned from the Moors – and a new agricultural model was imposed, based on single-crop cultivation: first sugar cane, then grapes.

The effect on the natural world was enormous. Large areas of thermophilous woodland and laurel forest were cleared for agriculture. The wood of the laurel forest was excellent for construction and heating so the profit from clearances was doubled, yielding both wood and arable land.

In keeping with the relatively high population density and advanced development, Tenerife's woodlands suffered much heavier blows than those on La Gomera. Sugar Cane became the most lucrative crop, followed by grapes and later bananas. Tenerife grew quickly to become a major trading hub between Spain and the colonies in South and Central America. Located conveniently to take advantage of trade winds between the old and the new world, ships logically made a stopover at the Canaries. Columbus, Von Humboldt and Charles Darwin all passed through before moving towards America. Columbus made a stop at San Sebastian de la Gomera and stayed in the town for a while. He returned to San Sebastian twice and there are rumours about him having a fling with the then ruler of the island, Beatriz de Bobadilla. The discoverer Von Humboldt explored the Canaries more thoroughly, and famously proclaimed the La Orotava valley 'the most beautiful in the world'. Near the town of La Orotava there is still a Von Humboldt viewpoint. Charles Darwin also visited the islands but sadly, never set foot on them. Much to his dismay (he had read the accounts of Von Humboldt), as the ship was quarantined and the crew denied access on land because of cholera in England. Imagine what would have happened if the architect of the theory of natural selection had explored the islands... Instead of Galapagos finches, we may now have talked about Darwin lizards, Darwin Marguerites or Darwin Houseleeks – all these species show speciation and adaptation processes similarly to the famous Darwin Finches.

Tenerife's economy benefited massively and grew more cosmopolitan thanks to its position astride the main trade routes. The Canary Islands maintained close relationships with Latin America. People from Tenerife crewed the ships that sailed to the New World, bringing back food and goods from there that today form part of the Canarian tradition. For example the famous *papas arrugadas* or wrinkly potatoes are from South America and are the signature dish of Canarian cuisine. The Canaries became an important 'half-way house' for crops and ornamental plants brought back from South America. They were planted on Tenerife in botanical gardens to prepare them for introduction to Europe. The second oldest botanical garden in Spain is that of Puerto de la Cruz (site C on page 170).

It is important to realise that all of this agricultural innovation took place on the northern side of Tenerife, where there was sufficient moisture to allow crop growth. This is why even today, the Oratava valley and the slopes above Icod are all terraced, right up to the start of the pine forest zone.

On southern Tenerife, terraces are more restricted to the barrancos. So communities here were much smaller and further apart as the land had little to offer. It was only when tourism boomed that this changed, and southern Tenerife became the densely populated land of the tourist resorts, while the north remained the place of historical towns and villages.

From the 17th century onwards, the link with the Americas, always so lucrative, started to backfire. Cheap produce – in particular sugar cane from Cuba – outcompeted the crops of Tenerife. As the economic situation

---

Canary Islands – Islands of dogs

The Canary Islands are not, as is often thought, named after the famous cage bird. The mistake is easily made, as the wild Canary is indeed native to the Canary Islands and is commonly seen all over Tenerife an La Gomera. However, it is the other way around – the bird is named after the islands.

The name Canary actually comes from the Latin *canus* – dog. It was given to the islands by the expedition of King Juba II because of the many ferocious dogs the crew discovered on the islands. This account is highly dubious, as it wasn't very likely there were dogs at all on the Canary Islands. So most probably, they referred to *Canus maritimus* – sea dog, or seal. In historic times, Lanzarote and Fuerteventura had large populations of Monk Seals on their beaches, which sadly disappeared in the 20th century.

deteriorated, many *Canarios* sought a better life in South America. The economic malaise and emigration continued into the 20th century. It was only after the Spanish Civil War ended in 1939, that people began to move back to Tenerife.

Developments on La Gomera

The turbulent developments on Tenerife clearly passed La Gomera by, leaving the island a relatively unaffected backwater. The genetic study carried out in 2011 that established the Berber genes of the Guanches, also revealed that, although present on all of the islands, the Berber background is particularly marked in the people of La Gomera. The indigenous people of the island were called *Gomeros* or *Gomeritas* and the name Gomera could derive from the *Ghomara*, a Berber tribe. By and large, the *Gomeros* carried on living in their traditional manner. Old traditions and beliefs, gradually morphing into a christianised version, persisted well into the 20th century. The historic and easy-does-it atmosphere is still very much part of the laid back feeling that is at the heart of the island. Some of their traditions have been preserved into the present day, the most famous being *El Silbo*, the language of whistles (see below). In 1492, Columbus visited San Sebastian de la Gomera on his famous journey to the New World, thereby meriting La Gomera its only footnote in global history.

Like Tenerife, but on a much more modest scale, La Gomera started to produce sugar cane and wine and do a little goat herding. Palm

---

El Silbo – language of whistles

The ruggedness of La Gomera, with its many deep barrancos, made travel across the island quite difficult. Even what is a short distance as the crow flies, could take a day of travel. Hence the locals created a language that could be whistled – *El Silbo*. The loud whistles easily carried over broad barrancos and made communication easy. The amazing thing about El Silbo is that it is a complete language, not just a couple of sounds that signal a few basic messages. The language has two vowels and four consonants that can be used to generate more than 4,000 words. Originally, El Silbo was developed by the Gomeran Guanches, but was later 'translated' into a Spanish version. In 2009, the El Silbo became part of UNESCO's list of oral and intangible world heritage.

El Silbo is still practised today – in some restaurants, bars and on some excursions you are treated to an El Silbo communiqué – best appreciated with earplugs or from a safe distance!

---

groves, above all, became important. More than any other island of the Archipelago, Date Palms and Canary Palms were planted on La Gomera. Today, over 120,000 palms grow in the island's valleys – they are all counted and protected as part of the identity of the island. The palms are used (though less than in previous times) for a variety of things, such as animal fodder and tools, but above all for the sugary sap *(guarapo)* of which palm syrup *(miel de palma)* is produced.

Recent history

Tenerife is a tourism island. The island's potential for tourism was discovered relatively early. Already by the late 19th century, a small tourism industry was developing around Puerto de la Cruz – remarkable, as this was well before the age of aeroplanes. The big attraction of Tenerife was the clean air and climate. In an early form of wellness tourism, tourists visited the island to recover from illnesses or to improve their health.

When commercial flights became affordable for a larger number of people, tourism took a huge leap forward and changed the face of the Canary Islands drastically. Tenerife and Gran Canaria were most affected. The perspective changed from medically inspired tourism to regular sun and sea worshipping. The big attraction of the Canaries in comparison to the Mediterranean are the year-round pleasing temperatures, making it the perfect escape from the dreary winter weather back home.

For this type of tourism, the southern side of the islands is better suited. With such an influx of tourism money, it was worth the investment of diverting water from the northern slopes to the new resorts in the south. A complex system of small channels reached deep into the most desert-like spots in the south.

With this new irrigation system in place, the level wastelands in the south were ready to be cultivated with a new crop: bananas! Bananas were actually one of the first crops brought back from South America and were grown on a small scale by the 16th or 17th century. The lower barranco valleys in northern Gomera and Tenerife offered good conditions to grow them, but these areas were small. In the south of Tenerife, there are large areas of more or less level terrain. With the aid of irrigation and nets that prevent evaporation, large banana plantations rose up in the south and south-west of the island. Together with the new Tenerife Sur airport and accompanying industry, this gives that part of Tenerife a rather shabby appearance. On the bright side though, Tenerife has preserved quite a lot of its charm in the north, because tourists mostly concentrate in the south.

Tenerife was not the only island that was booming in the 20th century – Gran Canaria was a main centre of commerce too. The rivalry between the cities of Las Palmas (Gran Canaria) and Santa Cruz (Tenerife) for the capital of the Canarias led to the division of the archipelago into two provinces in 1927 – the province of the eastern islands and that of the western islands, to which Tenerife and La Gomera belong.

After the establishment of a democratic government in Spain in 1978, the autonomous Community of the Canary Islands has its own president, its own parliament and two capitals (Las Palmas de Gran Canaria and Santa Cruz de Tenerife).

Over the last few decades, tourism has seen yet another spurt in growth. Two new developments are responsible for this. The rise of low-cost airlines, in combination with an increase of wealth of the middle classes, made a holiday to the Canaries available to the masses. This threatened to result in water shortage, but this problem was solved by new technology that desalinised sea water. With nothing standing in the way, tourism shot through the roof. This industry currently counts for 78% of Tenerife´s economy and nearly five million tourists visit the island every year.

With tourism came work and many *Canarios* that had moved to South America, migrated back to Tenerife. With a 36.7% growth in the period 1990 – 2010, the island saw the largest population increase in Spain. Apart from returning locals, pensionados from all over

Monocultures of bananas, partially covered in plastic to prevent evaporation, are both an important cash crop as well as a threat to the natural world.

Europe settled here and the Spanish from the Peninsula found work in the tourist industry.

La Gomera and El Hierro lie at the other end of the spectrum. Tourism largely passed by these islands, although La Gomera did develop a modest industry around green tourism, mainly for hikers. Being so close to Tenerife, many *Gomeros* moved to Tenerife (there are now more on Tenerife than on La Gomera) or commute between San Sebastian and Los Cristianos to work in the hotels.

Nature conservation

"Islands are evolutionary dead-end streets", wrote David Quammen in his book *Song of the Dodo*. On the one hand, it is where plants and animals evolve into unique species, and on the other, it is where they go extinct, because populations are too small and vulnerable.

Tenerife and La Gomera could not be better examples of this theory. Many species are restricted to such small areas that it wouldn't take much to wipe them off the face of the earth. Take the endemic Blue Chaffinch as an example: it is restricted to a single, large pine forest that clads the slopes of an active volcano, which is extremely susceptible to forest fires (such as those of 2023). That is asking for trouble. Clearly, the nature on Tenerife and La Gomera is very fragile.

If you consider the enormous number of tourists that fly in each year and set out to explore these fragile islands, it is quite amazing that so much of the original Canarian nature is still preserved. The situation on Tenerife is slightly different in this respect from that on La Gomera. Due to the size and topography, Tenerife has a more diverse nature, but La Gomera's ecosystems and landscapes are far more intact.

The relatively good state of the nature conservation is in part due to the rugged terrain that means large areas of land that are of little or no use to agriculture. It should also be appreciated though, that the necessity to conserve the unique nature of the Canary Islands was recognised at a fairly early stage. The Teide National Park was

Nature reserves on Tenerife and La Gomera. In dark green the National Parks of Cañadas del Teide and Garajonay. In light green all other reserves, like natural monuments, nature reserves and natural parks.

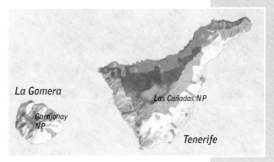

La Gomera

Garajonay NP

Las Cañadas NP

Tenerife

declared in 1954, well before the tourism boom. In 1981, the Garajonay National Park was established and in 1986 it was declared a World Heritage Site by the UNESCO.

The state of the laurel forests serves as an example of the difference between Tenerife and La Gomera. The current size of all Canarian laurel forests combined is roughly 16,500 ha. Of this, only about 6,000 ha are full-grown forests – the rest are secondary stands of scrub. On La Gomera, 52% of the original laurel forest remains, either as mature or as secondary woodland. On Tenerife, this figure is no more than 10%! The felling of laurel forest was stopped only recently, although since the 1950s the disturbance was relatively low.

A lot of nature conservation work was done in the 1980s, when comprehensive legislation was enforced roughly when mass tourism developed on the islands. Today, under the *Red Canaria de Espacios Naturales Protegidos* (protected areas network) there are 42 protected areas on Tenerife, amounting to granting 49% of the island some sort of protective status.

La Gomera designated 17 protected areas amounting to 33% of its surface. All waters surrounding La Gomera are included within the marine IBA (Important Bird Area) of La Gomera – Teno and seven marine areas around Tenerife fall under the EU Habitats Directive.

Economic development in these areas is mainly based on sustainable tourism and activities that are clearly damaging to nature are not allowed.

Time will tell if this is enough. Sadly, if any conclusions can be drawn from similar developments on comparable islands, the future does not look very bright. The island flora and fauna is too fragile.

Evolutionary naiveté is the term that describes the fragility of island flora and fauna best – species that evolved in relative isolation lost their fear, protective measures and competitive edge as they were of no evolutionary advantage in a world where no threats exist. They evolved to become ecologically naïve. The most helpless creatures became extinct in the early Guanche times: the dragon tree seed eating bird was flightless, the Giant Rat and the Giant Lizard had no natural enemies.

Today, one of the main problems are the invasive species. Weeds previously alien to the native flora, were brought in by visitors and tourists and are taking over from the native flora. The most eye-catching examples are Cape Sorrel from South America, Purple Viper's-bugloss from the Mediterranean and Prickly Pear (*Opuntia*) from Central America, which takes over in the succulent scrub.

The problem with invasive species is that they are competitively stronger than native species and are therefore capable of pushing them out. This usually happens after the soil is disturbed and the race for recolonising that patch begins. Therefore, vigorous growth of invasive species is often tied to disturbed areas.

Another threat (to Tenerife's nature in particular) is the relatively light protection of the coastal and succulent ecosystems. Like any other habitat, these are home to very special species, but somehow they have not been fully recognised as such. This area was never very attractive for human use, except for a bit of dry arable farming. Yet the combined developments of tourism resorts and irrigation methods for banana plantations make these fairly level areas suddenly of interest for development. Tourism is big business and the pressure is high to lift protection on sites like the Montaña Roja (site B on page 178) to develop it for tourism. As a result, many of these areas in southern Tenerife have been destroyed, bringing the populations of some desert birds – which never were very common here – to the brink of extinction.

El Medano, seen from the Montaña Roja nature reserve. Disturbance from tourism is a threat to this reserve, which boasts the only sandy semi-desert habitat and coastal lagoon of Tenerife.

FLORA AND FAUNA

The flora and fauna of the Canary Islands is unique in the world. As a result of isolation, a high number of species have evolved on the spot into distinct species or subspecies (see evolution chapter on page 24). Tenerife has the highest number of endemic species per square kilometre in the European Union, and La Gomera comes second! This is what makes the islands such exciting places for naturalists.

It is just one aspect that makes the islands unique. Another is the even, warm climate, dry on the southern slopes and moist on the north ones. This climate is not found in nearby areas on the continent, but is shared only with some other isolated, Atlantic Islands, namely those of the Salvages, Madeira, the Azores and the Cape Verde Islands. Together these islands form a distinct biological region, known as Macaronesia. A large number of species is found only on these islands – the Canary (the bird) is just one of many examples.

As the Macaronesian islands lie far apart, they are also isolated from one another. Only the Salvages and Madeira are fairly close to the Canaries, hence some species (Berthelot's Pipit for example) are shared only with these islands. Many more species occur only on the Canary Island archipelago, such as King Juba's Spurge (all Canary Islands), Bolle's and Laurel Pigeon (only Tenerife, La Gomera and La Palma) and Blue Chaffinch (Tenerife and Gran Canaria only). Often, these species occur on all of the islands where suitable habitat is present. Laurel forest species for example, are mainly shared between the western islands (El Hierro, La Palma, La Gomera and Tenerife) while the sub-alpine species of the caldera only occur on Tenerife and La Palma as these are the only islands high enough to sustain a montane ecosystem.

Some typical species of La Gomera and Tenerife have even smaller distribution ranges. This is most evident in the flora. La Gomera has its share of wildflowers that are unique to the island. These are mostly houseleeks, sow-thistles, viper's-buglosses, marguerites and pericallises – the plant groups that have seen an explosion of speciation. Separate species formed on each of the islands and often even split into different species for each ecosystem. Likewise, Tenerife has its own set of endemics. Some are even restricted to small areas on the island. Often these are either the Anaga mountains or the Teno mountains. The occurrence of these narrow endemics is not because the habitat is so radically

Monarch on a Rocket Viper's-bugloss*
(*Echium simplex*).
The flora and fauna of the Canary Islands consists largely of two extremes: local endemics that evolved on the spot (like the Rocket Viper's-bugloss) and cosmopolitans that are able to float in from the far corners of the world (like this Monarch Butterfly).

different there compared to elsewhere, but is better understood in the light of the geological history of Teno and Anaga. For millions of years, they were separate islands that only became connected when the Cañadas volcano laid down the lava that became the land bridge between the islands.
All these endemic species on Tenerife and La Gomera evolved from ancestral species that had to colonise the islands from somewhere. Both Europe and Africa provided the 'raw material' from which the Canarian flora and fauna emerged. The birds are clearly of European or North-African origin, with local variants of Chaffinches, Blue Tits, pigeons and Robins (see also page 29 and 93). Among the butterflies and the wildflowers there are some with more exotic lineages, such as the African tropics. The little Disc-leaved Fern* (*Adiantum reniforme*) is an example. A lot of those species were once much more widespread in the Tertiary era, when the climate was moister in southern Europe and North-Africa. Most, if not all the plants of the laurel forest originated from ancestral mainland species that long since became extinct there as the climate became drier. Only on the Macaronesian islands were they able to survive. Some have their closest relatives at the far southern or eastern end (tropical Africa or Asia) of the original range of the tertiary forests. A very good example is the Canary Pine, whose closest relative grows in the Himalayas.
After the colonisation by the Spanish, many new species were introduced to the Canary Islands. Most originate from the Mediterranean. A very common Mediterranean species is the Purple Viper's-bugloss which, together with the Cape Sorrel from South-Africa, can dominate in weedy fields. Stripeless Tree Frog and Iberian Water Frog are other widespread, introduced species. These introductions are cause of concern among conservationists, as these species can push out the native ones (see page 66).

The endemic wildlife can be quite inquisitive. Here an African Blue Tit exploring the remains of our espresso.

Mediterranean / European
Robin
(*Erithacus rubecula*)

Introduced
Stripeless Tree Frog
(*Hyla meridionalis*)

Tenerife

Macaronesia

La Gomera

Africa

Western islands endemic
Bolle's Pigeon
(*Columba bollii*)

African
Plain Tiger
(*Danaus chrysippus*)

North Tenerife endemic
Saucer-leaved Houseleek
(*Aeonium tabulaeforme*)

FLORA AND FAUNA

Flora

The succulent scrub and coastal flora is wonderful on routes 5, 9, 10, 11 and 12, and sites B on page 150 and A, B and D on page 178-180. North cliff flora is best explored on route 9, the Teno cliffs (on the way to site B (page 150) and site B on page 203. The flora of thermophilous woodlands and barrancos is best developed on routes 6, 7, 10, 13, 15 and 16, plus sites A on page 150 and F on page 153, sites A on 169 and F on 173 and sites I and L on pages 207-208. Wildflowers of the laurel forest are best enjoyed on routes 6, 8, 9, 13 and 14, and sites D, E, F and G on pages 204-206. For the flora of the Canary pine forest, route 1, 4 and site D on page 135 are excellent. Wildflowers of the subalpine zone are best enjoyed on routes 2 and 3 and site C on page 135.

The Canary Islands are sometimes called the *Galapagos of Botany* and justifiably so, as there are few places in the world where the flora has so many unique species, often with strange and exotic appearances. Within the archipelago, Tenerife and La Gomera combined have the most diverse flora. If wildflowers have your interest, then you've come to the right place. One word of warning though – there are so many endemic species that it may confuse and dazzle any first time visitor. As everything is new, many species are rare and a lot of them are spectacular, it becomes hard to focus. You may want to concentrate on a

The curious Brown Ceropegia (*Ceropegia fusca*) is one of the stranger wildflowers of the Canary Islands. The skeletal appearance of grey, jointed sticks sport dark red flowers after rains in spring. It grows on young lava and is – as so many other species – endemic to the Canary Islands.

few of the most interesting groups of species first (e.g. spurges, houseleeks, sow-thistles and viper's-buglosses). We've given these additional attention in the description that follows.

Endemism is what the flora of these islands is all about – species that occur only in a single spot. Biologists have pondered why some areas are more blessed with endemic wildflowers than others. They have discovered two very different mechanisms that cause endemism.

Many centres of endemism are the last remnants of a specific habitat that was once much more widespread. For a variety of reasons (many of which are related to us humans) species have disappeared everywhere, except in that last remaining locality. Such areas are like museums of relict species. Many of our protected sites and National Parks are exactly that – the final retreat of a natural world that elsewhere belongs to the past.

The other cause of hotspots of endemism is precisely the opposite. In certain isolated places, where plants arrive by chance, evolution works rapidly. The limited gene pool and different environmental condition forms the perfect recipe to create new species (see page 24). Such places are the power houses of diversity – factories of new species.

These two types of hotspots seem to be mutually exclusive – an area is either a museum of nature of the past, or it is a factory of new species. There are very few places in the world which are both. One of these are the Canary Island archipelago.

The Canaries, being isolated volcanic islands in the Atlantic, gave rise to a large variety of species which only occur here (see page 24). The superb, tall viper's-buglosses, the odd-shaped houseleeks and sow-thistles are unique to the Canary Islands. They evolved on the spot.

The museum element lies in the steady, moist, subtropical climate of the northern slopes of the islands, with their frequent fog and rain. In the tertiary period (before the series of ice ages) such environments were widespread across the Mediterranean basin and Near East (which had a

---

The odd plant world

The first thing that will strike is that plants frequently look radically different from the plants back home. Some have abnormally large flower stalks (e.g. Teide Viper's-bugloss). Others have grotesquely swollen stems out of which a flimsy bush of leaves emerges. Plants that would elsewhere have a basal rosette of leaves, suddenly sprout from a stick a metre high, while many species you know from Europe as a herb, have supersized into a bush – spurges, viper's-buglosses, sow thistles and bindweeds, are all shrubs or even small trees.

different shape and position back then). However, the climate changed throughout this area, except on the Atlantic islands of the Canaries, Madeira and the Azores. The entire laurel cloud forest ecosystem, including the bulk of its species, are relicts of a tertiary subtropical flora. Hence the Canary islands are an amazing place for wildflowers, with Tenerife and La Gomera the jewels in the Canary crown. The title *Galapagos of botany* is more than justified.

The wildflower hotspots of Tenerife and La Gomera

Stonecrops grow in abundance and in many varieties on Tenerife and La Gomera. This is the Loose-flowered Monanthes (Monanthes laxiflora), which frequents barranco walls.

Wildflower hotspots

In the first hours, or perhaps even days, that you spend on Tenerife or La Gomera, any place is a hotspot. Even an abandoned field close to the coast has Canarian attractions like Canary Aizoon, Shrubby Launaea, iceplants and Small-leaved Sea-lavender* *(Limonium pectinatum)*. On the motorway, you'll pass hectare after hectare of scrub full of the curious succulent plants, while any stone wall in the north will offer you a collection of Canarian specialities.

After a couple of days, you'll discover that such places usually produce the same set of species. Many of the rare and local endemics concentrate around a few botanical hotspots. Some of these are:

1. **Anaga Mountains** Particularly the barrancos and cliffs in the north have a high diversity, including a score of endemic species like the impressive Rocket Viper's-bugloss* *(Echium simplex)* – see page 68. The laurel forests of Anaga sport most of the unique species of this habitat. The many trails make this area relatively easy to explore (e.g. route 9 and 11).

2. **Guïmar cliffs** The massive cliffs and barranco of Guïmar are the result of a land slide that followed when the old Cañadas volcano collapsed (see page 18). The cliffs and valley sport a remnant laurel forest, which includes some endemic species that occur only in this valley. Unfortunately, there are no way-marked trails.

3. Esperanza forest The laurel forest of Esperanza grows on a cliff of simi-lar origin to the Güímar cliffs. There are various trails but they are all long and strenuous.

4. Teno mountains and barrancos This is perhaps the richest botanical region of Tenerife. The best parts are the north-facing cliffs, the laurel forests near Erjos and the barrancos (in particular the Barranco de Masca and Barranco de Cuevas Negras). Although many parts of Teno are hard to explore, those trails that do exist are a heaven for botanists (e.g. routes 6, 7, 8 and site A and B on page 150).

5. Cañadas del Teide The high altitude zone of the Cañadas is less diverse in species, but has the highest rate of endemics. Nearly all plants are either endemic to the Cañadas crater or shared only with the summits of the Canary Island of La Palma. The richest parts are around the crater rim at La Fortaleza (route 2) and Montaña de Guajara south of the Parador (site C on page 135). There are plenty of easy trails in the Cañadas.

6. Barranco del Infierno This easily explored barranco combines the widespread flora of the southern succulent scrub with a variety of bar-ranco species, including several endemic species of southwest Tenerife (site E on page 180).

The Gomera Blue Viper's-bugloss (*Echium acantho-carpum*) is locally common in clearings in the high parts of the Garajonay National Park.

7. Agulo and Vallehermoso The north-facing cliffs and slopes of La Gomera host many inter-esting species, ranging from Leafless Spurge to local endem-ic Cabbage-leaved Sea-lavender* *(Limonium brassicifolium).* Various trails near the villages enable you to explore the area.

8. Laurel forests of El Cedro and el Bailadero This is the largest laurel forest, with numerous wildflowers, including impres-sive endemics like Spoon-leaved Houseleek* *(Aeonium subplanum)* and Gomera Blue Viper's-bugloss* *(Echium acan-thocarpum).* There are plenty of trails in this area (e.g. route 14 and sites D, E, F and G on pages 204-206).

The wildflower season

The Canary islands are famed as the islands of eternal spring. Since spring is the season of wildflowers, this phrase fuels the expectation of a non-stop wildflower show...

Tenerife and La Gomera live up to this promise – at least to a large degree. Many species of wildflowers bloom over a long period and a good number always have a few specimens in flower outside the main flowering season. We've found Hedgehog-Pericallis* (*Pericallis echinata*) which usually starts flowering in January, in flower in November. We even found Canary Foxglove in bloom in November, while its season is from April to July!

This being said, the wildflowers in bloom do change during the course of the year. Autumn and winter (mid-October to early February) is an excellent season in the lower parts of the islands (up to the laurel cloud forests). It is the season for several of the orchids, for the wildflowers of the succulent scrub, the Canary Bellflower and, on La Gomera, the Gomera Blue Viper's-bugloss *(Echium acanthocarpum)*. Springtime (March-May) brings out many new wildflowers in the barrancos, such as sea-lavenders *(Limonium)*, spurges *(Euphorbia)*, the Ceropegia's and most of the Viper's-buglosses *(Echium)*. Higher up, rockroses start to bloom and later on, the Teide Viper's-bugloss. Also, several species of houseleeks flower in this period.

Late spring and early summer brings out many more houseleeks and a score of wildflowers in the Cañadas, but in August, these gradually finish. The islands are at their driest in late summer and early September, which is when the flora is least abundant. But not for long. In early October, the new season starts, heralded by the beautiful Canary Sea-daffodil.

The Hedgehog Pericallis* *(Pericallis echinata)* is one of the wildflowers which, although it has its prime flowering season in spring, can also be seen in bloom at other times of the year.

Flora of the coast and succulent scrub

The coast and the zone up to roughly 200 (on north-facing cliffs) to 700 metres (on south-facing slopes) is the realm of the drought-adapted flora. Many plant species are succulents: plants with thick stems and leaves that store moisture. Fleshy species of spurges *(Euphorbia)* dominate most of these lowland vegetations.

The succulent scrub is the first vegetation type you will see from up close, as the Tenerife Sur airport is situated within this vegetation zone. It is a vegetation well worth exploring, because many of the archetypical and very recognisable Canarian plants are found here.

The area under direct influence of salt spray is rather poor in species, but those that occur are unique to this zone. The dark lava is brightened with the yellowish leaves of the Canary Sea Fennel and the greyish, dome-like bushes of the Balsam Spurge. Between these bushes, hugging the ground, you may find Canary Aizoon, Common and Small-leaved Iceplant* *(Mesembryanthemum nodiflorum)* and Sea-heath.

Away from the direct influence of the sea, the lower slopes of Tenerife and La Gomera are covered with bushes of succulent plants, many of which are unique to the Canary islands. Spurges are particularly dominant here. In addition to the aforementioned Balsam Spurge (small, oval leaves), the Blunt-leaved Spurge (long, blunt-tipped leaves) and King Juba's Spurge (even longer, pointy-tipped leaves) and Canary Spurge (cactus-like, no leaves) occur on Tenerife. Some botanists class the spurges on La Gomera as different species to those on Tenerife, even though they look rather similar.

Teno Scrub-knapweed* *(Cheirolophus canariensis)* is confined to the cliffs of Teno.

Another very common plant is the Verode *(Kleinia neriifolia)*, a thick-stemmed miniature 'tree' that is a member of the daisy family. Like the spurges it produces a milky substance when the leaves or stems are bruised.

Other frequent species are Plocama (a large bush, endemic to the Canaries and belonging to the madder family), Canary Silk-vine, Canary Boxthorn and Shrubby Launaea. On recent lava fields *(Malpaís)* the vegetation is rather poor, but it is here that you'll find a very peculiar plant, endemic to Tenerife, La Palma and Gran Canaria: the Brown Ceropegia. It forms a bush of grey, leafless sticks, which, after rains in the winter time, produces bundles of dark-red flowers.

Leafless Spurge
(*Euphorbia aphyllum*;
top) and Viera (*Viera
laevigata*; bottom)
are two rare species
typical of north-facing
cliffs.

The succulent scrub on the rocky northern slopes of the Anaga and Teno mountains on Tenerife, and the northern slopes of La Gomera is quite different. They form one of the botanical hotspots on the islands. The old basalt formations, stemming from the tertiary era, harbour many species with a very small range. Many are endemic either to La Gomera's or Tenerife's northern slopes, or even to just a few mountain slopes on either of the islands. These sites are virtually impossible to reach or involve long and perilous hikes. But there are some easy routes (like route 5 and site B on page 150) on which you'll be able to find rarities like Leafless Spurge (a small bushy succulent without leaves, endemic to the central Canary islands), Teno Scrub-knapweed* (*Cheirolophus canariensis*; a tall bush with pretty pink flower heads, endemic to the Teno mountains), Viera (endemic to Tenerife) and Lugoa (a marguerite-like species endemic to the Anaga mountains).

Many of the above are members of the daisy family, but the north-facing slopes and cliffs are rich in rare sea-lavenders as well. Some again have ridiculously small ranges. The Large-leaved Sea-lavender* (*Limonium macrophyllum*) grows on rocks above the water line on Anaga and nowhere else in the world. The same holds true for the Shrubby Sea-lavender* (*Limonium fruticans*), which is restricted to similar sites on Teno. It is a spectacular plant of half a metre tall. On La Gomera, there is even a species, the Tree Sea-lavender* (*Limonium dendroides*) that grows up to 3 metres. The northern slopes are also the home of some interesting, very localised houseleeks, like the odd Saucer-leaved Houseleek* (*Aeonium tabulaeforme*; endemic to northern Tenerife), Stonecrop-leaved Houseleek *(Aeonium sedifolium)* and Lindley's Houseleek (*Aeonium lindleyi*; endemic to to the Anaga mountains).

Some conspicuous plants
Rocky sea shores Canary Sea Fennel (*Astydamia latifolia*), Balsam Spurge (*Euphorbia balsamifera*), Leafless Spurge (*Euphorbia aphylla*)[can], Canary Aizoon (*Aizoon canariense*), Common Iceplant (*Mesembryanthemum crystallinum*), Small-leaved Iceplant* (*Mesembryanthemum nodiflorum*), Sea-heath species (*Frankenia ssp*), Crystal Reichardia (*Reichardia crystallina*)[T], Teno Scrub-knapweed* (*Cheirolophus canariensis*)[T], Schizogyne (*Schizogyne sericea*)[mac], Lugoa (*Gonospermum revolutum*)[T]
Succulent scrub Balsam Spurge (*Euphorbia balsamifera*), Lamarck's Spurge (*Euphorbia lamarckii*)[T], Canary Spurge (*Euphorbia canariensis*)[can], Canary Boxthorn (*Lycium intricatum*), Shrubby Launaea (*Launaea arborescens*), Moon Dock (*Rumex lunaria*)[can], Canary Lavender (*Lavandula canariensis*)[mac], Small-leaved Sea-lavender* (*Limonium pectinatum*)[can], Hair-leaved Sowthistle* (*Sonchus capillaris*)[T], Shrubby Marguerite (*Argyranthemum frutescens*)[can], Brown Ceropegia (*Ceropegia fusca*)[T+P+GC], Justice Bush* (*Justicia hyssopifolia*)[T+G], Prickly Pear (*Opuntia spec.*), Canary Silk-vine (*Periploca laevigata*)[can], Plocama (*Plocama pendula*)[can], Bonnet's Viper's-bugloss (*Echium bonnetii*)[can], Pastor's Asparagus (*Asparagus pastorianus*)[mac]

mac = Macaronesian endemic; can = Canarian endemic; T, G, P, GC, H = Tenerife, La Gomera, La Palma, Gran Canaria and El Hierro respectively

Flora of thermophilous woods and barrancos
The climatically more benign thermophilous woods sport a very rich flora. Sadly, the original woodlands have disappeared in many places. In particular on Tenerife much of this habitat has been converted to allotments, where many of the original wildflowers of the evergreen woods found an alternative home on stone walls and in neglected corners.
This is the vegetation zone of the Dragon Tree, the Canary Palm and the realm of a large number of houseleeks that stick their fleshy disks out from between rock cracks, stone piles, terrace walls and even from between old roof tiles. In particular Tree (*Aeonium arboreum ssp. holochrysum*) and Rooftop Houseleeks* (*Aeonium urbicum*) are common, both of which are

stout species. On shady walls, the smaller Hairy Aichryson is frequent – one of the few houseleeks with downy leaves. Various sow-thistles grow alongside the houseleeks. On Tenerife the Stemless Sow-thistle is common. It has a giant, Dandelion-like rosette with a flower stalk of a metre or more high. The Canary Tree Sow-thistle is even larger, reaching over 3 metres. On La Gomera the Sow-thistles are represented by Gomera* (*Sonchus gomerensis*) and Hierro Sow-thistles* (*Sonchus hierriensis*).

The thermophilous woods form dense tangles of various species of shrubs. Again, shrubby relatives of familiar European herbs are frequent. As examples may serve the Willow-leaved Carline Thistle (a woody carline thistle of 2 m tall), Tree Bindweed, Canary St. John's-wort (up to 4 metres) and Dark-red Spurge.

This is also the realm of the bulk of the viper's-buglosses, in particular on Tenerife. Broad-leaved Viper's-bugloss* (*Echium strictum*) has wide leaves and pale blue flowers and prefers the barrancos. Giant Viper's-bugloss *(Echium giganteum)* is a tall bush with white flower clusters, endemic to Tenerife. The Anaga mountains host two other species: the Anaga Viper's-bugloss* (*Echium leucophaeum*) and the splendid Rocket Viper's-bugloss* (*Echium simplex*), which is like the Teide Viper's-bugloss, but with white flowers. The Rough-leaved Viper's-bugloss* (*Echium aculeatum*), recognisable by the spiny leave edges, is the only one that occurs on both islands.

Tree Bindweed (*Convolvulus floridus*) is a common species of the thermophile woodland.

Another group of wildflowers you will frequently encounter here are the Pericallises
– a group related to the ragworts *(Senecio)*
with purple or white flower heads. This
genus is endemic to the Macaronesian
islands. Of a total of 14 species, 12 occur
on the Canaries, of which 6 are found on
Tenerife and 4 on La Gomera. You'll find
Colt's-foot Pericallis* *(Pericallis tussilaginis)* and Hedgehog Pericallis* *(Pericallis
echinata)* frequently along roadsides.

Some conspicuous plants
Thermophilous woodland Dark-red Spurge
(Euphorbia atropurpurea)[T], Willow-leaved
Carline Thistle *(Carlina salicifolia)*[mac], Sea
Rosemary *(Campylanthus salsoloides)*[can],
Ceballosia *(Ceballosia fruticosa)*[can], Tree
Bindweed *(Convolvulus floridus)*[can], Rough-
leaved Viper's-bugloss* *(Echium aculeatum)*[can],
Giant Viper's-bugloss *(Echium giganteum)*[T],
Rocket Viper's-bugloss* *(Echium simplex)*[T],
Broad-leaved Viper's-bugloss* *(Echium strictum)*[can], Stemless Sow-thistle
(Sonchus acaulis)[T+GC], Canary Tree Sow-thistle *(Sonchus canariensis)*[T+GC],
Small-headed Sow-thistle* *(Sonchus leptocephalus)*[can], Dragon Tree *(Dracaena
draco)*[mac], Three-fingered Orchid *(Habenaria tridactylitis)*[can], Canary Dragon
Arum *(Dracunculus canariensis)*[can]

Walls, barrancos and cliffs Canary Houseleek *(Aeonium canariense)*[T], La
Palma Houseleek *(Aeonium palmense)*[G+P], Tree Houseleek *(Aeonium arbore-
um)*[can], Rooftop Houseleek* *(Aeonium urbicum)*[can], Loose-flowered Houseleek*
(Aeonium decorum)[G], Golden Greenovia *(Greenovia aurea)*[can], Saucer-leaved
Houseleek *(Aeonium tabulaeforme)*[T], Lindley's Houseleek *(Aeonium lindleyi)*[T],
Monanthes species[can], Hairy Aichryson *(Aichryson laxum)*[can], Cross-leaved St.
John's-wort* *(Hypericum reflexum)*[can], Bosea Laurel* *(Bosea yervamora)*[can],
Red Rock Mallow* *(Lavatera phoenicea)*[T], Wild Jasmin *(Jasminum oderatissi-
mus)*, Yellow Ceropegia *(Ceropegia dichotoma)*[can], Willow-leaved Globularia*
(Globularia salicina)[mac], Viera *(Vieraea laevigata)*[T], Woolly Pericallis*
(Pericallis lanata)[T], Colt's-foot Pericallis* *(Pericallis tussilaginis)*[T+GC], Cliff
Sow-thistle* *(Sonchus radicatus)*[T], Canary Squill *(Scilla haemorrhoidalis)*[can],
Broad-leaved Squill *(Scilla latifolia)*[mac], Brown Bluebell *(Dipcadi serotinum)*,
Canary Sea-daffodil *(Pancratium canariense)*[can], Allagopappus *(Allagopappus
canariensis)*[can]

Tree Houseleek
*(Aeonium arboreum
holochrysum)* –
a common plant of
rocks and stone walls
of northern Tenerife.

The Dragon Tree

According to legend the eleventh Labour of Hercules was to steal the 'golden apples' from the garden of the Hesperides located in the far west. To do so he had to kill the hundred-headed dragon, Ladon, that guarded the tree. As the beast died, trees miraculously sprang into being from the blood-soaked ground. The Canaries stand on the western rim of the ancient world and there

is found a distinctly strange tree that looks like no other. Stranger still, when wounded it 'bleeds' blood-red sap so it's scarcely surprising that they became known as the Dragon Tree and its genus *Dracaena* (from the Greek for dragon). The Dragon Tree is one of the Canary Island's most conspicuous native plants. The thick trunk and odd, umbrella-shaped canopy gives it an iconic appearance, which is why it has become a symbol of Tenerife. The oldest living specimen is the '1000 years old' Dragon Tree of Icod de los Vinos on Tenerife, which is a tourist attraction in itself (site D on page 152).

The Dragon Tree has (recently) been classified as belonging to the family of the Asparagus which is part of the large and diverse order of the lilies. It grows very slowly and can become very old. Precisely how old is unknown, as unlike 'true' trees it doesn't produce yearly rings. In fact the impressive 'cabled' trunk of old specimens is a result of aerial roots that grow down along the stem from the canopy into the ground. However, a good estimate can be made by the number of branches in the canopy. In a cycle of about 15 years, the tree produces a spike of flowers, after which it branches and grows further to the next cycle. By this method, the Icod Dragon tree has an estimated age of 'just' 300 years. The explorer von Humboldt (see history section) described another, much older Dragon Tree that was used by the Guanches as a shrine. Sadly, it was destroyed in a storm in 1868.

The Dragon Tree is endemic to the Canaries, Cape Verde Islands and a small area in Morocco, although there are relatives all over the world's tropics.

On Tenerife, Dragon Trees are frequently planted, but have become very rare in the wild. The reason behind its scarcity is not fully understood but one important theory involves an extinct bird. It is thought the seeds could only germinate after having passed the bird's gut.

The iconic Dragon Tree of Icod de los Vinos

Laurel cloud forest zone

The laurel cloud forest (*lauriselva* or *monte verde* in Spanish) is of great interest because it consists of species that are relicts of a once widespread forest that now is restricted to the western Canary islands, Madeira and the Azores.

The tall laurel trees largely belong to four species. The Canary Laurel (*Laurus novocanariensis*) is the most widespread and common one. Stink Laurel (*Ocotea foetens*) and Indian Laurel* (*Persea indica*) are common in the wettest areas, while Barbusano Laurel* (*Apallonias barbujana*) dominates the drier forest.

Other, less common species of the laurel forest are Heberdenia and Pleiomeris. They are not members of the laurel family, but of a group of tropical trees known as *Myrsinacea*. The leaves are very much like those of the laurels, being leathery and with smooth edges. The same goes for the Portuguese Laurel (*Prunus lusitanica*), a thick-leaved member of the cherry family.

Epiphytes – plants growing on tree branches – are a common feature of the laurel forest. Here, Hare's-foot Fern (*Davallia canariensis*) and Loose-flowered Monanthes (*M. laxiflora*) share a branch of a Canary Laurel.

The Honey Spurge* (*Euphorbia mellifera*) is the only spurge in the laurel forest and the only tree-sized member of the group (reaching up to 15 metres). It has now become very rare. With the exception of the Portuguese Laurel, all these species are endemic to the Macaronesian region.

The laurel cloud forest is also the realm of the ferns. The tall leaves of Woodwardia, the shade-loving Lady Fern, the Guanche Buckler-fern* (*Dryopteris guanchica*) and Canary Male-fern add to the jungle-like appearance of the forest. The Hare's-foot Fern is very common. It is a climber whose thick rhizomes with hair-like scales wrap around branches and creep through the cracks of rocks. It is locally joined, on shady rocks, by the odd Disc-leaved Fern* (*Adiantum reniforme*), Ivy-leaved Spleenwort* (*Asplenium hemionitis*) and Golden Rustyback Fern* (*Asplenium aureum*).

The laurel cloud forest is also home to some breath-taking wildflowers, but these mostly grow along roadsides, in clearings and on rocky outcrops. These are all places that benefit from the damp air of the forest, but also from light which is often in short supply in the deep forest.

Some conspicuous plants of the laurel forests

Trees and tall bushes Glandular St. John's-wort (*Hypericum glandulosum*)^mac, *Visnea mocanera*^mac, Canary Gale* (*Myrica faya*)^mac, Canary Laurel (*Laurus novocanariensis*)^can, Barbusano Laurel* (*Apollonias barbujana*)^mac, Indian Laurel*

(*Persea indica*)^mac, Stink Laurel (*Ocotea foetens*)^mac, Portuguese Laurel (*Prunus lusitanica*), Honey Spurge (*Euphorbia mellifera*)^mac, Maytenus *canariensis*^can, Canary Ivy (*Hedera canariensis*)^mac, Tree Heath (*Erica arborea*), Besom Heath (*Erica scoparia*), Canary Strawberry Tree (*Arbutus canariensis*)^can, Heberdenia (*Heberdenia excelsa*)^mac, Pleiomeris (*Pleiomeris canariensis*)^can, Picconia excelsa^mac, Canary Laurustinus (*Viburnum rigidum*)^can, Canary Elder (*Sambucus nigra palmensis*)^can

Herbs Disc-leaved Fern* (*Adiantum reniforme*), Macaronesian Polypody (*Polypodium macaronesicum*), Ivy-leaved Spleenwort (*Asplenium hemionitis*), Golden Rustyback Fern* (*Asplenium aureum*)^mac, Diplazium (*Diplazium caudatum*), Canary Male-fern (*Dryopteris oligodonta*), Hare's-foot Fern (*Davallia canariensis*), Woodwardia (*Woodwardia radicans*), Canary Buttercup (*Ranunculus cortusifolius*)^mac, Laurel Sea-kale* (*Crambe strigosa*)^can, Gomera Sea-kale (*Crambe gomerae*)^G, Pyramidal Houseleek* (*Aeonium cuneatum*)^T, Spoon-leaved Houseleek* (*Aeonium subplanum*)^G, Hairy Aichryson (*Aichryson laxum*)^can, Bush-burnet (*Bencomia caudata*)^can, Canary Crane's-bill (*Geranium reuteri*)^can, Canary Foxglove (*Isoplexis canariensis*)^T+G+P, Gomera Blue Viper's-bugloss (*Echium acanthocarpum*)^G, Canary Ironwort (*Sideritis canariensis*)^T, Canary Balm (*Cedronella canariensis*)^mac, Canary St. John's-wort (*Hypericum canariense*)^mac, Laurel Forest Gentian* (*Ixanthus viscosus*)^can, Noble Bush-madder* (*Phyllis nobla*)^mac, Broussonet's Marguerite (*Argyranthemum broussonetii*)^T+G, Hedgehog Pericallis* (*Pericallis echinata*)^T, Perfoliate Pericallis* (*Pericallis steetzii*)^G, Bloody Pericallis* (*Pericallis cruenta*)^can, Laurel Forest Sow-thistle* (*Sonchus congestus*)^T+GC, Hierro Sow-thistle* (*Sonchus hierrensis*)^G+P+H, Canary Smilax (*Smilax canariensis*)^mac, Climbing Butcher's-broom (*Semele androgyna*)^mac, Two-leaved Gennaria (*Gennaria diphylla*)

Ivy-leaved Spleenwort (*Asplenium hemionitis;* top) and Canary Foxglove (*Isoplexis canariensis;* bottom) are two typical species of the laurel forest.

In winter and early spring, the large (up to 7 centimetres long), bright orange bells of the Canary Bellflower are one of the highlights (page 4). It is a climbing plant that covers rocks and trees, and is frequent along trails. In the summer months, the Canary Foxglove, also with orange flowers, is another spectacular species. Very common are Canary Crane's-bill and Canary Buttercup.

Locally, the endemic Three-fingered Orchid (small and green) grows on moist rocky places and old walls. Another small green orchid, the Two-leaved Gennaria, forms large drifts, especially in the higher zone, dominated by Tree Heath and Canary Gale* *(Myrica faya)*. Rocky places inside this woodland type sport Canary Orchid and various houseleeks and greenovias (a genus of houseleeks). On La Gomera, these are the sites for the spectacular endemics Spoon-leaved Houseleek *(Aeonium subplanum)* and Gomera Blue

Orchids

With only 7 species, the orchids are one group that is not well-represented on the islands. All of them grow in the wetter parts in barrancos and laurel forests. The most numerous and widespread is the Three-fingered Orchid *(Habenaria tridactylitis)*, a small, green-flowered Canarian endemic of a genus that has many species in Africa and America, but not in Europe. It grows mostly on shady walls and cliffs and flowers from November to January. Two-leaved Gennaria (another small, green-flowered species) is locally common in the laurel forests and Tree Heath zone. It flowers from January to March. Another winter species is the extremely rare and localised Tenerife Giant Orchid* *(Himantoglossum metlesicsiana)*, which is confined to a few valleys around Santiago del Teide on Tenerife. From March to April, the pink Canary Orchid *(Orchis canariensis)* flowers on moist, rocky forest clearings.

The other orchids are Dense-flowered, Bumblebee and Small-flowered Tongue Orchid. They are all listed for both islands, but seem to be rare.

The Two-leaved Gennaria is a small orchid that sometimes forms large drifts in the upper laurel forest zone. There are thousands of them at los Barranquillos (site E on page 205).

Viper's-bugloss *(Echium acanthocarpum)*. The massive specimens of Tree Heath are amazing. Those who've seen this species in the Mediterranean, may remember it as a very tall bush. On Tenerife and La Gomera, this heath species grows out to a real tree, with trunks over a metre in diametre.

Canary pine forest zone

Apart from the endemic Canary Pine, the typical plant of the pine forests is the pink-flowered Canary Cistus. It can cover the entire forest floor, especially in the lower parts of the forest, where it meets with the Tree Heath (northern slopes) and succulent evergreen bush-forest (southern slopes). In such places keep an eye out for the parasitic Pink Hypocist, a small bundle of pink flowers growing on the roots of the cistus. The cistus shares its habitat with brooms and some bushes belonging to the bush-mints, genus *Bystropogon*.

In general the pine forests are rather poor in plant species, although there are a couple of attractive species to be found. In particular the lower, more open and moister parts of the forest are the richer wildflower haunts. This is where you may find various mountain teas, several species of endemic marguerites, and where houseleeks reach their altitudinal limit with Spade-leaved Houseleek* *(Aeonium spathulatum)* and Smith's

The Spade-leaved Houseleek *(Aeonium spathulatum)* is a common sight on rocks in north-facing pine forests. Together with Smith's Houseleek *(A. smithii)*, it is the only one that reaches so high into the mountain.

Houseleek *(A. smithii)* on the northern and southern slopes respectively. Moist rock slopes on the north side are the haunt of the rather uncommon Canary Orchid.

Another frequent pine forest plant is the stout Greenish Viper's-bug-loss* *(Echium viriscens)*, which is endemic to Tenerife.

Towards the upper zone of the Canary pine forest, the wildflower haunts are in the barrancos, where quite a few of the species of the subalpine zone intrude the forest zone.

Some conspicuous plants of the pine forests

Canary Cistus (*Cistus symphytifolius*)[can], Narrow-leaved Cistus (*Cistus mon-speliensis*), Large-flowered White Broom* (*Chamaecytisus proliferus*)[can], Leafy Broom* (*Adenocarpus foliolosus*)[can], Spade-leaved Houseleek* (*Aeonium spathulatum*)[can], Smith's Houseleek* (*Aeonium smithii*)[T], Golden Greenovia (*Greenovia aurea*)[can], Link's Fennel (*Ferula linkii*)[can], Greenish Viper's-bugloss* (*Echium viriscens*)[T], Tenerife Ironwort (*Sideritis orotener-iffae*)[T], Southern Ironwort* (*Sideritis soluta*)[T], *Bystropogon canariensis*[can], *Bystropogon origanifolius*[can], Vincent's Marguerite (*Argyranthemum vincen-tii*)[T], Graceful Marguerite (*Argyran-themum gracile*)[T], Pinewood Marguerite* (*Argyranthemum adauctum*)[T], Canary Orchid (*Orchis canariensis*)[can]

Subalpine zone

The Subalpine zone – the region of Tenerife that lies within the crater rim of the Cañadas del Teide – consist largely of endemic plants. Climatically, it is an island within the island which is why many species here are either unique to this part of Tenerife, or are shared with the island of La Palma – the only other Canary island which tops 2,000 metres. The flower season kicks off in March, with the pink Teide Wallflower *(Erisymum scoparium)*. Between May and July, the Cañadas are at their finest. Tenerife's most iconic wildflower, the Teide Viper's-bugloss *(Echium wildpretii)* flowers here at this time of year. It has a single inflorescence that grows up to 3 metres tall, with hundreds or even thousands of dark red flowers – a truly impressive plant. It is endemic to Tenerife and La Palma. Another viper's-bugloss, which is much rarer and has bright blue flowers, is the Auber's Viper's-bugloss* *(Echium auberianum)*. It is endemic to the caldera where it prefers tuff-stone areas.

Another highlight of this altitude zone are the dome-like Teide Brooms. When not in flower, their smooth forms look alien in the barren landscape. Its flowering season is in May and June and coincides with that of two other very common bushes: the Teide Scrub-scabious* *(Pterocephalus lasiospermus)* and Teide Flixweed *(Descurainia bourgeauana)*. In summer, when these plants have mostly finished, the yellow-flowered Teide Scrub-knapweed* *(Cheirolophus teydis)* comes into flower.

The branches of the Sticky Broom *(Adenocarpus visco-sus)* are tightly packed with small, sticky leaves. It is a typical plant of the Cañadas. Its close relative, the Leafy Broom* *(A. foliolosus)*, grows at lower altitudes.

The world distribution of the Teide Viper's-bugloss is confined to the Cañadas del Teide on Tenerife and the Caldera de Taburiente on La Palma.

The richest wildflower haunts are near and on cliffs. The entire eastern crater wall and the rock formation La Fortaleza in the north, are especially rich. The least diverse are the young lava fields and the slopes of the Teide and Pico Viejo.

As you climb up the slopes of the Teide, the landscape becomes more barren. Here only one species does well – the Teide Pansy, a pretty violet that is endemic to the Teide Volcano. It flowers in April and May and is found up to an altitude of 3500 m, although it prefers the base of the volcano – an altitude of about 2500 m.

Some conspicuous wildflowers of the Cañadas:
Teide Flixweed (*Descurainia bourgeauana*)[T], Teide Wallflower (*Erysimum scoparium*)[T], Teide Pansy (*Viola cheiranthifolia*)[T], Teide Broom (*Spartocytisus supranubius*)[T+P], Sticky Broom (*Adenocarpus viscosus*)[can], Teide Cistus* (*Cistus osbaekiaefolius*)[T], Teide Viper's-bugloss (*Echium wildpretii*)[T+P], Auber's Viper's-bugloss (*Echium auberianum*)[T], Teide Catmint (*Nepeta teydea*)[T+P], Teide Mint* (*Micromeria lachnophylla*)[T], Glabrous Figwort (*Scrophularia glabrata*)[T+P], Teide Marguerite (*Argyranthemum tenerifae*)[T], Teide Carline Thistle* (*Carlina xeranthemoides*)[T], Stemmacantha (*Stemmacantha cynaroides*)[T], Teide Scrub-knapweed* (*Cheirolophus teydis*)[can], Teide Scrub-scabious* (*Pterocephalus lasiospermus*)[T]

Mammals

Organised tours and ferry crossings are the best way to see dolphins and pilot whales (route 12, 13, site G on page 154, site A on page 203 and N on page 209. Bats are best seen in woodland clearings and near reservoirs.

Except for bats, all land mammals of Tenerife and La Gomera present today are introduced species. They include the Algerian Hedgehog, Rabbit, Black Rat, Brown Rat, House Mouse, Etruscan Pygmy Shrew and Mouflon. The only native land mammal, a very large species of rat, became extinct a long time ago (see page 90).
The Algerian Hedgehog and Etruscan Pygmy Shrew are most abundant in scrub and gardens at low altitudes. The latter has some fame for being the smallest and lightest mammal of the world – weighing only 1.8 grams! Neither species occurs on La Gomera. Black Rat, Brown Rat and House Mouse occur on both islands. They are common in towns and villages. Rabbits were introduced for hunting and still are important game animals, which is why they are so shy. They are widespread on both islands. The Mouflon was also introduced as game animal. In the 1970s, it was released in the Cañadas, where it is now a threat for the unique vegetation. Several herds still live in the central part of Tenerife. Fences have been erected to avoid damage while periodically, hunting campaigns control the population.

Bats
The isolation of the ocean-born islands has less effect on bats because they can fly. Seven species are found on Tenerife and four on La Gomera. Most are difficult to find, but if you have an ultrasonic bat detector with you, visit the small reservoirs at night. Bats come down here to pick up water from the surface in flight.
The small Madeira Pipistrelle is the most abundant bat. It lives on both islands and uses a variety of shelters, such as cracks, buildings and hollow trees in a wide range of habitats from sea level up to 2150 metres. Madeira Pipistrelle prefers foraging over reservoirs, woodland and farmland. The very similar Kuhl's Pipistrelle is possibly present on Tenerife too. Savi's Pipistrelle occurs on both islands and is a woodland species, just like Barbastelle and Lesser Noctule. The largest bat of the islands is the European Free-tailed Bat. It is believed that, because it is a strong flyer, it moves between islands, but this has not yet been confirmed.

The Tenerife Long-eared Bat (endemic to Tenerife, El Hierro, La Palma and perhaps on La Gomera) lives in woodlands between 100 and 2300 m. It is the only long-eared bat on the islands and roosts in volcanic caves, crevices and abandoned buildings. The population is estimated to be between 500 and 2000 individuals only.

Marine mammals

No less than 29 species of cetaceans (dolphins and whales) have been recorded in the waters around the Canary Islands. This is a very high number. In fact, these waters are said to be the richest in Europe for marine mammals, because the ocean around the islands marks the southern limit of cold water species and the northern limit for tropical cetaceans. Unfortunately, most species are rare or occur irregularly and are generally very hard to find.

From the ferry and by organised whale-watching trips you can frequently see the smaller species, Common and Bottlenose Dolphins and Short-finned Pilot Whale. There is a stable population of the latter of about 300 individuals off the Southwest coast of Tenerife, which marks the northern limit of its distribution range. They can also be seen from the southernmost point of Tenerife (route 12).

Several groups of Short-finned Pilot Whales live in the strait between Tenerife and La Gomera.

The extinct Tenerife Giant Rat

With a body about a metre long, the extinct Tenerife Giant Rat (*Canariomys bravoi*) was the biggest of the world's rats. It was endemic to Tenerife, where it inhabited all habitats from sea level up to the Cañadas del Teide. Fossilized remains have been found in caves and volcanic pipes (site E on page 152). The Giant Rat has the dubious honour of being the first known human-induced extinction in the Canary Islands. It is believed that it became extinct due to the arrival of the Guanches. The Museo de la Naturaleza y el Hombre in Santa Cruz exhibits fossil skulls and bones, and faithful reconstructions.

Birds

For birds of dry lands and deserts, try route 5, 12 and sites A and B on page 178 and M on page 209. Sea birds are best observed from the ferries, on 12 and 13, and site B on page 150, sites A, B and C on page 178-179, G on page 154 and N on page 209. The birds of gardens, allotments and thermophilous woods are present in many places, including routes 1, 4, 5, 7, 8, 9, 10 and 11. Route 5 and site M on page 209 are good for birds of dry plains. Laurel forest birds (including the pigeons) should be looked for on routes 7, 8, 9, 13 and 14, plus site E on page 136, A, B and D on pages 169-172 and D on page 204. The best route for birds of the pine forest is route 1. For (coastal) wetland birds, check out site E on page 172 and B on page 178 and K on page 208.

When, in the 1970s, flights became accessible to the wider public and, fortuitously, a new European field guide included the Canary Islands, birdwatchers started to visit Tenerife. Suddenly it was easy to add to your list eight endemic birds: the Blue Chaffinch (only occurring on Tenerife and a small population on Gran Canaria), Bolle's Pigeon, Laurel Pigeon and Canary Island Chiffchaff (all endemic to the western Canary Islands), Plain Swift and Berthelot's Pipit (only occurring on the Canary Islands and Madeira) and Canary, which is also found on the Azores. The final one is Barolo Shearwater, which occurs throughout the Macaronesian waters. All of them can be seen within a single holiday (spring-autumn). Add to this the wide availability of comfortable hotels, frequent flights, inexpensive living and superb weather and you'll appreciate the perks of Tenerife as a birdwatching destination. Moreover, it is a destination the non-birding part of the family does not object to either.

Apart from the aforementioned endemics, Tenerife and, to lesser extent, La Gomera support a number of Mediterranean and North-African birds which will quicken the heartbeat of the birdwatcher – birds like Barbary Partridge, Barbary Falcon, Trumpeter Finch, African Blue Tit and Spectacled Warbler. Next in line are the seabirds, of which several highly attractive and sought-after birds breed on the islands, although most of them can only be seen with luck and perseverance, and best in late summer. A final attraction of the islands is the occurrence of many local forms of familiar birds of Europe and north-Africa. The Tenerife Goldcrest and the Canarian forms of Robin, African Blue Tit, Great Spotted Woodpecker and that of the Chaffinch are clearly very different from those on the mainland. The taxonomic status of these birds remains unclear but they are clearly on their way to evolving into new endemic species.

Tenerife and La Gomera's birdlife in a nutshell

Canarian and Macaronesian endemics Macaronesian (Little) Shearwater, Madeiran Storm-petrel, Bolle's Pigeon, Laurel Pigeon, Plain Swift, Berthelot's Pipit, Canary Islands Chiffchaff, Blue Chaffinch, African Blue Tit, Canary

North-African and Mediterranean species Barbary Falcon, Barbary Partridge, Stone Curlew (rare), Kentish Plover (rare), Pallid Swift, Hoopoe, Spectacled Warbler, Sardinian Warbler, Southern Grey Shrike, Lesser Short-toed Lark (rare), Spanish Sparrow, Trumpeter Finch (rare)

Other specialities Bulwer's Petrel, Cory's Shearwater, Manx Shearwater, European Storm-petrel, Osprey, distinct subspecies of Robin, Buzzard, Chaffinch, Goldcrest, Great Spotted Woodpecker, Raven, etcetera

Nevertheless, Tenerife has only a limited number of birds. Its small size in combination with an isolated position in the Atlantic makes for a low bird diversity. This holds true even more so for La Gomera, which is decidedly poor in birds. This was already the case when the naturalist Bannerman visited the island in 1920: *"I know of few places so entirely shut away from the world, and which convey such an impression of complete isolation... From an ornithologist's standpoint the valley of San Sebastian is terribly disappointing, birds being very scarce and confined to a few species only."*

Most birdwatchers come in winter, escaping from bad weather in their homelands. However, all months are good for finding the characteristic island species, though (late) summer is best for seabirds. Note that Plain Swift is scarce in mid-winter.

Sardinian Warblers breed in scrublands and gardens on both islands.

Birds of the succulent scrub and dry fields of the south

The desert and semi-desert birdlife forms a great attraction on Lanzarote and Fuerteventura, but on Tenerife and La Gomera there are only small and dwindling populations. Most desert birds require sizeable areas of relatively flat, arid land which is in short supply on Tenerife and even more so on La Gomera. Unfortunately, most suitable terrain in southern Tenerife has fallen prey to urban and tourist

Bird subspecies and their characteristics

Not only do Tenerife and La Gomera support a number of clearly distinct birds that are endemic to the Canary Islands, they also host various familiar birds which look (or sound) only a little different from those found elsewhere. These 'subspecies', as they are called, are listed below.

Sparrowhawk (Macaronesian subspecies *granti*) Darker above, thicker barring below.
Buzzard (Canary subspecies *insularum*) Smaller, lighter, underside more streaked.
Kestrel (West Canary subspecies *canariensis*) darker, male's head is darker.
Stone Curlew (West Canary subspecies *distinctus*) paler, heavy dark streaks.
Yellow-legged Gull (Macaronesian subspecies *atlantis*) – Generally darker and smaller.
Long-eared Owl (West Canary subspecies *canariensis*) darker and smaller.
Great Spotted Woodpecker (Canary subspecies *canariensis*) Underparts buff, bill longer.
Robin (West Canary subspecies *superbus*) larger, breast deeper red, underparts whiter, clearly separated from breast.
Blackcap (West Canary subspecies *heineken*) Smaller and darker.
African Blue Tit (West Canary subspecies *teneriffae*).
Tenerife Goldcrest (West Canary subspecies *teneriffae*) Deeper buff below and (like Fire-crest) black head stripes meet on forehead. Sometimes considered a full species.
Chaffinch (West Canary subspecies *canariensis*) Male upperparts deep slate-blue, rump bright green. Similar to North-African birds, which are sometimes considered a full species.
Great Grey Shrike (Canary subspecies *koenigi*) Smaller. Taxonomy and status under debate.
Raven (Canary / African subspecies *tingitanus*) Much smaller, higher call, brownish plumage.

The Canarian subspecies of Raven has a brown neck and is much smaller than its European relative.

developments and agriculture, in particular those ugly, walled banana plantations. So, never numerous to begin with, the semi-desert birds on Tenerife and La Gomera are close to extinction. The curtain has fallen for the Cream-coloured Courser, while Lesser Short-toed Lark and Trumpeter Finch have become very rare.

But it is not all gloom and doom. If you can stomach crossing some garbage-strewn wastelands and are not affected by the tristesse of derelict
sheds, there are some fine birds to discover.
The most common bird of the dry lowlands is the Berthelot's Pipit. This
endemic of the Canaries and Madeira is common in any dry open terrain. It is a small bird, but stands tall on its legs. Its Spanish name
Bisbita caminero – the striding pipit – is well-chosen. The Berthelot's
Pipit runs in sudden spurts from place to place.
The Berthelot's Pipit shares its territory with Kestrel (rather common),
Great Grey Shrike (locally common only in the south of Tenerife), Stone
Curlew (rare and hard to find), Hoopoe (fairly frequent), Linnet (fairly
frequent), Spectacled Warbler (locally common in scattered low bushes,
mostly in southern Tenerife) and Spanish Sparrow (near buildings).
Occasionally, Barbary Falcons come down to hunt.
A sought-after bird of dry semi-desert fields and barrancos is the
Trumpeter Finch. This small finch is, with its big red bill and funny,
nasal call, a lovely bird. It is now restricted to a single small area in
Tenerife (if it is still there) and another in La Gomera.
The more densely vegetated areas of succulent scrub, usually higher up
the slope, have little birdlife to offer. Locally though, these can be good
areas to find Barbary Partridge, especially where arable fields are nearby.

Seabirds and cliff breeders
The seabird colonies are mostly hidden on inaccessible sea cliffs and
steep, inland barrancos. Tenerife holds important colonies of Bulwer's
Petrel on its north coast, from the Roques de Anaga to Garachico. In the
south and west of La Gomera there are some smaller colonies.
The most common seabird, after the abundant Yellow-legged Gull, is the
Cory's Shearwater. It breeds on many places on the coasts and can be
seen without much difficulty (except in winter) from any viewpoint and
from the ferries (see box on page 96). Barolo Shearwater (formerly known
as Macaronesian or Little Shearwater) breeds on Tenerife and is most
easily seen in summer and autumn. Birds are seen from the Punta de
Teno (site B on page 150), Punta de la Rasca (route 12) and from the ferry.
Manx Shearwater breeds in ravines in the laurel forest, up to a height of
1000 m. Madeiran Storm-petrels breed on both islands, while European
Storm-petrels nest on Tenerife only. The only realistic hope of seeing
them, as is the case with the White-faced Storm-petrel, is out at sea. Very
exciting is the recent increase in sightings of the spectacular Red-billed
Tropicbird. It was confirmed to breed in 2013 on Lanzarote and seems

Between March
and October, Cory's
Shearwaters are
common at sea around
the islands. The ferry
between Tenerife and
La Gomera is an ex-
cellent way to see and
photograph them.

to be increasing slowly. Although too early to tell, it may yet become an established bird on Tenerife.

The only terns that are regular in the coastal waters are the Sandwich Tern and, in fluctuating numbers, the Common Tern. Sandwich Tern can be found in small numbers all along the coasts, especially in winter and during migration. Common Tern is sometimes seen from the ferries or in the harbours during summer and autumn. It nests sporadically on Tenerife and La Gomera.

Apart from these species, the coastal cliffs also host raptors. Osprey breeds exclusively on the coast and fishes over the sea. Both Tenerife (in the northwest) and La Gomera (in the south) hold several pairs. Barbary Falcon also breeds at sea cliffs, as do Raven and Rock Dove.

The skerries and tidal pools at the coast attract numerous waders during migration and in winter. In suitable places all along the coast you can find Whimbrel, Grey Plover and Turnstone commonly, while Greenshank, Common Sandpiper and Green Sandpiper are less common. Sanderling is scarce but regular on the beaches of the islands. Near the Montaña Roja in southern Tenerife (site B on page 178), a handful of Little Ringed and Kentish Plovers and the occasional Black-winged Stilt breed. Yellow-legged Gull has established fairly sizeable colonies and Grey Heron and Little Egret are also frequent at the coast, although they don't breed.

Presence of breeding seabirds on the Canary Islands

Species	Observation period	Location
Cory's Shearwater ***	Feb-mid Nov	Tenerife, La Gomera
Manx Shearwater *	Feb-June	Tenerife, La Gomera
Macaronesian Shearwater **	Jan-Dec	Tenerife, La Gomera?
Bulwer's Petrel **	Feb-Sept	Tenerife, La Gomera
European Storm-petrel ***	June-Oct	Tenerife
Madeiran Storm-petrel **	Sept-mid Feb	Tenerife, La Gomera
Yellow-legged Gull ***	Jan-Dec	Tenerife, La Gomera
Common Tern *	March-Nov	incidental Tenerife

*: less than 100 pairs, **: less than 1,000 pairs, ***: more than 1,000 pairs

Birds of the resorts, villages, the allotment zone and dry fields

The ring of built-up areas and agricultural land in the lower part of Tenerife is of interest to birdwatchers too. You might not have to leave your hotel to spot Canary, Grey Wagtail, Canary Islands Chiffchaff, African Blue Tit, Blackbird, Robin, Sardinian Warbler, Blackcap, Plain Swift and Spanish Sparrow.

Better still are the terraced allotments on the north side of Tenerife and La Gomera. Because it is so green and the small vegetable gardens offer plenty of food, birds abound here – another reason to consider staying on the north side of the islands. If you bring a telephoto lens, you can take more than decent shots of African Blue Tit, Canary Islands Chiffchaff, Robin and Canary from your breakfast table. During an evening stroll, look out for Barn Owl and Long-eared Owl, both of which are found in the villages of northern Tenerife and La Gomera. The Long-eared Owl is the more common of the two and is seen quite often.

The Canary is the most common bird in the vegetable gardens and rural villages. Its song immediately reminds of the familiar cage bird, although the appearance of the wild Canary is quite different. The green, streaked bird is indeed the wild ancestor of the yellow pet Canary. It is native to Madeira, the Azores and the Canary Islands. Canaries can often be seen on overhead wires, in gardens or feeding on sow-thistles and fig trees. It outnumbers by far the Goldfinch and the Greenfinch, which occur in small numbers the agricultural plots in the north of both

The wild Canary, the ancestor of the familiar yellow cagebird, but has a very different plumage. Its song is a little different too, but just as cheerful.

islands. The Serin is even rarer, being restricted to villages and in agricultural landscape of
north-eastern Tenerife.

The Turtle Dove is a common breeding bird of
cultivated land. It is, together with Plain Swift,
Quail and a couple of seabirds, among the few
migratory birds that spend the winter further
south. As in mainland Europe, the Turtle Dove
is a bird of the countryside, while Collared
Dove and Feral Pigeon occupy the towns,
just like Spanish Sparrow, the only sparrow
breeding on the islands. It takes a particular
liking for breeding in palm trees. In some
towns (e.g. La Laguna and Puerto de la Cruz),
Ring-necked and Monk Parakeets breed in the
parks. They were recently introduced.

In former days, cereals were grown in some uplands and terraces. Today,
such dry arable lands are still present near Teno Alto and in various parts
of La Gomera (e.g. near Chipude and near the airport). Such fields offer home to a variety of birds, such as Quail, Corn Bunting, Hoopoe,
Kestrel and Raven. Very typical species of these old agricultural lands are
Buzzard, Rock Sparrow, Barbary Partridge and Corn Bunting.

The African Blue Tit
is a common bird in
gardens and open
woodlands. It is the
only tit species on the
islands.

The extinct Red Kite

The Red Kite, once common on the Canary Islands, became extinct in 1967. The
German naturalist Carl August Bolle (after whom the pigeon is named) stated
in 1854 that it was the most abundant raptor of Tenerife. His famous British
colleague David Bannerman used to see it frequently on his visits to the islands
between 1912 and 1920, but when he returned in 1959 he was perplexed by its
scarceness.

A study based on interviews with the oldest inhabitants concluded that the Red
Kite was a common bird until the middle of the 20th century. The abuelos also
remembered a massive influx of the Desert Locust. Invasions of desert locusts
happen occasionally when plagues in the Sahara coincide with strong easterly
winds. But the locust invasion on the 14th of October 1954 was the worst ever – a
front of more than 200 km wide reached the islands. The government decided to
combat the locusts with the chemical Lindane. Within two months, about 150
tonnes of this particularly nasty toxin were applied. The use of Lindane is probably what did the Red Kites in. Since 2009, the use of Lindane is forbidden - too
late for the Red Kite.

Birds of the laurel forest

The laurel cloud forests are home to two of the most characteristic and sought-after birds of the Canary Islands: the endemic Bolle´s Pigeon and Laurel Pigeon. The latter is sometimes called White-tailed Pigeon because its light tail contrasts starkly with the dark body.

Both species feed on the berries of various species of laurels and other bushes and trees associated with the laurel forest. They live a rather secretive life and rarely emerge from the canopy. Hence they are hard to find and most observations are of birds that break cover as they fly from tree top to tree top.

Both pigeons breed in the laurel forest zone with a preference for the oldest stands. Laurel Pigeons breed on rock ledges on steep, well vegetated precipes while Bolle's make elaborate nests on branches. This may be the reason that Laurel Pigeons are more often seen in steep barrancos with laurel forest vegetation (even outside the area of unbroken laurel forest) whereas Bolle's Pigeon is more common in extensive forests. DNA research revealed that both species evolved from an ancestral type of Wood Pigeon, which colonised the islands at least twice. The first colonisation, some 20 million years ago, gave rise to the Laurel Pigeon and a more recent one (5 million years ago) started the lineage of today's Bolle's Pigeon.

Bolle's Pigeon. Just like its relative, the Laurel Pigeon, Bolle's rarely leaves the crowns of the laurel trees and is a shy and difficult to find bird.

Both species are known to visit nearby agricultural fields and orchards to feed, particularly during the summer months when their food in the forests has become scarce.

Bolle´s Pigeon is the most abundant of the two pigeons, particularly on Tenerife, where the Laurel Pigeon is rare and restricted to the Teno Mountains and Esperanza forest. On La Gomera both pigeons occur throughout the Garajonay National Park.

The pigeons share their forest with a number of familiar temperate-European birds, each of which having a distinct form on the Canary Islands. The Chaffinch, Blackbird, Canary Islands Chiffchaff, African Blue Tit and Tenerife Goldcrest are all frequent inhabitants of the laurel forest. The latter seems to be tied to stands of Tree Heath, which dominates woodland edges and young forests, where it can be very common.

Much less frequently seen is the Sparrowhawk and even harder to track down is the Woodcock, of which a resident population persists in the deepest forests.

Bolle´s and Laurel Pigeon populations

Intensive exploitation of the forests since the 15th Century has resulted in population decline of Bolle´s and Laurel Pigeon. However, from the end of the 20th century the extent of forest loss has slowed down and populations are thought to be stable or even slightly increasing. There are more than 2,000 Bolle´s pigeons on Tenerife (2007) and over 1000 birds in the Garajonay National Park on La Gomera. Laurel Pigeon is estimated at 3,000-7,500 individuals for the Canary Islands as a whole, the largest population is found on La Palma. Only a few hundred birds live on Tenerife and La Gomera respectively.

Birds of the Canary Pine forest and the upper Teide

The pine forests and sub-alpine zone of the central Caldera form the next great attraction for birdwatchers, mainly because this is where the amazing, endemic Blue Chaffinch occurs. It lives exclusively in Canary Pine forests between 1,200 and 2,200 m. The subspecies *teydea* lives in Tenerife, where roughly between 1,800 to 4,500 individuals occur, while on Gran Canaria there are only 150 birds left, belonging to the *polatzeki* subspecies.

In spite of these numbers, the Blue Chaffinch remains a scarce bird in the Tenerife pine forests. Since it is not very shy and comes to picnic sites for food and water, it is not very hard to find. A thorough look around the picnic sites mentioned in route 1 will reveal it sooner rather than later

The Blue Chaffinch is endemic to the pine forests of Tenerife and Gran Canaria. It frequently visits picnic sites in these forests and that is where you'll find them most easily.

(our first encounter was within 10 seconds on arrival at such a site; less than a minute later we took the picture on this page!).

A very typical pine forest bird, besides the Blue Chaffinch, is the Tenerife Great Spotted Woodpecker. It is also confined to Tenerife and Gran Canaria, frequenting the mature and well-preserved pines between 800 and 1800 m. It is a fairly rare bird with a world population that does not exceed a few hundred pairs.

Other birds in the pine forests are Robin, Canary Islands Chiffchaff, Canary, African Blue Tit, Tenerife Goldcrest, Plain Swift, Kestrel, Sparrowhawk and even Berthelot's Pipit – all birds that occur in other habitats too, and reappear in the pine forests in low numbers.

Higher up in the treeless interior of the Teide crater, the birdlife changes once again. This cold and desolate landscape does not allow a rich birdlife and there are no bird species specific of this zone.

The Berthelot´s Pipit is the most abundant bird of the caldera. It occurs all over the highlands, even quite high up the slopes of the Teide itself. It is especially tame near the Cañada Blanca parador (route 1). Other birds that can regularly be seen are cliff breeders like Kestrel, Rock Dove, Raven, Plain Swift and Barbary Falcon. They breed in low numbers in the Caldera wall. In the Teide Broom scrub, there are low numbers of Great Grey Shrike, Barbary Partridge, Spectacled and Sardinian Warblers and Canary.

Birds of the barrancos and cliffs

Barrancos are frequently the best places to find birds. It is in the barrancos that you'll find the best remnants of laurel forests, and therefore the endemic pigeons. They also form an important retreat for Barbary Partridge and all sorts of small woodland and scrubland birds.

There are also a number of birds that are typical breeders of cliff faces. In barrancos the lion's share of the Barbary Falcons and Kestrels breed, while above them large numbers of Plain Swifts perform their aerial acrobatics.

Plain Swifts are not restricted to barrancos though. They breed all over Tenerife and La Gomera and can be seen from virtually any point of the islands. Most migrate to Africa in winter and return in March. Only a few birds remain in winter. The Pallid Swift, another migrant, is quite rare, but a few small colonies exist on Tenerife's east coast.

Rock / Feral Pigeon also breed on inland cliffs and in gorges. Flocks of up to several hundred can be seen. Finally, and perhaps unexpectedly, the Cory's, Macaronesian and Manx Shearwaters are also breeding birds of inland barrancos. They only come to land at night and produce mysterious noises from deep within the ravines.

Birds of reservoirs and tidal ponds

The reservoirs on the islands are quite small and have little vegetation. Moorhen and Coot are the only breeding species of waterfowl. Any duck or heron you may see is a vagrant, migrant or winter visitor. Nevertheless, reservoirs are interesting birdwatching sites because they attract waders during migration and in winter. You may regularly find species as Redshank, Greenshank, Green and Common Sandpiper and Snipe, albeit generally in low numbers. Some reservoirs attract waterfowl and herons during migration and in winter. Grey Heron and Little Egret, Teal and Pochard are frequent too, and reservoirs often turn up a rarity or two. Most of them are vagrants from Europe, but American and African birds are seen regularly too. The best pools are near La Rasca, but they are closed to visitors now.

It is a somewhat odd sight for people from northern Europe to see waders, like this Grey Plover, resting on and feeding between the lava rocks (left). The *Atlantis* subspecies of the Yellow-legged Gull is small and has a rather dark back (right).

Reptiles and amphibians

Tenerife Lizards are everywhere on the island, but particularly common in winter on route 12 and site B on page 150, while later in the year, the botanical garden of Las Cañadas (route 1,2) has tame specimens. Route 10 and 11 are good for finding West Canary Skink (although it occurs elsewhere too). Tenerife and Gomera Gecko are common in the lowlands of each island respectively. Site L (page 208) is good for finding reptiles on La Gomera.

The Canary Islands were colonised naturally by a lizard, a skink and a gecko. These three reptiles spread on the Canary Islands and evolved into 14 species of reptiles in total. Most islands have their own species of skink, lizard and gecko – all closely related.
On Tenerife and La Gomera, the situation is a little different: one species of skink occurs on both islands (although the populations of each island are now sometimes regarded as two species). Each island has its own gecko species plus two distinct species of lizard.

Canary Island lizards
All lizards belong the the genus *Galliota*, or Canary Island Lizards. The genus is endemic to the Canary Islands and most closely related to the *Psammodromus* Lizards which are common in north-Africa.
On Tenerife, the commonest lizard is called rather to the point Tenerife Lizard. The males are impressive beasts, measuring up to 50 cms (snout to tailtip) with heavy heads. They are slaty black and some specimens have bright yellow and blue spots and a bright blue throat. The females are usually (dark) brown with lots of yellowish spots on the back. The lizards in the south of Tenerife *(ssp galloti)* are a little smaller and less colourful than the subspecies *eisentrauti* of northern Tenerife.
The Tenerife Lizard is widespread, abundant and highly visible. It occupies all sunny habitats from the coast up to the Cañadas del Teide. In the lower regions, the lizards remain active all year. In mid-winter, the coastal rocks sport large numbers of them, while in summer, you'll encounter them plentifully high up in the mountains as well. The lizard feeds on invertebrates and seeds, fruits and flowers alike and can be quite tame in gardens and holiday resorts.
The lizard is a so-called keystone species: an animal that plays a key role in the original ecosystem. It is staple food for Kestrels, Buzzards, Ravens and Great Grey Shrikes.

The common Lizard on La Gomera (and El Hierro) is the Boettger's Lizard. It is much smaller and lighter in colour than the Tenerife Lizard, but equally numerous and important in the ecosystem.

Apart from these species, both islands also hosted a giant lizard. The one on Tenerife belonged to the species *Gallotia goliath* and was believed to have grown to at least one metre long. Fossils and mummified remains have been found in volcanic caves of Tenerife. It was written about in the 15th century, so extinction presumably occurred in the years after the Spanish conquest of the Canary Islands.

There is also a giant lizard on La Gomera. It was considered extinct, but was fortunately rediscovered in 1999! It grows up to half a metre long and is easily distinguished by the intense white colour in the neck, chest and around the mouth, contrasting with its brown back. It is thought to have once ranged throughout La Gomera, but today, it is restricted to dry cliffs with sparse vegetation in the natural park Valle Gran Rey. There is a recovery station for this lizard at the northwestern end of the village, just below the cliffs where it occurs naturally.

A little earlier, there was also a new lizard species discovered on Tenerife. Similar to the Gomera

In the mating season, the males of the Tenerife Lizard are almost black (left). The rediscovery of the Gomera Giant Lizard in 1999, which survived on a steep cliff north of Valle Gran Rey (right), was as spectacular as it was unexpected.

Giant Lizard, the Tenerife Speckled Lizard is confined to a few steep slopes in the northern Teno Mountains.

Geckos and West Canary Skink

The skink is widespread on both islands, but in contrast to the lizards, rather hard to find. It spends most of its time underground, safe from predators. West Canary Skinks are found in most habitats, but have a preference to the warmer, lower slopes with slightly moist soils and a well-developed layer of soil and leaf litter. Fields, gardens and barrancos are preferred sites.

The Tenerife Gecko also lives under stones. It is also widespread and inhabits rocky areas, rural gardens and urban areas. It also frequents buildings where it uses the light of street lights to catch insects. Like the skink, it prefers the warm, lower vegetation zones of the islands, in particular stone walls, sheds and farms. Like the other reptiles, the Gecko is rare in the relatively cold and shady Laurel Forests.

La Gomera has its own gecko, the Gomera Gecko, which is most common on the warm south side.

Amphibians

Amphibians have soft skins that cannot withstand salt water. This is why they are unable to colonise isolated volcanic islands without the aid of humans. The presence or absence of amphibians is quite a reliable litmus test to tell the true oceanic islands from the ones that were once connected to the mainland. Hence naturally, there were no amphibians on the Canary Islands.

The two frog species that occur on Tenerife and La Gomera were both recently introduced. Both the Iberian Water Frog and the Stripeless Tree Frog occur in fresh-water habitats. Their distribution is not fully known, but the loud treefrogs are present all over the north coast of Tenerife, where they live both in the barrancos and in the countless wells and small water reservoirs that are present all over the allotment zone.

The Gomera Gecko is a champion in hiding in cracks and underneath rocks. It takes a real effort to find one.

Insects and other invertebrates

Good routes for butterflies are routes 1, 2, 7, 8, 9, 10, 11, 15 and 16, and sites B and C on page 134-135, sites A, D and F on pages 150-153, sites A, C and F on pages 169-173, and sites B, C, and L on pages 203-208. For dragonflies, check out routes 6, 9, and 12, site E on page 180 and site K on page 208. For grasshoppers and praying mantises, we advise routes 5 and sites A and B on page 178.

Among the Canarian butterflies and dragonflies, there are again a number of endemic species, although the diversity is not as marked as that of the flora. Many of them are strong fliers, which arrived on the islands via the air. Among them is a fair number of African species, which are either completely absent from Europe, or occur only in small pockets on the Spanish south coast. The presence of a number of Canary endemics plus the good deal of African migrants (there is even a butterfly named African Migrant), makes the archipelago an interesting place to visit for those with an interest in butterflies and dragonflies. It should come as no surprise that Tenerife, being the largest and ecologically most diverse island, has the largest variety of species.

The Canary Islands Large White is closely related to the familiar Large White, but has big black spots on the forewing.

Butterflies

In keeping with the saying that the Canaries are the islands of eternal spring, butterflies can be seen all year. Nevertheless, winter clearly is the 'low season', in which many species fly either in lower numbers or in specific lowland sites. A fair number of species do not fly in winter at all and should be looked for in the (second half of) spring and summer. It is interesting to note that whilst some species have evolved into endemic species, those that are strong fliers and thus are able to disperse rapidly, occur throughout Europe. As a result, the sought-after local species fly happily side by side with the very common butterflies you know from your garden back home.

In winter, the southern lowlands boasts plenty of Bath Whites, sometimes mixed with a Painted Lady or Canary Blue. The diversity on the northern slopes – the barrancos and the gardens – is higher, with Canary Speckled Wood, Common and Canary Red Admiral, Small Copper and Common Blue.

Numbers and diversity greatly increase as the season proceeds. In early spring, Canary Islands Large White and Canary Cleopatra are common in the barrancos, in some places joined by Canary Blue. In the second half of spring, when the high slopes of the Cañadas del Teide are in bloom, this is a superb area for butterfly watching. Tenerife Green-striped White, Tenerife Grayling and Cardinal are all common, but none of them occur in the numbers in which you'll see the Canary Blue. This is one of the star species of the Canary Islands. At last, this is a species of blue that is clearly recognisable from all the other species!

The Canary Red Admiral is frequent by roadsides and in flowery fields (top). A Canary Blue on Teide Broom (bottom).

Canary Blues – another evolutionary puzzle

The Canary Blue belongs to a genus – *Cyclyrius* – that has only two species: one on the Canary Islands and another on the other side of Africa, on Mauritius. It has long puzzled evolutionary biologists how this was possible. The leading theory was that the parent species of both of them was widespread in Africa but went extinct. The problem with this theory is that the Canary Blue is a butterfly that seems to do well in an enormous variety of habitats – hardly a candidate for swift extinction.

Recent research indicates that Canary Blues become very picky in their habitat as soon as other blues enter the scene. Probably, other blues form strong competitors, so perhaps it is their absence on the Canaries that allows the Canary Blue to be abundant. On the mainland, the Canary Blue's parent species was pushed out by the competition.

Butterflies at various vegetation zones

Many butterflies on Tenerife and La Gomera are tied to one or two specific vegetation zones. Here are some typical species for each vegetation, plus their most prominent flying season. If no season is given, butterflies are on the wing year-round (although a lot less numerous in the winter moths).

Allotments, clearings in thermophilous scrub Canary Skipper (may-aug), Red Admiral, Canary Red Admiral, Small White, Bath White, Clouded Yellow, Meadow Brown (spring-summer), Small Copper, Common Blue, Long-tailed Blue, Gomera Grayling (spring-summer)

Barrancos and clearings in laurel forests Canary Speckled Wood, Canary Red Admiral, Red Admiral, Plain Tiger, Canary Islands Large White (march-sept), Canary Cleopatra (mar-sept), Canary Blue (feb-oct), Gomera Grayling (may-sept; Gomera only), Spanish Brown Argus

Cañadas del Teide and gullies in the pine forests Tenerife Green-striped White (mar-june); Canary Blue (may-aug; very common), Tenerife Grayling (april-sept), Cardinal (summer)

Lowland gardens and parks Monarch, Plain Tiger, African Migrant (some years), Geranium Bronze, African Grass Blue, Small White, Canary Speckled Wood

Dragonflies

The porous volcanic bedrock has, by its nature, little surface water. Therefore, dragonflies are few and restricted to specific sites. There are no local species, with the exception of the Island Darter, which is unique to the Canaries and Madeira. There are quite a few African dragonflies that do not occur in Europe, or only very locally. These are highly attractive species like Ringed Cascader, Red-veined Dropwing and Sahara Bluetail. Most of them are restricted to the few permanent streams on Tenerife, such as the Barranco de Afur (route 10) and Barranco del Infierno (site E on page 180). These are the dragonfly hotspots. In the vegetation and on rocks in the streambed, large numbers of brilliantly red Red-veined

Bath Whites are common on the hot, south-facing lowlands.

There are only a few dragonfly species on Tenerife and La Gomera. Two attractive species you'll encounter frequently along small channels and streams, are the Epaulet Skimmer (left) and the Red-veined Dropwing (opposite page).

Dropwings sit side by side the blue Epaulet Skimmers. Red-veined Darter and Broad Scarlet are, like the Red-veined Dropwing, fairly small, red-bodied dragonflies so take care distinguishing them.

With the construction of new irrigation systems and its hundreds of kilometres of pipes and small concrete channels in the second half of the 20th century (see page 63), a new freshwater habitat was created. However, the bare channels are only suited for pioneer species that are not very demanding, like Sahara Bluetail, Broad Scarlet and Red-veined

Species	Scientific name	habitat	frequency
Sahara Bluetail	Ischnura saharensis	channels, reservoirs	uncommon
Ubiquitous Bluetail	Ischnura senegalensis	reservoir	only Callao Salvaje
Vagrant Emperor	Anax ephippiger	any habitat	vagrant
Blue Emperor	Anax imperator	reservoirs	fairly common
Lesser Emperor	Anax parthenope	reservoirs	fairly common
Broad Scarlet	Crocothemis erythraea	any habitat	fairly common
Epaulet Skimmer	Orthetrum chrysostigma	barrancos, channels	fairly common
Red-veined Darter	Sympetrum fonscolombii	any habitat	common
Island Darter	Sympetrum nigrifemur	any habitat	rare
Red-veined Dropwing	Trithemis arteriosa	barrancos	locally common
Ringed Cascader	Zygonyx torridus	barrancos	local

Darter. Likewise, newly constructed water basins are readily accepted and colonised by dragonflies and damselflies. The greater availability of habitats appears to be encouraging new colonists. The latest arrival is the Ubiquitous Bluetail at the reservoir of Callao Salvaje. The name of this rather unremarkable-looking damselfly is interesting – it is indeed ubiquitous in tropical Africa, but, for now, it is only found in this one site on Tenerife's west coast.

The males of the Redveined Dropwing are brilliantly coloured. The females look radically different (see page 164).

Other invertebrates

The Canary Islands in general and Tenerife in particular, have a relatively high number of praying mantises (although the precise number has been obscured by mis-identifications and taxonomic arguments). This group is quite invisible though, except during the summer months (June-September). Quite spectacular is the large, broad-bodied *Blepharopsis mendica* and the slender-bodied, hooded *Hypsocorypha gracilis*. Both occur, like the other species in dry, bushy vegetation, especially in the lower reaches (although both are recorded in the Cañadas crater too).

There are several interesting, endemic grasshoppers on the islands. Among them is the Tenerife Sand Grasshopper, *Sphingonotus picteti*, endemic to Tenerife, where it only occurs in hottest semi-arid areas close to the coast. It is rare and endangered, occurring principally in the last remaining patches of semi- desert areas like the Malpaís de La Rasca (route 12) and Montaña Roja (site B on page 178). This small grasshopper performs a visual courtship display with the male climbing on a pebble and flagging with its hind leg to attract the female. The grasshopper genus *Canariola*, consisting of two species, is unique to the Canary Islands and live exclusively in the laurel forests.

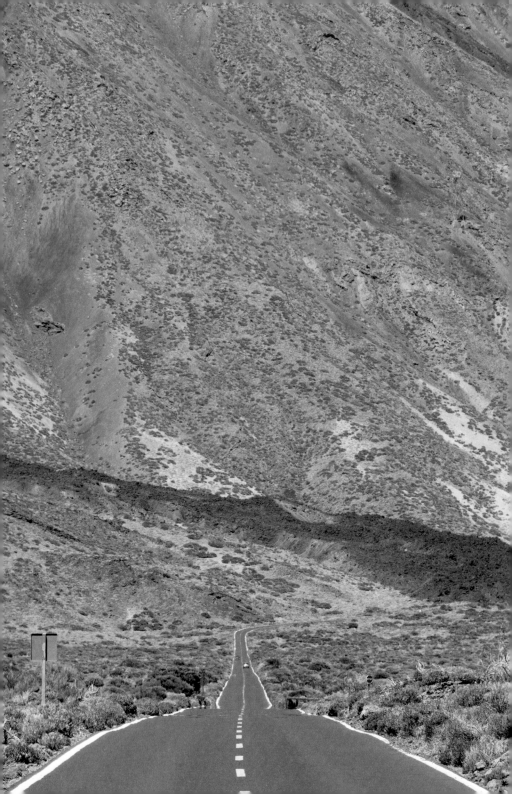

PRACTICAL PART

An increasing number of naturalists and hikers have discovered Tenerife and La Gomera. Tenerife is the more popular of the two, which is understandable as it is much larger and, due to the high Teide mountain, there are habitats you won't find on La Gomera. It is on Tenerife that you'll find the large pinewoods and the superb high altitude lava deserts of las Cañadas del Teide. The diversity of species – breeding birds, plants, insects – on Tenerife is the highest of any of the Canary Islands.

In contrast, the much smaller island of La Gomera attracts hikers and those who seek peace and tranquility. La Gomera is rugged, wild, green and much quieter and more pristine than its larger cousin. La Gomera is famous for having the largest laurel cloud forests of the Canaries. Much less known is the fact that the barrancos and succulent scrub of the southern half of the island are beautiful and intact.

A visitor to the islands will soon discover that the best way to fully appreciate their nature is by lacing up their boots and start walking. Both islands have an excellent network of wonderful trails – enough to keep you occupied, even mesmerised, for weeks. However, given the steepness and rockiness of the terrain, there is a lack of short and easy circuits. Many of the most beautiful trails are linear routes that go down (or worse, up) a steep barranco, meaning that you have to either walk or take a bus back to where you started. Another strategy by which you can explore the islands is to drive around and stop at various points to look for wildlife. This is a better way to find most of the island's rare birds and plants, but makes it more difficult to connect with the landscape and appreciate the special ecological characteristics of the islands. Car routes inevitably offer mere telegramatic summaries of a natural environment that deserves closer attention.

In our selection of routes, we have tried to create a balance between the two. The car routes serve both as an introduction to an area and as a means to find some of the more sought-after species. We have included one or two short and easy walks within each of the car routes to get a better feel for the area. Subsequently, we have described some more walks to truly get to know the area. We have sought out the easier walks and put the emphasis on the surroundings rather than piling on the miles. Finally, we have added a large number of sites and walks which are great to explore the islands further. The islands are divided in smaller regions: central (page 112), north-west (page 137), north-east (page 152) and south Tenerife (page 167) and La Gomera (page 176).

The open dry landscape makes driving through the Cañadas feel like something out of an American road movie.

Routes and sites on central Tenerife – El Teide

The centre of Tenerife is dominated by the massive crater of Las Cañadas. Two nature reserves together cover the entire central part of Tenerife: the nature park of *La Corona Forestal* which lies in a belt around the
National Park Cañadas del Teide.

The Corona Forestal is exactly what the name suggests: a crown of forest
(consisting of Canary Pines) around the bald head of El Teide.

The forest grows up to the edge of a huge, half-circular crater at about
2,200 m. This caldera and its interior plains are known as the Cañadas.
In the middle rises another volcano, El Teide. At 3,717 m, it is Spain's
highest mountain – surpassing both the Pyrenees and Sierra Nevada on
the mainland.

Both the Corona and the Cañadas are very special for naturalists. The
Corona Forestal harbours the largest pine forest of the Canary Islands,
while the subalpine world of the Cañadas del Teide, including its flora and
fauna is nearly exclusive to Tenerife. Only on La Palma, there is a small
area of mountains high enough to boast a similar habitat. Hence, central
Tenerife is like an island within an island. Inside the main caldera you
find yourself in a different world – one in which most species are either
endemic to Tenerife or shared only with the highest zone of La Palma.
These include sought-after attractions like Teide Viper's-bugloss, Tenerife Green-striped White and, in the Corona Forestal, Blue Chaffinch.

There are only four roads that lead up from the coast to the top, one from
every direction. Each of these four roads cross the forest belt before arriving in the Cañadas. In route 1 (next page), we have described stops on
each one of them. This is the best introduction to the area and the perfect
way to see a lot of special species in a short time. Routes 2 and 3 are fairly
easy walking routes. Each focusses on another landscape type in the

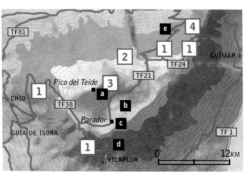

caldera, while route 4
leads through a won-
derful area of pine
forest.

Both in the forest, as
in the caldera, there
are many more walk-
ing options. Some of
them are briefly de-
scribed on page 134-
135.

Route 1: The Cañadas del Teide National Park

FULL DAY OR MORE
EASY

Best season
May-July
Of interest
Year-round

This is the must see part of Tenerife.
Stunning scenery and endemic flora and fauna.
All the good sites to see the endemic
Blue Chaffinch.

Habitats: Allotments, pine forest, high altitude desert
Selected species: Teide Viper's-bugloss, Teide Broom, Canary Strawberry
Tree, Tenerife Green-striped White, Blue Chaffinch, Bolle's Pigeon,
Berthelot's Pipit, Barbary Partridge, Spectacled Warbler

A visit to the Cañadas del Teide National Park, the huge crater of El Teide, is a highlight that no-one should skip. It is worth exploring this unique mountain thoroughly on foot (see next routes and sites A, B, C and D on pages 134-136), but to get an initial general impression we recommend this car route from the foot of the mountain up to the caldera, stopping for short walks in the various vegetation zones on the way up.

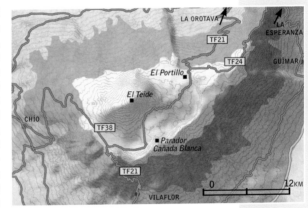

There are four roads up the mountain: from Chío in the west, La Orotava in the north, La Esperanza in the north-east, and Vilaflor in the south. Naturally, which one you take up will depend on where you are based, but we suggest to take a different one coming down. In the following description, we treat each ascent separately before describing the sites in the caldera.
The scenery on any of these ascents is downright spectacular, and all of them give a great insight into the diversity of habitats in Tenerife.

Teide Flixweed with El Teide in the background. The Cañadas landscape appears otherwordly, as does the flora and fauna here. Nearly all species are endemics – unique to the Teide.

The various short walks offer you the easiest views of some of Tenerife highlights like Teide Viper's-bugloss, Blue Chaffinch, Tenerife Goldcrest, and Canary Blue. If this isn't enough, this route also offers the most spectacular geology and landscapes, with recent lava fields, a spectacular crater cliff, pumice deserts and much more. Note that on the main roads, it is difficult (and illegal!) to pull over, except at special lay-bys and car parks.

Ascent from the north – La Orotava

The ascent from La Orotava is the most diverse, leading through orchards, fields and remnants of laurel forest before entering the pinewoods. This entire area burnt down in 2023 (see box).

Take the TF 21 that winds up the mountain. At Chasna, turn right onto a small road that leads to Palo Blanco and Benijos. Pull over at the valley some 300 metres ahead. Follow the road a little further on foot.

1 This stop allows you to have a proper look down the Orotava valley which is, according to the famous explorer Von Humboldt, one of the most beautiful spots in the world. One wonders what it looked like when he was here in 1799, because, although pretty, it is not spectacular. The terraced plots are planted with groves of Sweet Chestnut, testimony to the cool and humid micro-climate of this valley, which receives the highest rainfall on Tenerife. Chestnuts are not native to the Canaries, but were planted to provide food for the villagers. Originally, this was all covered in laurel forest, small patches of which still remain. The small barranco where you parked is one of them, and from here you have a good view over the trees so look out for Bolle's Pigeon which often overfly the area. Continue on foot for a few hundred metres to get a taste of the area. The arable plots and bramble thickets hold Canary Islands Chiffchaff, Canary, Chaffinch, Blackcap and Sardinian Warbler.

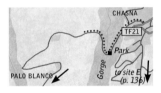

Back in the car, continue along the TF 21, pass the La Caldera recreational area (route 4) and enter the pine forest. Continue until you arrive at the *Ramon Caminero area recreativa.*

2 Stop at the *Ramon Caminero area recreativa.* At this large picnic spot in the middle of the forest, look for African Blue Tit, Blue Chaffinch and Great Spotted Woodpecker, which are drawn here by water sources and the leftovers from the picnickers. Just beyond the picnic spot is a broad barranco, which supports some interesting wildflowers. In spring, you can find the bright yellow Spade-leaved Houseleek* *(Aeonium spathulatum),* Teide Carline Thistle* *(Carlina xeranthemoides)* and Tenerife Ironwort* *(Sidiritis oroteneriffae).*

Continue along the TF 21 until you reach the junction with the TF 24 from La Esperanza. There is a bar at the junction and 100 metres ahead in the crater lies the information centre of El Portillo.

> **2023 Forest fires**
> In late summer 2023, just after the research for this edition of the book was completed, a large forest fire swept over the northwestern part of the Corona forestal. **Large parts of the forests of this northern and eastern ascents were affected**, but it is as of yet unclear to what extent. Canray Pine trees are known for their remarkable resilience against fire. Therefore, we have maintained the original text. Be aware, that the actual situation is likely to be very different than description given here.

Ascent from the east – La Esperanza

The ascent from La Esperanza is quite long and leads through an extensive stretch of pine forest (sadly destroyed by the 2023 wildfire) and some splendid Teide Broom scrub. There are superb volcanic ash landscapes.

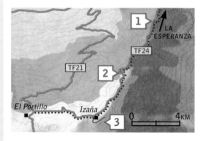

Follow the TF 24 to El Teide. After a longish drive, turn right to Chipeque and Chimague and drive on to the final viewpoint.

1 From the viewpoint, you have excellent views of mount Teide and, to the left, your ascent towards it. Closer at hand, look for birds like Great Spotted Woodpecker and Blue Chaffinch. The latter is not as easy to find as it is on other sites (e.g. El Portillo, Las Lajas and Pinar Chío) but there are several pairs around. The undergrowth consists of two of the most typical bushes of the pine forest: Leafy Broom* *(Adenocarpus foliolosus)* and Canary Cistus. Note the odd shapes of the trees here – thin and vertical, almost entirely lacking branches. This is the result of a forest fire. The Canary Pine Forest is naturally resilient to fires. The flames kill all the lateral branches, but the tree sprouts again from the trunk.

Usually above the clouds and away from air pollution, the astronomy station of Izaña takes advantage of one of the clearest skies in the world.

Continue along the TF 24. At the mirador *Margarita de Piedra* you leave the forest and enter the subalpine zone with lots of Teide Broom and Teide Flixweed. Stop at the viewpoint at km 32.

2 From here you have extensive views over the Teide and the wildfire area. During the course of the morning, you usually see clouds forming on the north side which contrasts with the clear skies on the south side.

Inside the crater of Las Cañadas.

Close by, the dark slopes contrast sharply with the Teide Broom bushes, especially when they are in flower. In the bend, the road works have cut through the various layers of soft pumice, some very dark, some almost white.

Continue and turn left to the meteorological station of Izaña.

3 The futuristic buildings of Izaña consist of a meteorological and astronomical station. The very clear skies at this altitude, away from pollution and water vapour, offer the most perfect conditions for astronomy.

On the stretch of road towards Izaña, park and look out over the hill that slopes down towards the south-east. The slopes are covered in Teide broom and Teide Flixweed. In spring, this is a very good place to track down Spectacled Warbler, several pairs of which breed here.

Continue until you reach El Portillo visitors' centre at the junction with the TF 21.

PRACTICAL PART

Ascent from the south – Vilaflor

The ascent from Vilaflor is characterised by aridity – the south-facing, open woodlands offer some excellent birdwatching opportunities and several interesting wildflowers.

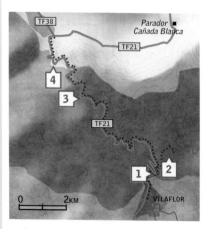

Vilaflor is a pretty mountain village with two fine restaurants with Canarian food and Teide Viper's-bugloss near the church – planted and flowering as early as March. From the village, follow the TF 21 up the mountain.

1 The pine forest just above the Vilaflor holds some stunning, large specimens of Canary Pine trees, which are worth stopping for. Just above the village is a mirador called *Pino Gordo*, literally fat pine – and that's exactly what you see from this point. The Pino Gordo has a circumference of over 9 metres and is 46 metres tall.

At the 4th hairpin above the village, a track forks off to the right. Park somewhere along this track and walk the track for about a kilometre.

2 This track gives a good insight into the bone-dry and open pine forest of the south-facing slope. The open patches along the track hold some interesting plant species, such as Smith's Houseleek (endemic to the dry pinewoods of Tenerife and recognisable by the hairy base of the stem), Greenish Viper's-bugloss* *(Echium virescens)*, Southern Ironwort *(Sideritis soluta)*, Canary Tree Sow-thistle, Teide Carline Thistle* *(Carlina xeranthemoides)*, Large-flowered White Broom* *(Chamaecytisus proliferus)*, Leafy Broom *(Adenocarpus foliolosus)* and even Teide Viper's-bugloss.

3 Continue along the TF 21 until you find after km post 59 and on the left hand side, *Las Lajas área recreativa*. This large picnic site is one of the best places on Tenerife to see the magnificent Blue Chaffinch. It is attracted to the crumbs left by picnicking families, and by the water in the drinking fountains here. Stroll around and search for the places with a high bird activity. Other common birds here are Canary, Great Spotted Woodpecker, African Blue Tit and Tenerife Goldcrest.

4 Continue. As you climb, you pass an area which burnt down in 2012, a testimony to the fire sensitivity of these forests, but also of its resilience: while most of the trees lost all their branches to the fire, their trunks survived. At present, you'll need to look closely to see traces of the event. This gives a little hope for the pinewoods in the northwestern part of the forests (see previous points) which were affected so badly in 2023. The views become increasingly impressive and culminate when you cross the crater rim. In May, masses of Teide Catmint* (*Nepeta teydea*) and Teide Viper's-bugloss grace the roadside. It's tempting to stop and look around – if you do, make sure you find a good spot to park, well off the road.

Continue over the crater rim (what a view!) and a little further on, you reach the crossing with the TF 38.

Greenish Viper's-bugloss (top) and Blue Chaffich (bottom) – two endemics of the pine forest zone. Both can be seen when ascending the Cañadas from Vilaflor.

Ascent from the west – Chío

The ascent from Chío is characterised by its very young lava and extremely sparse vegetation cover, but despite this there are good opportunities for birdwatching.

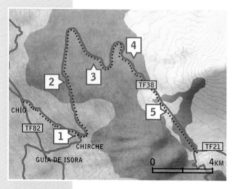

Follow the TF 38 up to El Teide (sign-posted). After 5 km, turn right towards Chirche and Aripe. Park at the viewpoint.

1 You are now, at an altitude of 1,000 metres, in the thermophilous scrub zone, but one of a special kind. The entire area here is covered in young lava. The flora is special, with many tall Rooftop Houseleeks* *(Aeonium urbicum)*, Tree Sow-thistle, Greenish Viper's-bugloss* *(Echium virescens)*, Lamarck's Spurge, Tree Houseleek* *(Aeonium arboreum)*, Graceful Marguerite and Canary Silk-vine.

Return to the TF 38 and turn right to start the climb onto El Teide. The extremely rare Tenerife Giant Orchid* *(Himantoglossum metlesicsiana)* is reputed to grow in this general area.

2 Note how in the first few kilometres, all the wildflowers disappear from the forest, leaving only pine trees and bare rock. The young lava can't support anything else but this sparse growth of Canary pines. As you climb, you'll pass several lava streams where even trees can't grow.

After km 13, turn right to the *Chío Pinar recreational area.*

3 The *área recreativa* is a picnic site in a very open pine forest in a landscape of volcanic ash. There is no undergrowth at all, giving the weird sensation of walking through a computer model of a landscape rather than the real thing.

There are several drinking fountains that attract forest birds. Take your time to observe these spots and you may find Great Spotted Woodpecker, Canary, Berthelot's Pipit and, the grand prize, Blue Chaffinch.

Continue up the mountain.

4 Just before km 7, there is a car park on the left, from which several walks start. It is worth walking a short part of the trail, just to experience the bizarre landscape.
You are now at the upper edge of the pine forest zone where the pine trees are stunted and the needles of an unhealthy yellowish colour – a reflection of the winter cold and extreme dryness of the young lava field. The yellow trees stand out against the black lava, which makes for an extraordinary sight. The first bushes of the Cañada zone appear here – Teide Broom and Teide Scrub-scabious* *(Pterocephalus lasiospermus)*.

5 A little further and you have left the zone of pine forests to enter the barren open expanse of El Teide crater. Just before km 2 is a viewpoint on the left, which overlooks a giant lava field. The lava is nearly black, indicating that it hasn't yet oxidized (which would turn it reddish-brown as you'll see further into the crater). This lava flow is from the second latest eruption in Tenerife, which was in 1798. You can even see the crater from which the lava flowed. Nothing grows on these barren chunks of lava, which looks a little like a giant, ploughed field of clay, but from the humble perspective of a beetle.

Two kilometre ahead you reach the junction with the TF 21.

At the very edge of the pine forest zone. The drought and poor soils make growth impossible, even for the sturdy Canary Pine.

Inside the the Cañadas del Teide

The main attraction of this excursion is the interior of a large crater– the Cañadas del Teide. From the TF 21 – TF 38 junction in the south to the TF 21 – TF 24 junction in the north, these are the attractive sites:

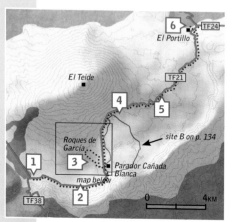

1 The viewpoint at the TF 38 – TF 21 junction offers beautiful views of El Teide and two massive flows of lava, one from the middle ages and a more recent one from the 1798 eruption. There isn't much life here, although Raven and Berthelot's Pipit may show themselves, while a pair of Barbary Falcons breed on the crater cliffs above the viewpoint. The big brooms in front of you are the endemic Teide Brooms.

2 Just east of the junction of the TF 38 and TF 21 you pass a large dry, sandy plain with a scattering of the endemic Teide broom bushes – the *Llano de Ucanca*. This plain is the drainage basin for Teide mountain. When snow melts on the southern slopes of El Teide, the water runs down onto this plain. However, since the evaporation is much higher than the precipitation, the 'lake' is a dust-dry plain for most of the year. With the crater rim on your right and the desert plain and el Teide on your left, this is a scenically superb spot.

3 The Cañada Blanca is one of the two main visitors' centres of the Cañadas del Teide. Several trails start from here and we suggest

the walk around the conspicuous rock garden on the other side of the road – the *Roques de García*. This 2-hour, moderately difficult walk is deservedly very popular, so if you like a quiet walk, do this early in the day and avoid weekends.

Along the walk, you'll see streams of solidified lava. There are the famous wind-swept rocks (see photo) and gigantic walls of basalt. Apart

from the geology and scenery, this loop offers a rich flora. Nearly all plants you encounter here are endemic to the Cañadas del Teide, and include Teide Viper's-bugloss, Teide Wallflower, Teide Scrub-scabious* (*Pterocephalus lasiospermus*) and Teide Broom. Butterflies frequent here are Tenerife Green-striped White (a butterfly endemic to the crater which flies from March to June), Canary Blue (April to September) and Tenerife Grayling (mid-May to September).

Among the birds, only Berthelot's Pipit is likely to be present. There are some tame ones close to the visitor's centre. Kestrel, Raven and Barbary Partridge may turn up if you are lucky – the latter only when there are few people around.

The impressive Roques de García are wind-sculpted remains of the former Cañadas volcano (see page 18).

Beyond the visitors' centre, you continue a few hundred metres through the broom scrub before entering the bizarre rockscapes of the young lava fields. You can't park at the side of the road but there are two car parks from which you can stroll around.

4 The first car park, *Tabonal Negro*, is on the right just beyond the cable lift car park. It offers sublime views over the young lava, and has many specimens of Teide Viper's-bugloss growing around the viewpoint.

When walking the loop around the Roques de García (top), the Tenerife Green-striped White (bottom) is a frequent sight. This butterfly flies only in the Cañada crater.

5 The second is called *Minas de San José* and lies beyond the start of the trail up to the summit (see route 3 and site A on page 134). Park on either side of the road. The surroundings of this viewpoint are desert-like, with just a few black rocks standing out of the sand-coloured volcanic gravel. Note the flow of ropey lava on the slope on the left side of the road. There are plenty of Teide Marguerites here.

The final stop is on the northern edge of the crater, where the second visitors' centre, *El Portillo*, is located.

6 El Portillo has a great exhibition on the geology of El Teide. Right next to it is a botanical garden with all the main species that grow in the Cañadas National Park. Birdwatchers will want to head straight to the small pond at the back, close to where the pine forest begins. African Blue Tit, Canary, Chiffchaff, Blue Chaffinch and even Great Spotted Woodpecker flit back and forth to drink here, particularly early in the morning. From spring until autumn, when the Tenerife Lizards are active at this altitude, there are dozens of very tame individuals around. They will take small chunks of fruit straight from your hand.

It pays to be here early, before other visitors arrive.

Route 2: La Fortaleza

5 HOURS
EASY-MODERATE

Beautiful walk to one of the Cañada's botanical treasure troves.

Habitats: Teide Broom scrub, volcanic sandy desert, cliffs
Selected species: Teide Viper's-bugloss, Teide Broom, Teide Scrub-Scabious*, Mouflon, Barbary Partridge, Berthelot's Pipit, Blue Chaffinch, Canary Blue, Tenerife Green-striped White, Tenerife Grayling

!
No shade

At the time of writing, the trail was closed on Tuesdays and Thursdays

Best season
May-July
Of interest
Year-round

This route offers a more in-depth exploration of the superb nature of El Teide caldera. It takes you through the lava and pumice fields to the isolated plateau of La Fortaleza. La Fortaleza is one of the botanical highlights of the crater and attracts a good number of butterflies, but to appreciate this, you need to be here in late spring or summer. This route is also quite good for birdwatching, with a fair chance on finding Barbary Partridge and, in the botanical garden at the start of this route, various forest birds, including Blue Chaffinch. The scenery *en route* is stunning, as everywhere in the Caldera.

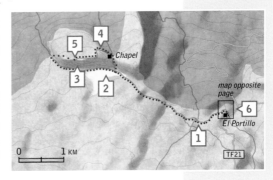

To beat the crowds to La Fortaleza, visit the visitors' centre upon your return.

Starting point Visitors' centre El Portillo (GPS: 28.304408, -16.566512)

Follow the trail that runs directly left past the visitors' centre. At the T-junction turn left.

1 The path you are following is the National Park trail number 1. Ignore the side tracks, with different numbers. You walk through hilly lava fields and light-coloured pumice. The Teide is constantly more or less in front of you.

Teide Viper's-buglosses flower en masse at the base of La Fortaleza in May and June.

In this section, there are many Sticky Broom, Teide Broom, Teide Flixweed, Teide Wallflower, Teide Marguerite and Teide Mint* (*Satureja lachnophylla*), all of which are endemic to the subalpine zone of Tenerife, or shared only with La Palma. In spring and summer, there are plenty of butterflies. Most frequent are Teide Green-striped White, Canary Blue (very common!), Clouded Yellow and Tenerife Grayling.

The birdlife is scarce, but Berteloth's Pipit is around and Plain Swifts wheel overhead. Keep an eye open for Barbary Partridge which are frequently seen. Lizards dart out in front of you, seeking shelter underneath the bushes.

You may also come across Mouflon here – this introduced species (see page 89) is not common but nevertheless poses a threat to the rare flora of the caldera. In fact, the trail is closed during Tuesdays and Thursdays to allow for Mouflon 'control'.

2 The trail drops down to a large sandy plain with the cliffs of La Fortaleza to the right. This is an outwash plain of volcanic sand and gravel brought down by the annual thaw of snow on the Teide's slopes. Except for Teide Flixweed, nothing grows here.

3 The flanks of La Fortaleza provide a contrast with the plain, as here you'll find a rich flora with many Teide Viper's-bugloss and Link's Fennel (*Ferula linkii*). A large part of the slope is fenced off, except for the far ends of the cliff, where you can get close to the plants. Kestrel breeds on the cliff.

Continue to the first trees for a picnic (the only shady spot on the route; GPS: 28.315226, -16.606221). The very agile may attempt to climb the short, but difficult, trail that starts just before the first tree on your right and climbs straight up the Fortaleza. Otherwise, return over the sandy plain and turn left to the small chapel of Ermita *Cruz de Fregel* (GPS: 28.314600, -16.592172).

4 The area around the chapel was seriously affected by a forest fire in 2007. This is why the tree line in this section is so abrupt. The plants that took their place – mostly Teide Scrub-scabious* *(Pterocephalus lasiospermus)* – attract many butterflies. Apart from the aforementioned species (see point 1), we found Cardinal and Canary Red Admiral here.

Continue the broad track behind the chapel which comes to an end 500 metres further on. Continue along the stone-lined trail to the left. It leads to the edge of the cliff.

5 From the end of the trail, you have splendid views over El Teide and you can see the course of the meltwater down to the plain in front of the cliff. Keep an eye out for plants near the cliff as well. This is a good spot for Teide Carline Thistle* *(Carlina xeranthemoides)*, another endemic plant to the Cañadas.

Afterwards, return to the El Portillo visitors' centre.

6 At El Portillo, enjoy the wonderful exhibition on the geology of Tenerife. Don't forget to visit the botanical garden, where you can see most native wildflowers of the Cañadas del Teide with convenient labels stating their names. Take some time at the small pond in the back of the centre where Blue Chaffinch, Canary, Chiffchaff, African Blue Tit and Great Spotted Woodpecker come to drink right in front of you, offering excellent opportunities for photography.

Chiffchaffs, Robins, Blue Chaffinches, African Blue Tits and this Canary frequently come down to drink in the small pool in botanical garden of El Portillo.

Route 3: The Teide Eggs

5 HOURS
EASY-MODERATE

Surreal desert landscape at the foot of El Teide.
Site for the rare and localised Teide Pansy and Auber's Viper's-bugloss.

Geological features: Volcanic glass, pumice fields, teide eggs, ropey lava, block lava
Habitats: Pumice slopes of the highest altitude zone
Selected species: Teide Marguerite, Auber's Viper's-bugloss, Teide Pansy, Teide Catmint

!

No shade

Best season
late May-June

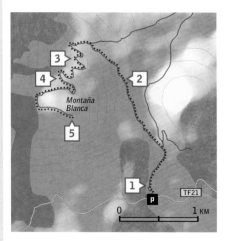

This linear walk to the Montaña Blanca brings you into Tenerife's highest vegetation zone (see illustration on page 31) – a spectacular, desert world that appears to be almost devoid of plant growth. Nevertheless, there are several rarities to be found here – extremely specialist species that have adapted to the harsh climate of the summit of El Teide. They occur only in higher parts of the Teide Caldera and are rare even here.

Otherwise, there is nothing here but silence. This may well be the first walk you've ever taken on which you don't see a single bird!

This walk is not just about the living world. The clear atmosphere, deep blue sky, light-coloured pumice fields and brown layers of block lava produce an amazing landscape. The odd *Huevos del Teide* (Teide eggs) – large, black boulders in the middle of the white pumice are a scenic highlight of this route.

Starting point car park of the Montaña Blanca (GPS: 28.259466, -16.603307; 2.5 km east of the parking for the cable car).

1 On the first 50 metres of the trail, you'll encounter already some of the key features of this route. The young lava is laced with threads and spots of volcanic glass (obsidian) – curious chunks of black glass formed from lava that cooled down very rapidly. There are few flowers here, but they clearly stand out in the barren landscape: Teide Scrub-scabious* *(Pterocephalus lasiospermus)*, Teide Marguerite, Teide Wallflower, Teide Flixweed and, a little ahead, Teide Catmint. All, except the latter (which also grows on La Palma), are endemic plants of the Cañadas.

2 Follow the track, keeping left at each turning. You cross fields of sand-coloured pumice – volcanic rock honey-combed with tiny gas bubbles, which makes it very light. The pumice fields alternate with large areas of brown block lava, which originated from a more fluid lava stream. On the hillside on the right, you see a good example of a ropey lava, which stems from more viscous material. Look carefully for the first Auber's Viper's-bugloss* (*Echium auberiana*), a beautiful plant that grows only on these high slopes of the Teide.

The 'Teide Eggs' are huge lava balls that broke off from a half-solidified lava flow and rolled downhill onto the pumice fields, thereby obtaining their round form.

130

At the junction (GPS: 28.276515, -16.610607), turn left towards the Montaña Blanca.

3 The trail winds along the remarkable Teide eggs – black boulders of basalt which, half solidified, broke loose from the lava stream above and rolled downhill as a ball of hot stone. The pumice debris around the Teide eggs is where you find the Teide Pansy, flowering in late May and June.

4 The track then winds round the bend, passes a notice board explaining the origin of El Teide eggs. At the bend beyond, there are many more of the rare Auber's Viper's-bugloss*.

5 Continue to the viewpoint with superb views towards the east and south over the outer caldera wall.

Return via the same way.

Auber's Viper's-bugloss (top) and Teide Pansy (bottom), two very rare endemic wildflowers of the highest vegetation zone of Tenerife. Both can be found on this walk.

Route 4: The pine forests of Los Organos

4-5 HOURS
EASY-MODERATE

Best season
March-April
Of interest
Year-round

Pretty walk through a tall, shady pine forest.
Attractive flora and birdlife.

Habitats: Pine forest, allotments, laurel forest remnants
Selected species: Canary Orchid, Dense-flowered Orchid, Golden Greenovia, Spade-leaved Houseleek, Greenish Viper's-bugloss*, Red-leaved Monanthes*, Tenerife Goldcrest, Canary, Bolle's Pigeon, Blue Chaffinch, Canary Red Admiral

This easy walk leads through what up to the summer of 2023 was one of the loveliest pine forests of Tenerife. Set beneath the steep cliffs of *Los Organos* in the upper Orotava valley, it follows a track, with several options for more strenuous loops that lead you deeper into the forest.

The route is located at the lower edge of the pine forest zone. In the barrancos, there are many plants from the laurel forest zone. This blend of two habitats is also noticeable in the birdlife: both Bolle's Pigeon (typical of the laurel forest) and Blue Chaffinch (an inhabitant of the pine forest) occur alongside each other.

The return trail leads through the chestnut groves of the upper Orotava valley, where Canaries, Chiffchaffs, Robins and Blackbirds are the common birds.

Starting point La Caldera recreational area (GPS: 28.357997, -16.501159)

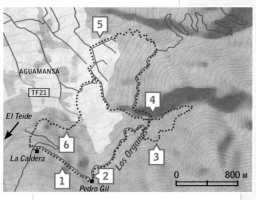

2023 Forest fires

In late summer 2023, a wildfire destroyed the northwestern part of the forest belt of Tenerife. The area of Los Organos lies at the western end of the affected area. As the fire took place shortly before this book went to print, we have not been able to verify how badly this route is affected by the fire. This route description maintains the original text describing the situation prior to the forest fires. Undoubtedly, the situation on the ground will be different, and will change strongly in the course of the following years.

Getting there From La Orotava, follow the TF 21 up to the Teide. After the last village, just beyond km 16, turn left towards *La Caldera* and *Los Organos*. Continue and park at the car park of La Caldera.

1 The first section up to the hut of *Pedro Gil* (at the first bridge) passes through a majestic pine forest, with tall trees whose branches are covered by the long threads of beard lichens. This part of the pine forest is often shrouded in fog and the beard lichens profit from the moisture. If you are here when it is foggy, note how the tall pine needles capture the droplets and collect them at the tip from which they fall to the ground. This *llúvia horizontal* is very important for the forest ecosystems of the Canaries (see page 43).
The undergrowth is dominated by Canary Cistus, Canary Laurustinus, Canary Gale* *(Myrica faya)* and Tree Heath. Tenerife Goldcrest is common and Blue Chaffinch is sometimes present. The small Dense-flowered Orchid grows in ones and twos in the forest here and further on.

2 Beyond *Pedro Gil*, follow *Casa del Agua / Pinolere*. You pass a cliff with Spade-leaved Houseleek* *(Aeonium spathulatum)*, This is the common houseleek of the north-facing pine forests. Crenulated and Hairy Aichrysons are also common and if you look carefully, you'll find the inconspicuous Loose-flowered and Red-leaved Monantheses as well. The tall bushes of the Greenish Viper's-bugloss* *(Echium virescens)* bear large spikes of flowers in early spring.

Just before the next barranco, a trail leaves to your left for the village of Aguamansa (GPS: 28.360336, -16.487864). Take this if you just wish to make a short loop. It brings you down to the chestnut groves, before climbing back up to *La Caldera*.

3 Go right onto the *Ruta del Agua* for the long route. This narrow and steep trail (but one with a sturdy handrail to grip for the nervous or less sure-footed) leads through a rocky part of the forest. The tall rosettes of the Stemless Sow-thistles are impressive. It takes you an hour or less to complete this loop, which returns just a little further along on the main track. Turn right.

4 The bridge over the barranco is a good spot for a short break. The sunny spots (rare here on the north slope) are appreciated by Canary Red Admirals and Canary Speckled Woods. Scan the rocky outcrops on the south side of the barranco. In summer, you'll see many Golden Greenovias in flower on the rocks, while the rare Canary Orchid flowers here in April. If you follow the half-overgrown trail a bit into the barranco upslope, you'll find more of these pretty flowers.

Continue along the track through another section of pine forest. At the fork, take the righthand track. At the *Choza del Topo* (GPS: 28.368870, -16.486340; a picnic table between two walls), a track leads to the left, signposted *Pinaleris* and *La Florida*.

As you descend, more and more laurel forest species appear in the woodland. At the next fork, go right and at the following turning, take the second left – the one that leads further downwards (GPS: 28.37044 -16.48999).

5 As soon as you reach the tarmac, the woodland is replaced with a pretty landscape of terraced fields and chestnut groves. Look across the barranco to the right, where Bolle's Pigeon may be seen. Otherwise, this is the world of Canaries and African Blue Tits, and that of many Tenerife Lizards which take shelter in the stone walls along the road.

The rare Canary Orchid can be found on this route.

The Teide seen through the canopy.

At the junction by the shrine, go left. Subsequently, go right (Aguamansa) and then right again. At the second barranco, go left onto a trail, signposted *Casa Forestal* and *Barranco de la Arena* (GPS: 28.37044 -16.48999).

6 When you come to the road, follow it round the bend and then take the trail to the left, back towards *La Caldera*. This is another section where we found Blue Chaffinch.

Additional sites on Cañadas del Teide

A – Climbing mount Teide

Of interest
Year-round

Only ascend when
the weather is good

  There are two reasons to climb Mount Teide. The first is to get to the highest peak of Tenerife, indeed of the whole of Spain! The second is to experience the breath-taking views you have from this amazing crater. In terms of wildlife or wild-flowers, there is little cause to start this ascent. The Teide Pansy will be your only living companion in this barren world – apart from the other climbers of course.

You can go up the peak via the trail on the east side of the volcanco, or via the cable car (tickets online at **www.reservasparquesnacionales.es** or on the spot, on the car park of the cable car). The cable doesn't bring you all the way to the top. The final ascent of 163 metres is closed unless you have applied for a special permit, which needs to be arranged well in advance (best several weeks before; see **www.reservasparquesnacionales.es**). Another option is to spend the night in the mountain hut *Refugio de Altavista* and make the climb very early in the morning to see the sun come up on the Teide. This is an unforgettable experience, but tough, and one that requires proper preparations (torch and sufficient water and food – there is no food in the refuge).

B – Las Cañadas walk

Best season
April-June

    GPS: 28.223796, -16.627291. You can do an easy circuit in the Cañadas del Teide, offering great hiking, views, flora and butterflies.

On an evening on the upper Orotava valley, you may well find yourself standing on the shore of a sea of clouds. The altitude here is 1050 m.

Most of the typical Cañadas wild-flowers (e.g. Teide Catmint, Teide Marguerite, Teide Viper's-bugloss) are here, while Tenerife Green-striped White and Canary Blue are common butterflies en route. Birds are few, as everywhere within the crater, but Berthelot's Pipit, Sardinian Warbler, Kestrel, Barbary Falcon and Barbary Partridge are all possible. From the Cañada Blanca visitors' centre, follow National Park trail number 5 in the direction of the Teide. It runs parallel to the TF 21 until it ends at a track. From here, go right following the track to a *Sanatorio* and further on to the parador (see map on page 122).

The Teide Wallflower (top) is among the earliest flowers to appear in the Cañadas. You can find it in bloom in late March. The Berthelot's Pipit is the most common bird in the Cañadas del Teide (bottom).

C – Climbing the Guajara

GPS: 28.223796, -16.627291. From the Cañada Blanca visitors' centre a trail leads to the third-highest peak of Tenerife and the highest point of the outer Caldera: the Montaña de Guajara (2712 m). This mountain is a botanical delight and there are many butterflies, especially in early summer, such as Canary Blue, Tenerife Grayling, Cardinal and Tenerife Green-striped White. The walk is short, but fairly strenuous.
Start at the Parador bus station roundabout and follow the walking route 4. Where it reaches a road, you turn left (GPS: 28.220673, -16.622324). At the edge of a plain, go right onto the way-marked ascent to the Guajara (GPS: 28.223450, -16.605488).

Best season
April-June

D – The lunar landscape

GPS: 28.189874, -16.603487. North-east of Vilaflor, in the middle of the pine forest belt, lies an extraordinary spot known as the lunar landscape. It is a badland of soft pumice, covered by a thin, hard crust of lava. The crust is broken in places

Best season
April-June

136

and the soft underlying material eroded, leaving odd pillars of pumice. A trail leaves from the centre of Vilaflor and climbs about 600 metres to the lunar landscape in a fairly long and strenuous walk, especially when it is warm and sunny. You can start a bit closer by driving up towards the Teide, turn right in the 4th switchback (GPS: 28.165202, -16.634339) and drive on for 3.6 kms to the start of the trail (GPS: 28.171468, -16.619940). The route mostly runs through open, south-facing pinewoods with an interesting flora (e.g. Smith's Houseleek and Teide Viper's-bugloss).

E – Bolle's Pigeons at Camino de Chasna

Of interest
Year-round

 GPS: 28.359733, -16.530280. Birdwatchers in search of Bolle's Pigeons may get lucky at the barranco de Chasna. A path crosses the gorge, passes a shrine and, on to the other side of the gorge, leads along some fields. Both on these fields and in the gorge, Bolle's Pigeons are frequently seen and (in a refreshing deviation from its normal, shy behaviour) it sometimes perches conspicuously on branches, even allowing itself to be photographed.

As you drive along the TF 21 up towards the Teide, pass through the village of Camino de Chasna and, beyond the turn to Benijos and Palo Blanco, take the first small road upwards (on the right). After 800 metres, there is a car park next to the barranco, from which you can walk to the shrine in 2 minutes, and it takes another 2 to get to the fields on the other side. Note that the 800 m stretch of road is extremely steep and that walking is perhaps a wiser option.

F – Stargazing on the Teide

Of interest
Year-round

 Well above the clouds and in a dry part of the world, the night skies of Tenerife's Cañadas are extraordinarily clear. This is one of the best places in the world for star gazing.

You can go by yourself or join a guided tour. The advantage of going by yourself is the alienating experience of the countless stars in combination with the silence and the impressive landscape. The *Roques de García* in front of the visitors' centre are a favourite night-time destination, but elsewhere is just as wonderful. The perks of an organised tour (e.g. www.astroamigos.com and www.elcardon.com) is the equipment and specialist guide, who will be able to show you constellations, the milky way, nebulas and detailed views of the moon. Companies to check out for booking your stellar adventure are

In either case, dress warmly and pack your bins and telescope.

Northwest Tenerife

Tenerife's Northwest is dominated by the Teno mountains, a very jagged and heavily eroded mountain range with very steep barrancos and sea cliffs. Teno is together with Anaga, one of the oldest parts of Tenerife (see page 18). They are made of tertiary volcanic rock, whose dramatic topography stems from a long period of erosion. In the interior part of the mountains, there are traditional villages and on the north slopes there are important areas of remnant laurel cloud forests. In this, the Teno mountains are similar to the Anaga mountains in the north-east, which also originated in the Tertiary era. The Teno mountains differ in having some upland plains (site B on page 147) and a large coastal plain at the Punta Teno (route 5), both of which support a rich birdlife.

The Teno mountains are a highlight for naturalists, bird-watchers and hikers. There are various species of wildflowers that are unique to this area.

A proper exploration of the Teno mountains involves long hikes in the steep gorges of the massif, such as the famous Masca gorge, which is at present rather difficult to access (see page 150). A great alternative is the barranco south of Los Silos (route 7). In contrast, route 6 explores the jagged crests of the Teno mountains.

Teno's laurel cloud forests are know as the Monte del Agua, and are the subject of route 8, while the bird-rich coastal areas, which are also very rich in wildflowers, are covered on route 5.

The main towns of northwest Tenerife lie just outside the Teno mountains. Icod de los Vinos and Garachico (sites C and D on page 148-149) are pretty towns on the north coast, each with their own natural attractions. Garachico and Punta Teno offer good opportunities for snorkelling. From Garachico the main circular road around the island climbs the saddle between Teno and El Teide, passing the villages of Erjos and Santiago del Teide along the way. At the southern end of Teno, overlooking its giant coastal cliffs, lies the resort of Los Gigantes from where many whale-watching trips depart (see G on page 151).

Route 5: From Teno Alto to Punta Teno

FULL DAY
MODERATE-STRENUOUS

!

No shade

Best season
Oct-June

Good bird watching with species of dry
farmlands.
Tenerife lizards and sea birds on Punta Teno.

Habitats: Abandoned farmland, coastal scrub, thermophile forest, barranco
Selected species: Dark-red Spurge, Osprey, Barbary Partridge, Berthelot's
Pipit, Canary, Corn Bunting, Raven, Spectacled Warbler, Tenerife Lizard

This scenic walk leads from the Teno plateau down to the coast and passes a wonderful range of habitats along the way. There are open grasslands and farmland on top, hosting a rich birdlife. From there you descend through a barranco along a hamlet (las Cuevas) with an endemic flora growing on abandoned terraces. The coastal zone further down has a beautifully zoned vegetation. Ultimately you end up at Punta Teno, where you can admire Tenerife Lizard, shearwaters and if you are lucky some dolphins or an Osprey. Combined this walk is scenically beautiful and has a rich flora and birdlife. Note that all the climbing takes place on your way back.

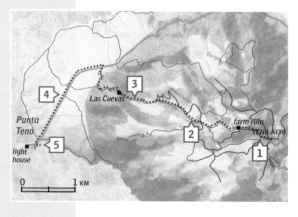

Starting point Teno Alto
(GPS: 28.3435169, -16.8767762)
Follow the trail to Punta de
Teno (signposted).

1 Just outside the village, you walk through scrubland with open grasslands, sometimes combined with a patchwork of tree heath, broom and cistus vegetation. Much of this was farmland, sometimes on terraces, but is now abandoned. This habitat houses many birds. Canary, Corn Bunting, Kestrel,

Berthelot's Pipit and Spectacled Warbler are easily to observe here. Along the way you can find some typical endemic plants of dry scrubland: Spiny Starwort* (*Pallenis spinosa*), Purple and Rough-leaved Viper's-bugloss* (*Echium aculateum*) and the Stemless Sow-thistle.

The road forks near a farm ruin. Take the right track following the yellow/white PR route. After 1 km you reach a small road and the first houses of the hamlet Las Cuevas. Cross the road and follow the trail to Punta de Teno.

2 On the right the terraced farmland dominates the view; on the left you look into the beautiful barranco. The Teno-bound endemic Dark-red Spurge grows between Lamarck's and Balsam Spurge, Prickly Pear, Agave and a number of field and roadside plants like Pelargonium and the white poppy *Papaver somniferum*. Further on the landscape becomes more open and rocky. This is the place where the Tenerife Lizard can be found. The birdlife remains rich, with Berthelot's Pipit, Buzzard, Raven and Barbary Partridge all frequently present.

3 The trail descends and as you walk down, the sea influence on vegetation becomes visible. Plants like Sea-heath, Canary Sea Fennel, Small-leaved Sea Lavender and Schyzogyne – all classics of the coastal scrubland – can be found here. They are well adapted to drought and salt, which comes as rain in drops from the sea, the so called salt spray. You'll still find some plants that were dominant in the barranco, such as Lamarck's Spurge and Prickly Pear, but here they are far less vital due to their low tolerance towards salt spray.

The terraced farmlands, now abandoned, are attractive for bird species like Buzzard, Raven, Corn Bunting and Barbary Partridge.

The trail ends at the road to Punta Teno, which is a little further to the left.

PRACTICAL PART

4 The walk along the road is a good opportunity to spot some characteristic birds like Rock Sparrow, Berthelot's Pipit, Corn Bunting and in winter also the Spectacled Warbler. Notice on your left the beautiful, colourful slope dominated by Canary and Dark-red Spurge and salt tolerating species that are typical for the coastal dry scrubland: Sea heath, Canary Sea Fennel, Small-leaved Sea Lavender and Schyzogyne.

5 On the small car park you can take a rest and enjoy the Tenerife Lizard which are abundant throughout the year. From here you have impressive views of the cliffs (acantilados) and in the distance the village of Los Gigantes. It is in the inaccessible crevices of these cliffs that the Tenerife Speckled (or Giant) Lizard lives, a species that is recently rediscovered (see page 103-104). End your tour by walking the beautiful boardwalk towards the ocean which gives you the opportunity to see the shearwaters and may be the Osprey that breeds here. When you are lucky you see some dolphins jumping out of the water.

Return the same way back.

In spring, the males of the Tenerife Giant Lizard have spectacular colours.

The coastal plain of Punta de Teno is covered in a beautiful, pristine succulent scrub.

Route 6: Cumbre de Baracán

4 HOURS
EASY

Best season
February -April
Of interest
Year-round

Pleasant walk with breath-taking views.
Dramatic difference between north and south slopes.
Rich flora and birdlife.

Habitat:s Tree heath forest, thermophilous scrub, fields
Selected species: Hedgehog Pericallis, *Greenovia dodrentale*, Haworth's Houseleek, Canary Squill, Three-fingered Orchid, Two-leaved Gennaria, Canary, Buzzard, Tenerife lizard

This dramatic crest walk leads from the Teno Alto to the TF-436 (Masca) road. Along the way you get a good taste of the great differences between the north and south-facing slope of the mountain. Although wide vistas into the deep barrancos are the main theme, this walk is quite diverse. You traverse dry scrubland, cross old tree heath forest, visit remnant

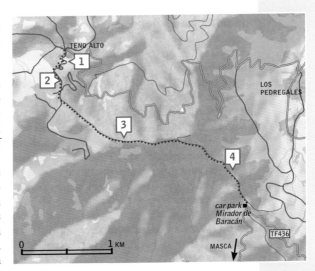

patches of laurel forests and enjoy a rich undergrowth of endemic plants. The rich flora is accompanied by a good range of reptiles, butterflies and birds.

You can also do this route the other way around starting at the parking facility at Mirador de Baracán.

Starting point Teno Alto (GPS: 28.3435169, -16.8767762)

The trail follows the crest known as Cumbre de Baracán (top). Notice the dramatic difference in vegetation between the north and south-facing slope. In spring, Plain Swift is a common bird along the trail (bottom).

1 *Cumbre* means mountain crest and that is exactly where you're headed to. On your climb out of the village, you pass scattered houses and fields, which are partially abandoned. Canary, Plain Swift, Corn Bunting and the local forms of Buzzard and Kestrel are frequently found here. As you leave these fields behind you, more and more remains of the original laurel forest show up. There are patches of Canary Gale, Canary Broom, Canary St. John's-wort, Canary Strawberry Tree and some interesting endemics like the Hedgehog Pericallis and Stemless Sow-thistle.

2 After ca 1 km the road turns into a track and all of a sudden the landscape changes completely as you enter the Roque membrillo, a red-coloured step-wise entrance to a closed tree heath forest. Its name is derived from the red colour of membrillo (a pasta of quinces, that is a traditional additive to tapas). The colour reflects the high content of iron oxide. This type of soils is very sensitive to erosion as you can see as you walk up the stairs. Once you are in the tree heath forest you will feel its magic: the very old tree heath branches are twisted by the wind and the closed canopy gives you a real forest experience, reinforced by the typical forest undergrowth with the winter-flowering orchid Two-leaved Gennaria, and the beautiful Canary Squill.

3 Once out of the forest you come on the crest (cumbre) where the trail alternates between the north and the south slope. Notice the differences between them. On the north slope you can clearly distinguish the dense, more forest-like vegetation. There are two endemic houseleeks here, *Aeonium haworthi* and *Greenovia dodrentale*. You may also find the small, endemic Three-fingered Orchid here, flowering in winter until April.

On the south side a shrubby, thermophile vegetation dominates. Narrow-leaved Cistus is particularly common. There are also lots of Tenerife Lizards, butterflies, and sometimes birds of prey that follow the ridge where they glide on the warm, rising air.

Looking further in the distance, past the the deep barrancos around Masca, you recognise La Gomera and La Palma on the horizon. From the north slope the most remarkable landscape feature is the Montaña de El Palmar, an ancient volcano that was dug out several decades ago leaving the deep quarries.

4 At the end of the crest you descend to the road at Mirador de Baracán. Along the path again you have some spectacular views into the deep barrancos and the ocean.

Return the same way back.

Red soils of the Roque Membrillo (left). The endemic Canary Squill (right).

Route 7: From Los Silos to Erjos

Best season
February -April
Of interest
Year-round

FULL DAY
MODERATE-STRENUOUS

Beautiful walk through intact thermophile forests and laurel cloud forests.
Very rich flora and birdlife.

Habitats: Laurel forest, thermophile forest, barranco, Fish Ponds
Selected species: Canary Bellflower, Canary Dragon Arum, Giant Viper's-bugloss, Bolle's Pigeon, Tenerife Goldcrest, Plain Swift, Kestrel, Barbary Falcon, Stripeless Tree Frog, Tenerife Lizard, Canary Islands Large White, Epaulet Skimmer

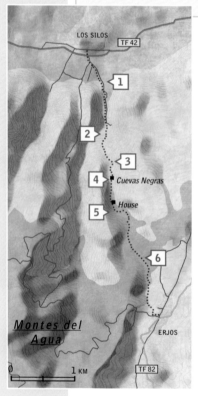

The walk proposed here leads up from roughly sea level, through steep barrancos to the laurel cloud forests and ends in the village of Erjos at 1,000 metres altitude, from where you can either walk back or take a bus. Along the way, you'll enjoy a truly wonderful flora with a large number of Tenerife endemics, as well as a good selection of butterflies. The entire stretch described is rather strenuous. However, the best part, both for wildflowers and for the scenery, is the first third of the route, up to Cuevas Negras.

Starting point Church of Los Silos. Cross the Los Silos bypass (TF 42) and follow the small road signposted *Senderos Erjos* and *Cuevas Negras*.

1 The first short section leads through partially walled banana plantations and later alongside a small stream. There are many Tenerife Lizards hiding in the stone walls. Along the stream in the irrigation ditches, look for the Epaulet Skimmer (a dragonfly). You'll probably see the first Canary Speckled Woods.

Keep an eye out for Stripeless Tree Frogs, which are common in the streambed vegetation, but hide between the leaves.

2 Where the track ends, continue via a trail into the Barranco. You now enter a nature reserve. Among the many species typical of the thermophilous forest, there is Giant Viper's-bugloss, Broad-leaved Viper's-bugloss,* *(Echium structum)* Lamarck's Spurge, Canary St. John's-wort, Canary Palm, Wild Jasmine, Willow-leaved Globularia* *(Globularia salicina)* and Stemless Sow-thistle (recognisable by the downy flower heads). Further up there are even some specimens of the Dragon Tree – a rarity in the wild.

There are not many birds, but keep an eye open for Chiffchaff, Plain Swift, African Blue Tit, Kestrel, Buzzard, Raven and Barbary Falcon. In spring, there are many butterflies along the path. Canary Islands Large White (with big black patches on the wing) is most frequent, but look out too, for the Canary Cleopatra and Canary Red Admiral.

3 Where the path passes beneath some cliffs (there is a sign '7' here), there are more interesting plants, such as Loose-flowered and Leafy Monanthes* *(Monanthes polyphylla)*, Saucer-leaved Houseleek and the showy Bush Sealavender* *(Limonium arborescens)*, which is endemic to the

The barranco of Cuevas Negras (left) is home to a massive number of rare and attractive wild-flowers. One of them is the stout Canarian Dragon Arum (top), which grows in wet patches along the trail.

Leafy (top) and Miniature Monanthes (bottom) grow on the cliffs at point 3. Both belong to the Monanthes genus, all of which are endemic to the Canary Islands and Madeira.

Teno mountains. There are many Yellow Ceropegias and Cliff Sow-thistle* (*Sonchus radicatus*), endemic to Tenerife.

4 A little further on, you come to a stone wall to your left, where Hare's-foot Fern and Disc-leaved Fern* (*Adiantum reniforme*) grow. You are now close to the ruins of the hamlet of Cuevas Negras, with its giant Barbusano Laurel* (*Apollonias barbujana*), the first sign of the laurel forest zone in the barranco (see also page 55). Just beyond the ruins, you cross the barranco – a wonderful shady spot where in May, numerous Canary Dragon Arums flower. If you want to make this route less strenuous, this is a good end point.

5 Continue through the barranco and enjoy the scenery, which gradually becomes more forested and shady. The laurel forest clearly penetrates the lower altitudes in the barranco – as you look up the slopes, you'll note they are still devoid of trees. Along the trail, in the small concrete channel, Canary Dragon Arum is frequent, while Canary Foxglove appears along the trail and Canary Bellflower becomes increasingly frequent. The latter grows particularly prettily where you pass a small house with a pergola that arches over the track. The Bellflowers hang from this pergola.

6 As you move upwards, you find yourself in a gallery forest of tall heath. Keep an eye out for Tenerife Goldcrest and note the many Hairy Aichrysons and Hare's-foot Ferns on the stone walls.

As you pass the sign that you are leaving the protected area, you reach the cultivations on the edge of Erjos village. Prepare for a final 600 metres of steep climbing.

Additional remarks
The very fit can return via another way. Follow route 7 of this book. At point 6 of that route, you can descend back to Los Silos, a walk which is comparable in length and difficulty to this one.

Route 8: Monte del Agua laurel cloud forest

4 HOURS
EASY

Beautiful walk through intact thermophile forests and laurel cloud forests.
Rich flora and birdlife.

Best season
April - June
Of interest
Year-round

Habitats: Laurel forest, allotments
Selected species: Canary Bellflower, Canary Foxglove, Golden Rustyback
Fern, Laurel Forest Gentian, Canary Laurel, Bolle's Pigeon, Tenerife
Goldcrest, Plain Swift, Buzzard, Chaffinch

The forest of Monte del Agua (water mountains) is, together with the Anaga mountains and La Esperanza, Tenerife's last remaining intact laurel cloud forest. It is a rich area for both plants and birds, including the sought-after Bolle's Pigeon – a unique species of the laurel forest.

This linear and level route runs over an old forest track straight through the mountains, connecting open viewpoints (best for finding the pigeons) with stretches of forest, which are best for seeing the other forest birds and wildflowers. This route is very rich in species, but lacks the mossy, jungle-like atmosphere of the laurel cloud forest of Anaga and La Gomera.

Note that the fog can rise up at any time, but in general it is more frequent at midday, while most pigeon activity can be expected in the first and last hours of the day.

Starting point

Erjos church. There is sufficient parking next to the bar-mini-market on the main TF 82 road, in front of the church.

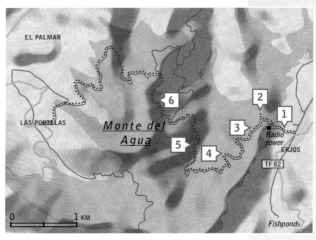

Follow the footpath signposted *Las Portelas / Monte del Agua.*

1 The first short stretch runs through partially abandoned, flowery fields with lots of butterflies, all belonging to the more common species (e.g. Meadow Brown, Canary Speckled Wood, Canary Red Admiral and Small Copper). Canaries are very common, as are Plain Swift, Buzzard and Kestrel while Barbary Partridge, Sardinian Warbler and Barbary Falcon may well make their appearance too.

Note that the larger trees were all burnt when, in 2012, the most recent forest fire swept across Erjos. Fortunately it spared the larger part of the laurel forest and should be a warning to everyone to be very careful with fire in the forest.

The trail reaches a track near a radio tower where you go right. A few metres further, go right towards a conspicuous hill.

Right beside the track there are large numbers of wildflowers (top).
The patches of Cedronella flowers attract butterflies like a magnet. Besides this Canary Cleopatra, Canary Speckled Wood and Laurel White are frequently seen (bottom).

2 The hill is right at the edge of the forest. You overlook the canopy through the burnt trees. This is a primary site to look for Bolle's Pigeon.

Follow the main trail into the forest.

3 You only need to walk a few metres into the forest to see the first of the wildflowers for which this habitat is famous: Canary Crane's-bill, Canary Buttercup, Bloody Pericallis* *(Pericallis cruenta)* and Hairy Aichryson. Note the typical smell of the laurel forest: fresh, somewhat sweet-scented, but in some places marred by the foul-smelling flowers of the Canary Laurustinus bushes.

The gently sloping track remains parallel to the main ridge, zigzagging from outcrop to side valley. The densest forest, dominated by Canary Laurel, is found in the valley, where shorter stands of Tree Heath and Canary Gale* *(Myrica faya)* dominate the crests.

En route, there is a fantastic show of wildflowers, including Laurel Sea-kale* *(Crambe strigosa)*, Laurel Forest Gentian* *(Ixanthus viscosus)*, Bloody Pericallis* *(Pericallis cruenta)*, Smith's Figwort and Canary Balm. The latter attracts many Canary Speckled Woods, Canary Cleopatra and Canary Islands Large Whites. Every now and then, you'll hear some pigeons crashing through the foliage and flying out of the canopy, but frustratingly, they mostly remain out of sight. The birds that are visible are Chaffinch, Chiffchaff, Tenerife Goldcrest and African Blue Tit.

4 After 500 metres, at a sign with a 7 on it, there is a short trail to an exposed rocky outcrop. This is another viewpoint for the pigeons – better than the first. Just stay here a while and wait for them to fly up from the canopy. On favourable moments in morning and evening, it is possible to see dozens of pigeons fly over the canopy in an hour or so. Most, probably all, will be Bolle's Pigeon.

5 Continue along the track which is, like before, choc-a-block with lots of interesting wildflowers. In some places, the track runs along some open areas, which are again good for seeing the pigeons, but also for some other wildflowers that prefer more sunlight. These include Willow-leaved Carline Thistle, Canary Foxglove, Canary Bellflower, Stemless, Laurel* and Small-headed* Sow-thistles *(Sonchus acaulis, S. congestus, S. leptocephalus)* and various rock-dwelling ferns.

6 After about 4 km from Erjos, a track branches off to the right, sign-posted for *Los Moradas* and *Los Silos*. Walk on for another kilometre until you see a conspicuous rock on your right. This is another good vantage point for the pigeons.

From here, you can either return or continue through the forest (which gradually turns into a heath thicket) to the village of Portelas.

Additional remarks

Just south of Erjos village, are some old fishponds (see map). The bushy vegetation around the ponds is home to good numbers of Canaries, some Linnets, Sardinian Warblers, Chiffchaffs, African Blue Tits, Grey Wagtails and, in summer, Turtle Doves. The ponds themselves support a population of Coots and Moorhens and attract waders during migration.

Additional sites and routes in north-west Tenerife

A – Barranco de Masca

Of interest
Year-round,
best spring

   GPS: 28.304372, -16.840502. The descent through the Barranco de Masca is the most famous walk on Tenerife. The small village of Masca, dramatically situated high up in the Teno mountains, is a superb site. Monarch butterfly can be found here, and the area is good for Rock Sparrow, Buzzard, Raven and Barbary Partridge.

The descent down the Masca gorge is beautiful but nowadays not so easy to undertake. At the time of writing, only is a limited number of visitors allowed, which means that you have to reserve in advance (see **www.caminobarrancodemasca.com**). Unfortunetely, in most cases, all tickets are reserved by local guide companies, which means that often-times, you can only book a ticket with them and join their organised walk (see 'collaborating companies' at the bottom of the abovementioned website). Furthermore, the boat service to Los Gigantes, which

The spectacular, winding road to Masca.

once made it possible to connect with the taxi service to Masca and save you the strenuous walk back up the gorge, no longer exists. So if you decide to do this marvellous hike, be aware that you have to walk up the same way; a height difference of 600 m!

Scenically and botanically the Masca gorge is top notch. It has such a special micro-climate that it enabled the evolution of species of plants which are unique to this particular gorge.

B – Punta Teno

Of interest
Year-round

  GPS: 28.344165, -16.919242. Punta Teno (the end point of route 5) forms the northwestern tip of Tenerife. It is a well-known beauty spot for naturalists and general visitors alike. The seabirds, dolphins, the succulent coastal vegetation and the tame Berthelot's Pipits and Tenerife Lizards are the main draw.

Because of its popularity, the road to Punta Teno is now closed for motorised traffic, except on Monday to Wednesday during the daytime. If you want to visit Punta Teno at other times, you can walk (see route 5) or take a bus from Buenavista.

C – Roque and *Piscina Natural* de Garachico

151

GPS: 28.373655, -16.766094. The *piscinas naturales* at the seaside by Garachico are natural tidal pools with a few adjustments made to accommodate swimmers. The pools are the result of a lava flow of an eruption in 1706, which famously halted just before the town. At the time, the lava was a great threat, but now, solidified as *piscinas naturales* they are are a major attraction.

Of interest
Year-round

Small paths through the rocks to facilitate walking from one pool to next. Walls were erected to shield the basins from the worst tidal action. The tidal pools are next to the restaurant-lined promenade making this an ideal and laid-back bathing spot.

The pools, with their natural rocky sea floors and open connection to the sea are the perfect place to snorkel. There is a high diversity of colourful marine life, which benefits from the relative calm of the seawater in the tidal pools – a condition which also enhances the visibility. The *piscina natural* of Garachico is perhaps the best and simplest place to enjoy marine life with the help of nothing but a pair of goggles.

In front of the *Piscina natural* lies de Roque de Garachico. This islet is just about a hundred metres from the village boulevard. Plain Swift breed, the

The brightly coloured Red Rock Crab* (*Pachygraphus marmoratus*) is common on the rocks of the Garachico tidal pools.

The *piscinas naturales* at Garachico offers safe bathing and snorkeling on an otherwise rough coastline.

152

(Atlantic) Yellow-legged Gulls are easily spotted near their nests and in winter, Little Egret and Grey Heron have a roost here. The real importance of this piece of rock is found in its small colony of rare seabirds: Bulwer´s Petrel, Madeiran Petrel and Macaronesian Shearwater breed, but frustratingly, they only come to land when it gets dark.

Garachico itself is a pleasant town – sufficiently laid-back to fit the wishes of naturalists who like it quiet.

D – Icod de los Vinos

Of interest
Year-round

GPS: 28.367128, -16.722043. The town of Icod de los Vinos is famous for its *Drago milenario*, or 1000 year old Dragon Tree (see page 82). The age of the tree is subject of debate – some claim it is several hundreds of years old, while other (Spanish) sources estimate it to be about 1000 years. None of this matters when you get a good look at it: it is a magnificent specimen. With its gnarled multi-pillared trunk (which makes it so hard to estimate the exact age) it looks more an artist's fantastical drawing of an Ent in Tolkien's books than a conventional tree. It is the oldest living Dragon Tree and its appearance lives up to this billing.

Bulwer's Petrel breeds on the Roque de Garachico, but is not easy to spot from land.

You overlook the Dragon Tree from a small park, with several impressive Ficus trees. This little park is the best place to look for the beautiful Monarch Butterfly, which is sometimes joined by its smaller cousin, the Plain Tiger.

A visit to Icod is easily combined with a visit to the Cueva del Viento (site E) and the orchid trail (site F).

E – Cueva del Viento

GPS: 28.352125, -16.704184. The Cueva del Viento (cave of the wind) is Europe's most elaborate lava tunnel system. It was formed 27,000 years ago when the Pico Viejo (next to El Teide) erupted. When a lava stream cooled off and its exterior solidified, the interior remained fluid and flowed down to the sea, leaving a hollow tube: the lava tunnel of Cueva del Viento.

The Cueva has 17 km of tunnels, making it the 4th most elaborate lava cave system in the world. A small section is open to the public (under supervision).

The cave is not only a geological masterpiece, it has also played an important role in understanding the ecological and evolutionary history of the island. It is here that the skeletons of the long extinct Giant Rats were found, as well as an ancient species of Giant Lizards measuring up to 1.5 metres (without tail!). Even the remains of a Houbara Bustard has been found here – an extraordinary find as currently, there is no suitable habitat for this species anywhere near.

Present-day fauna within the cave consists of 190 species, of which about 50 are strictly cave-dwelling, blind invertebrates.

To get to the cave follow the TF 366 above (south) of Icod and drive up (south) towards the Cueva el Viento (signposted). The address is Calle de los Piquetes 51. Entrance costs € 20,-.

Reserve in advance at **www.cuevadelviento.net**

153

F – The Orchid walk

GPS: 28.352125, -16.704184. We dubbed this walk the orchid walk because of the high numbers of Three-fingered Orchid we found here, and the presence of another species here, the Two-leaved Gennaria. We discovered this loop by chance, and it is not part of any way-marked route on the island. However, it offers a fine stroll through the allotment zone and lower Canary pine zone, with its rich flora and its many Tenerife birds, which include Tenerife Goldcrest, Canary, Chaffinch, Canary Islands Chiffchaff, Robin, Great Spotted Woodpecker, Turtle Dove, Plain Swift, Kestrel and Sardinian Warbler. It is very easy to combine with a visit to the Cueva del Viento from which' car park this walk starts.

From the *Calle de los Piquetes* (the Cueva del Viento car park) walk further south (uphill) along the street and at the Y-fork, take the left-hand branch (GPS: 28.350107, -16.702794). Pass *Las Breveritas casa rural* and

Top: Three-fingered Orchid

Best season
December-February

continue uphill. The terraced fields support the aforementioned birds plus butterflies like Canary Red Admiral and Canary Speckled Wood. Continue a little higher and in the stone walls, between the Hare's-foot Ferns, there are many Three-fingered Orchids in flower in January and February. Where the paved road ends, continue to search for the Two-leaved Gennaria in the pinewoods.

G – Whale-watching from Los Gigantes

 The tourist town of Los Gigantes has a beautiful beach that overlooks the steep cliffs of Teno. It is these gigantic cliffs that gave the town its name. Los Gigantes is also the whale-watching capital of Tenerife.

If whale-watching brings up images of tall flukes and whales that break the surface of a wild ocean, you'd better temper your expectations. Although there is a large number of species in the Canary waters, the average whale-watching trip brings you to a family group of Short-finned Pilot Whales (a small species of whale, measuring up to 7 metres), which laze on the water's surface. They are the same species you can see from the ferry to La Gomera, but now at close range. Sometimes, groups of dolphins are seen, as are Tenerife's seabirds. With the usual lovely weather this is, all in all, a pleasant rather than a spectacular excursion.

There are several companies offering whale-watching trips, such as Katrin (**www.whalesanddolphinsoftenerife.org**) and Flipper Uno (**www.flipperuno.com**). If you drive down to the harbour, you can arrange a trip on the spot.

Whalewatching Canarian style is laid-back and relaxing.

North-east Tenerife

The north-east of Tenerife is an area of extremes – on the one hand it encompasses the densely inhabited cultural heart of the island and on the other hand, some of the wildest and most difficult-to-travel terrain is found here. The island's capital of Santa Cruz lies in this section, not far from the important towns of La Laguna, Tacoronte, La Orotava, Puerto de la Cruz and Güimar.

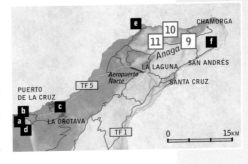

Although close to the main towns as the crow flies, the extremely rugged terrain of the Anaga mountains ensure that the unspoilt villages here are very isolated, even today.

Anaga harbours the largest area of laurel forest on Tenerife and is home to a rich flora. Like the Teno mountains in the north-west, Anaga's bedrock is much older than central Tenerife, and supports a number of endemic wildflowers that occur exclusively in Anaga or are shared only with Teno.

The Anaga mountains are a delight for hikers. It is also the place in Tenerife where the dramatic climatic differences between the windy and misty north slopes and sunny and warm south slopes are most tangible, both 'on the skin' as in the vegetation. This is very visible on route 9, which is also a good route to explore the laurel cloud forest. Route 19 explores another special Anaga habitat: a freshwater brook that carries water year-round. Route 11 has more laurel forest and thermophilous woodlands.

At the base of the Anaga peninsula, facing the southern sun, lies the pleasant, lively old town of Santa Cruz. It is perfect as a destination for a city break and has an excellent Natural History museum. From Santa Cruz, it is easy to get on the TF 1 motorway, and in an instance, you are at the lavafields of Güimar (site D on page 175) and the large dry slopes of southern Tenerife.

Taking the TF 5 northbound past La Laguna and the northern airport, you are on the way to the town Puerto de la Cruz. Just beyond this historic town, there are a number of pristine barrancos with a superb flora and rich birdlife (sites A, B and D on pages 162-163).

Both from La Orotava and La Laguna there are ways up the Teide (see route 1), so all in all, the north-east is, from a naturalist's point-of-view, perhaps the best base from which to explore the island.

Route 9: Anaga mountains – a first exploration

FULL DAY OR MORE
EASY

!
Cold and wet weather possible. Dress accordingly.

Of interest
Year-round

The best introduction to Anaga and the nature of Tenerife in general.
Splendid scenery, a large variety of habitats and rich flora.

Habitats: Succulent scrub, thermophilous scrub, laurel cloud forest
Selected species: Two-leaved Gennaria, Anaga Violet, Canary Bellflower, Woodwardia, Pyramidal Houseleek*, Canary Foxglove, Laurel Forest Gentian*, Bolle's Pigeon, Tenerife Goldcrest, African Blue Tit, West Canary Skink, Canary Blue, Canary Cleopatra

This route is set up as an introduction to the wild and rugged Anaga mountains, but serves very well as an ecological excursion into the habitats of Tenerife in general. Nowhere else on the island can you see the striking differences between the sun-drenched southern slopes and foggy cloud forests of the northern slopes over such a small distance as here in Anaga. Hence this is the best trip to come to grips with the fascinating game of sun and clouds that has created the natural diversity of Tenerife. Stops and short walks have been chosen to show the wide variety of

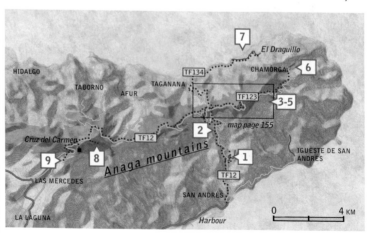

habitats albeit with an emphasis on the magnificent laurel forest. Along the way, you'll encounter a large number of wildflowers, some excellent spots to look for birds and good opportunities to see some reptiles, butterflies and dragonflies.

Starting point Roundabout of San Andrés. GPS: 28.503078, -16.193070

Follow the TF 12 north, signposted *Taganana* and *El Bailadero*. This road climbs from sea level up to roughly 750 metres and along the way you will witness the vegetation change from succulent to thermophilous scrub and, on the crest itself, laurel cloud forest.

After 2.7 kms, turn right onto a narrow tarmacked road (GPS: 28.521824, -16.193560; there is a bus stop here). Drive down into the valley and stop at the barranco (you can park a little beyond the barranco).

The fairytale laurel forests of the north slope of Anaga (bottom) is the sole area where the small Anaga Violet grows (top).

1 You are now firmly in the succulent zone. Plocama, Verode, Lamarck's and Canary Spurges are the common plants here, joined by Rooftop Houseleek* *(Aeonium urbicum)* and Lindley's Houseleek *(A. lidleyi).* The latter is endemic to the Anaga mountains. All except Plocama are succulent plants.

There is a trail following the barranco up on the east bank. It leads by stands of Giant Reed to some agricultural plots and there is a possibility to go down to the stream itself. Along this small trail there are many Canary Speckled Woods and a few Canary Blues. The stream holds water during a large part of the year, so keep an eye open for interesting dragonflies (even though we found only Red-veined Darters and Blue Emperors). The bushes along the stream hold plenty of Blackcaps, Sardinian Warblers, African Blue Tits and Turtle Doves, while Moorhen breeds in the streambed.

Return to the TF 12 and turn right.

View over the Anaga massif from the TF-12 road. Note how jagged these mountains are – the result of millions of years of erosion.

2 As you wind up the mountain the vegetation gradually changes: the succulents disappear while evergreen shrubs like Wild Jasmine, Tree Heath, Canary St. John's-wort and Anaga Viper's-bugloss* *(Echium leucophaeum)* enter the scene. It is not easy to stop, but you can pull over at km 6 (GPS: 28.541714, -16.199354) and walk back a little, where there is a small trail to the right.

Continue, ignoring the turn to Taganana, and go right to El Bailadero and Chamorga. Stop at El Bailadero.

3 El Bailadero lies in the laurel cloud forest zone and is exactly on the crest of Anaga. From here you have superb views on both the north and the south side. On the ridge, the wind is strong, blowing the fog over from the north to the south side, where it dissolves. Often, the conditions here are such that you are in the fog on the north side of the road, while you can look underneath it on the other side, down at the south coast bathing in sunshine just 10 kilometres away.

159

Rocket Viper's-bugloss (*Echium simplex*) on the roadside near Chamorga.

4 Continue and over the next four kilometres, make regular stops in the many small layby's along the narrow road. The cloud forest is superb here. The wind creates a special kind of forest – the crest forest or *Lauriselva de la Cumbre*. Tree Heath and Canary Gale* *(Myrica faya)* dominate in the forest, while on rocks the large Pyramidal Houseleeks* *(Aeonium cuneatum)* grow, together with Loose-flowered Monanthes and Laurel Forest Sow-thistle* *(Sochus congestus)*. The nearby fields hold many songbirds including Chaffinch, African Blue Tit, Goldfinch and Canary.

After km 4, there is an obvious car park in the forest on the left. This is the starting point for the laurel forest walk of El Pijaral, for which you need a special permit. If you don't have it. Stop anyway and walk along the road in eastern direction.

El Pijaral walk
4
El Bailadero   Park
TF123   5
3

5 This area is covered in a particularly attractive forest with a dazzling variety of wildflowers. Within a few hundred metres, you can find along the road Laurel Forest Sow-thistle* *(Sonchus congestus)*, Canary Foxglove, Canary Crane's-bill, Canary Buttercup, Black Spleenwort, Ivy-leaved Spleenwort *(Asplenium hemiotis)*, Chain Fern, Large-leaved St. John's-wort, Canary Balm, Canary Bellflower, Hairy Aichryson, Climbing Butcher's-broom, Noble Bush-madder* *(Phyllis nobla)* and and Bush Pellitory* *(Gesnouinia arborea)*. And this is not a complete list!

Note that this section of the road lies on the leeward side of the mountain – sheltered from the wind. Trees grow much taller here and are heavily draped in mosses, lichens and various epiphytic plants (growing-on-trees).

Take the car and continue all the way to the picturesque village of Chamorga (note the many Canary Foxgloves along the way).

6 Chamorga is an original Anaga village – isolated even today in this age of cars. It is not difficult to see how hard it was to get here when travel was limited to small trails through the forest. The surroundings and the hamlet offer chances of finding Rock Sparrow, Sardinian Warbler, Sparrowhawk and African Blue Tit. The West Canary Skink can be found in moist patches near the river. There are plenty of Dragon Trees in and around the village, while the spectacular Rocket Viper's-bugloss* *(Echium simplex)* grows next to the road at the village' entrance (flowering March-May). There are various hiking trails departing from Chamorga.

A dragon Tree in the hamlet of El Draguillo.

Return to El Bailadero and turn left at the junction and then left again, following the signs to Taganana. From Taganana drive further to the hamlet of Benijo. Turn left at the municipal waste bins and find a spot to park. Walk the coastal track that leaves here for El Draguillo.

7 The trail offers sublime views over the rocky north coast of Anaga with before you the *Roques de Anaga*. The large islet of *Roque Dentro* (or *Roque de Tierra*), which has wild Dragon Trees growing on its north slope, is barely tethered to the coastline. Beyond it, surrounded by the ocean, is *Roque de Fuera*. These rocks are plugs of ancient volcanoes that eroded over the years and form a natural reserve with important breeding sites for sea birds, like Bulwers Petrel, Madeiran Storm-petrel and

Macaronesian Shearwater. Cory's Shearwater and European Storm-petrel also breed. Unfortunately, they only come to land at night, making them very hard to see.
The cliffs along which you walk were unfortunately burnt in a recent fire, although the shrubby coastal vegetation, dominated by Balsam Spurge, Canary Sea Fennel and Shrubby Marguerite, is coming back. The very rare marguerite-like Lugoa, endemic to Anaga, also grows alongside the trail. Further towards El Draguillo, Lindley's Houseleek and Yellow Ceropegia can be found.There are plenty of Dragon Trees in the village.

Return all the way to the TF 12 and turn right and then straight towards Las Mercedes, Cruz del Carmen and La Laguna. Beyond Casas del Cumbre, after about 10 km from El Bailadero, turn left to the Pico del Inglés. (GPS: 28.533131, -16.264073).

The up to 2 metre tall Laurel Forest Gentian (*Ixanthus viscosus*) is locally common in forest clearings.

8 The touristic viewpoint *Pico del Inglés* overlooks the laurel forest and is one of the best places to spot Bolle´s Pigeon in flight – if you are lucky they even perch in the canopy and show themselves better. This is also a good lookout for Sparrowhawk, Plain Swift and, in summer, Pallid Swift.
Retracing your steps, there is a small road to your right, carved into the ridge. Follow it for some 200 metres and in spring, you have a flowery roadside where many Cleopatras are drawn to the Canary Balm flowers.

Continue towards las Mercedes, pass the Cruz del Carmen information point (see route 11), marvell at the last stretch of wonderful cloud forest and stop at the last viewpoint of this route: La Jardina.

9 This viewpoint marks the west end of the Anaga mountains. You have great views towards the west over the Teide. Usually you see the clouds in front of you coming in from the north and evaporating as they drift south towards Santa Cruz.

162

Route 10: Barranco de Afur

Best season
February -June
Of interest
Year-round

4 HOURS OR FULL DAY
MODERATE-STRENUOUS

Splendid walk in a remote part of the Anaga mountains.
One of the few permanent streams of Tenerife; great for dragonflies.

Habitats: Stream, barranco, thermophilous scrub, coastal cliffs
Selected species: Red Rock Mallow*, Lindley's Houseleek, Rocket Viper's-bugloss*, Grey Wagtail, West Canary Skink, Ringed Cascader, Red-veined Dropwing, Epaulet Skimmer, Broad Scarlet, Canary Blue, Canary Islands Large White

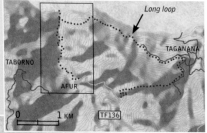

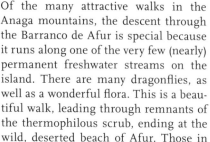

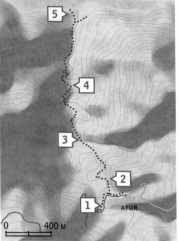

Of the many attractive walks in the Anaga mountains, the descent through the Barranco de Afur is special because it runs along one of the very few (nearly) permanent freshwater streams on the island. There are many dragonflies, as well as a wonderful flora. This is a beautiful walk, leading through remnants of the thermophilous scrub, ending at the wild, deserted beach of Afur. Those in for a long, day-filling and strenuous walk could follow a coastal path to Taganana, from where you can return to Afur.

Starting point Afur. Drive all the way down to the car park at the end of the street where the walk starts. GPS: 28.555549, -16.248274.
Follow the trail. Before following the sign Tamadiste into the barranco, first continue to the bridge.

1 Along the track, you may already have seen a number of dragonflies. From the bridge scan the rocks next to the water for Red-veined Dropwing, Epaulet Skimmer, Blue Emperor, Red-veined Darter, Broad Scarlet and, in late spring

A number of dykes (veins of very resistant lava) run across the valley of Afur. They function as natural dams that retain water in the valley which is, as a result, one of the few permanent streams on Tenerife.

and summer, Ringed Cascader. Many of these dragonflies will accompany you along the entire trail down to the sea.

The same holds true for the birds: Kestrel, African Blue Tit, Chiffchaff, and Grey Wagtail are all frequent here. The butterflies are mostly Canary Cleopatra and Canary Speckled Wood, but keep an eye out for Canary Islands Large White and Canary Blue as well. Finally, look up to the hillsides on the other side of the barranco and note the many Juniper bushes. The valley of Afur holds Tenerife's last sizable population of Junipers – a key species of the thermophilous scrub which is more common on La Gomera and El Hierro.

Return and turn left to Tamadiste.

2 The trail runs along a cliff with a conspicuous line of basalt rock. Here and a bit further on, there are plenty of Tenerife Lavender *(Lavandula buchii)*, Lindley's Houseleek, Saucer-leaved House-leek* *(Aeonium tabulaeforme)*, Allagopappus, Cross-leaved St.-John's-wort* *(Hypericum reflexum)*, Lugoa (looking like a marguerite and endemic to Anaga) and, in autumn, Canary Sea-daffodil.

3 The trail descends steeply towards the stream and crosses it. This is again an excellent spot to look for dragonflies. The skimmers, dropwings and Broad Scarlets frequently rest on the rocks, showing themselves very well.

The trail leads through brushwood and comes to a conspicuous, linear outcrop that runs across the valley at right angles. It creates a small terrace in the riverbed from which the stream drops down as a small waterfall.

This is yet another good place for dragonflies, but the rock formation in itself is interesting too. It is a basalt intrusion or *dyke*. As lava gradually cools down, it cracks. In a later eruption, the lava fills these cracks. Being of a different chemical composition and having solidified under higher pressure, it has a different, harder structure than the surrounding bedrock. Hence it erodes more slowly.

You'll see several more dykes crossing the river bed, which divides the brook in deeper sections separated by faster flowing parts. Look higher up on the hillsides and you'll see these dykes are frequently exposed.

4 A bit further on you arrive at some man-made terraces on your left, cut into the steep slope. The lower ones are still in use – testimony of how people made a living in these remote, distant parts of Tenerife. Look around here for the magnificent Rocket Viper's-bugloss* *(Echium simplex)*, flowering from March to May. Keep an eye out for the lizards too. Apart from the numerous Tenerife Lizards, we found geckos in the stone walls and skinks near the wet patches a little further on.

Two spectacular dragonflies of the Afur stream: Ringend Cascader (top) and a female Red-winged Dropwing (bottom).

5 Just before reaching the small beach, the influence of the sea becomes clear in the vegetation. The orange-leaved Canary Sea Fennel is very common here, together with Small-leaved Sea-lavender* *(Limonium pectinatum)*, Crystal Reichardia and Sea-heath. This last section of the stream is a site for Eel, a very unlikely fish for the Islands.

Just before the beach, a trail leads to the right and connects with the village of Taganana from where you can cross a pass back to Afur. This is a splendid but strenuous walk. To give you some idea – sofar you have completed about 15% of the long circuit.

Route 11: Through the laurel forest to Chinamada

**4 HOURS OR FULL DAY
MODERATE-STRENUOUS**

Best season
February -June
Of interest
Year-round

Beautiful walk from laurel forest to open barrancos.

Habitats: Laurel forest, farmland, thermophile woodland, barrancos
Selected species: Laurel Pigeon, Bolles Pigeon, Disc-leaved Fern, Milky
Cineraria, *Marcetella moquiniana*, Lindley's Houseleek, *Aeonium ciliatum*

This walk offers a splendid opportunity to get a good impression of the
laurel forest and its transition into the more open woodlands and barrancos. It is a very beautiful walk
with lots of great views. The steep
barrancos either north- or south-
facing reveal the broad variety of
species, not only plants but also
birds, reptiles and butterflies. On
the way you pass a number of landscape types and typical villages
where caves were used for living or
local industry.

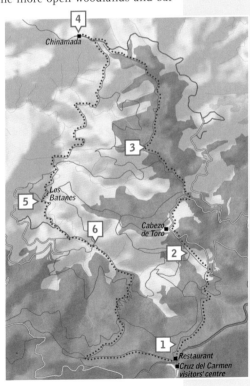

Starting point Centro de Visitantes Cruz del Carmen.
(GPS: 28.5308997, -16.2799207)

From the car park you have a beautiful view over the valley behind
the cross.
Cross the road and follow the PR
TF10, direction Punta de Hidalgo,
which starts right next to a café.

1 The path immediately plunges
into the dense and dark laurel
forest. There are only few spots where
the light breaks through and here

you'll find some fine plants like Laurel Forest Gentian, Large-leaved St. John's wort, Milky Cineraria* (*Pericallis appendiculata*) and Noble Bush-madder* (*Phyllis nobla*). In the heart of the laurel forest the atmosphere is humid and mild and here some beautiful Indian Laurel trees grow, one of the most typical trees of the laurel forest. You recognise it by the fallen leaves, which are bright red, large and leathery.

The slopes around Los Batanes are terraced, indicating former former agricultural use (top). The Disc-leaved Fern grows locally on cliffs along the trail (bottom).

2 The transition from forest to open terrain is sudden. Follow the track straight ahead along small fields where black potatoes are grown, typical for Tenerife. After passing two houses (Casas del Rio) remnants of laurel forest grow along the path. In the valley below terraces and farmland dominate. Chaffinch, Canary Island Chiffchaff, African Blue Tit and Canary are typical birds in areas like these. Any pigeons should be checked, as Bolle's Pigeon breeds in the surrounding laurel forest.

When you enter the road, keep following the signs PR TF10. After another 10 min you arrive at a bus stop (GPS: 28.546917, -16.279167), where the trail turns left and descends down the slope.

3 Laurel Forest Sow Thistle, White False Sage, Canary bellflower and the beautiful tiny Anaga Monanthes* (*Monanthes anagensis*) are among the botanical attractions here. On the right you see the impressive Roque de Taborno, often called Tenerife's Matterhorn for reasons that become immediately obvious once you lay eyes on this conspicuous peak.

Some 100 m further at a fork take the path to the left direction Chinamada and Punta Hidalgo. The Rooftop Houseleek grows on the cliff on the right. Further down you enter an open woodland with remnants of laurel forest and typical undergrowth like Tree Bindweed and Canary Foxglove. Note the Disc-leaved Fern (*Adiantum reniforme*) with kidney-shaped leaves which grows on shady banks or in the crevices. This fern is one of the few plants native plants that originates from the tropics (see page 70).

Among the birds, Sardinian warbler is frequent here. Also look out for Sparrowhawk, Plain Swift, Blackcap, Laurel and Bolle's Pigeons. The path leads over a slope, some steep walls and banks. Further on, the landscape is dominated by remnants of laurel forest with some shrubs like Sticky broom and Canary Whin* (*Teline canariensis*), later on by rocky outcrops with some beautiful vertical rock layers. This is the site of two endemic houseleeks not seen on this route before – Lindley's Houseleek and *Aeonium ciliatum*.

The entire stretch offers unimpeded and spectacular views into the barranco and afar Punto Hidalgo.

Thermophile woodland with ferns, alder and gale (top). Canary foxglove is commonly found in woodland edges (bottom).

Just before arriving at Chinamada, the path turns sharp to the left, sign-posted Batan/Cruz del Carmen. This is your route back, but first consider walking down to Chinamada.

4 Chinamada is an attractive village with many cave houses cut into the soft volcanic rock. Here you can enjoy some refreshments in the restaurant.
Walk back and follow the path to Batan / Cruz del Carmen. You now enter an exposed, south-facing slope with a wealthy growth of Prickly Pear and Agave, and many Tenerife Lizards. You cross two barrancos with more cave houses, the first of which is the location of the rare pimpernel-like burnet *Marcetella moquiniana*.

After crossing over the second barranco take the left path (not the right steep path up) to Batan de Abajo.

The conspicuous Dragon Tree in Los Batanes.

5 You walk through the old hamlet of Los Batanes, where in the centre an old Dragon tree is prominent. The hamlet is peculiar for its historic linen textile industry. The large cave (Cueva de Lino) was used for drying the flax. Information shields along the road give details on this interesting history.

After passing the transport lift to the hamlet of Batan de Abajo go left in the sharp curve over the PR TF11 direction Batan de Arriba.

6 Soon you walk along a beautiful stream (Barranco del Rio) with woodland. Here lot of butterflies can be found like Clouded yellow, Canary speckled Wood, Canary Cleopatra and Canary Blue.

At the end of the track go right over the road and after 50 m left up, again into the dense laurel forest and after a climb the last stretch is over a landscaped path through the forest before reaching Cruz del Carmen.

Additional sites and routes in north-east Tenerife

A – Barranco de Ruiz

GPS: 28.391400, -16.626361. The Barranco de Ruiz is a steep gorge in the central north of the island. It contains an important pocket of original thermophilous forest and, higher up, patches of laurel forest. The gorge is renowned for its flora, which includes Wild Jasmin, Saucer-leaved* *(Aeonium tabulaeforme)*, Canary and Tree Houseleeks* *(A. arboreum)* and lots of Tree Bindweed and Canary Silk-vine. There are plenty of butterflies (e.g. Canary Islands Large White, Canary Red Admiral, Cleopatra and Speckled Wood). It is also a great place for birdwatching. The barranco holds Laurel Pigeons, which can be seen on the first km of the trail that runs through the gorge. They fly in and around the deeper part of the gorge. Although they are quite distant, if you find yourself a good vantage point, they may show themselves quite well (even perched!). At least one pair of Barbary Falcon breeds and there are plenty of Kestrels, Canaries, Chiffchaffs, Blackcaps and African Blue Tits.

Access to the gorge is easy. Two kilometres east of San Juan de la Rambla, the main TF 5 Icod – Puerto de la Cruz road crosses the barranco.

Best season
January-April

A large specimen of Canary Houseleek (*Aeonium canariense*)

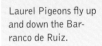
Laurel Pigeons fly up and down the Barranco de Ruiz.

170

The Canarian sub-species of the Chaffinch is common in the Anaga mountains.

There is a picnic spot signposted *Barranco de Ruiz* on the main road where you can park. Coming from the west, you can turn off directly onto the picnic spot. If you come from the east, turn right onto the road on the other side of the picnic spot before crossing the busy road.

A lovely trail, upgraded in 2014 with fencing, starts besides the bar (recommended for its simple but lovely Canarian food). You get a very good look of the barranco and its wildlife by walking the first kilometre or so to some overhanging rocks which form a good vantage point. For the entire walk, set aside at least 3 hours. The trail is narrow and steep in places, but well maintained. This site is easily combined with the Mirador La Grimona, less than 2 km to the east.

B – Mirador La Grimona

Of interest
Year-round

GPS: 28.392766, -16.608737. The Mirador La Grimona has recently acquired some fame among birdwatchers for its views of Laurel Pigeon and – less commonly – Bolle's Pigeon. At first glance it is an unlikely spot, right on the busy main TF 5 road, but the cliffs here provide the safe nesting sites that Laurel Pigeons need. During our visits the Laurel Pigeons were virtually unmissable, displaying most actively between 17:30-18:30 on the cliffs on the other (south) side of the road. Bolle's pigeons were also present, and at times both species were perched and visible through the telescope.

Acces is very easy when travelling from the east. Beyond Puerto de la Cruz, the TF 5 passes through two tunnels. The Mirador (actually a small parking area) is right after the second tunnel, and is well signposted. This site is easily combined with a visit to the Barranco de Ruiz (site A).

C – Puerto de la Cruz botanical garden

Of interest
Year-round

GPS: 28.411614, -16.535870. The botanical garden in Puerto de la Cruz (entrance 3 euros) is a lush tropical oasis. It was established by Carlos III in 1788 to acclimatise exotic plants from his American

Barbary Partridges occur in the shrubby areas in the lower zones of Anaga.

territories and destined for his palace in Madrid, but it has since become one of the world's most important botanical gardens.

Today, there are many superb trees and tropical flowers here from all over the world, with a giant *Ficus macrophylla* from Australia as the centre piece. Among the native fauna, Grey Wagtail, African Blue Tit, Blackcap, Robin and Blackbird live in the park and have accustomed themselves to visitors. Also of interest are the Monarch butterflies which flutter graciously through the canopy. The town itself has a small harbour with a *piscina natural* (good for snorkeling). A walk along the shoreline may produce Yellow-legged Gull, Sandwich Tern, Little Egret, Turnstone and other kinds of waders (best in winter and early spring).

D – Mirador El Lance

GPS: 28.38505, -16.60356.

This is the more famous site for watching the elusive Bolle's and Laurel Pigeons – the endemic pigeon species of the Canary Islands.

Mirador el Lance lies on the TF 342 west of Los Realejos. It overlooks the edge of a great fold near the village Icod el Alto. The viewpoint (with a bar next to it) overlooks the ocean, but, close by, there are remnant pockets of laurel and thermophilous woods. The pigeons drop

Of interest
Year-round

Barbary Falcons breed in many barrancos in northern Tenerife and can be seen in the Barranco de Ruiz and at the Mirador de los Lances (site A and D on the previous pages, amongst others).

The tidal pools at Punta de Hidalgo (top) are attractive not only for birdwatching, but also for exploring sea life. At times, the jellyfish-like Portuguese Man-o-War is washed ashore here (bottom). This strange organism is actually a colony of various types of polyps, attached to a gas-filled jellyfish, known as a pneumatophore.

down to the cultivated fields to search for food. Wait patiently and you will see both species flying in and out of the vegetation below the viewpoint and/or along the cliff a little east and above the mirador. Barbary Falcon and Buzzard may also show up.

E – Punta de Hidalgo

Of interest
Year-round

Punta de Hidalgo is a resort that is now past its prime. In spite of the somewhat tacky buildings, it is set beautifully on the north-western tip of the Anaga mountains and has a number of things to offer naturalists. Punta de Hidalgo has no beach, but a broad rocky coastline with *piscinas naturales* (rocky, seawater filled basins) and hundreds of tidal pools at low tide. The *piscinas naturales* are a good place to snorkel (although not as good as Garachico – see site C on page 148). The tidal pools attract more waders than elsewhere along the Tenerife coast. In winter and during migration, you may find

Whimbrels are frequent waders on the coast, such as at Punta de Hidalgo.

Grey Plover, Ringed Plover, Whimbrel, Common Sandpiper, Turnstone and Grey Heron and Little Egret. The best pools are beyond the light-house on the eastern side of the site. Later in spring and summer, Punta de Hidalgo is also a reasonably good point for seawatching. Looking to-wards the east, you can see the isolated rocks of *Roque Dentro* and *Roque de Fuera*, on which so many of the rare seabirds of Tenerife breed. From Punta de Hidalgo check for shearwaters. Cory's is the most frequent species, but keep an eye out for the rarer Macaronesian Shearwater too, especially during onshore winds.

Finally, there is a great hiking trail from Punta Hidalgo through the Anaga mountains to Cruz del Carmen (see next page). This trail has a wonderful scenery and rich flora – somewhat comparable to route 9 but without the stream. All in all, Punta de Hidalgo is a great place to spend an hour of birdwatching and/or a couple of hours of walking.

Access to these sites is easy – the *piscina natural* is signposted from the road (see map). The walking trail starts at the end of the main road.

F – Barranco de Igueste de San Andrés

GPS: 28.540088, -16.156041. At the far eastern end of the Anaga mountains, the beautiful valley of San Andrés intices you for a splendid hike. This area is of great interest botanically, in par-ticular because of the presence of many wild Dragon Trees.

Of interest
Year-round

From Igueste de San Andrés, drive to the hamlet of Lomo Bermejo. Here, a small concrete road branches off to the right. Some 60 m futher, after a hairpin bend, the trail (marked white-yellow) goes left into the valley.

South Tenerife

The large area we cover here as 'southern Tenerife', comprises the western, southern and eastern coastal lowlands and dry, south-facing slopes of El Teide, up to Vilaflor. This is the driest part of the island, largely covered in succulent scrub, some exposed lava fields, patches of thermophilous forest, and a lot of disturbed wastelands, agriculture and built-up areas. The big tourist complexes are here, mostly centred around the twin resort of Los Cristianos-Las Américas.

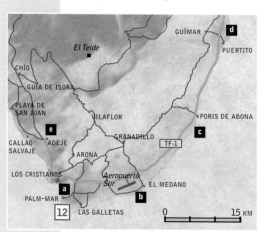

There are important agricultural areas along the west and south coasts. As Tenerife's main international airport is here, your first experience of the island is most likely here in this dry landscape.

Southern Tenerife is much less attractive for naturalists than the other regions. Partly, this is because of the natural environment. This is a relatively gentle, low-lying area with a drier climate that tends to favour a single vegetation zone: succulent scrub. An important second factor is the human impact. This is the sunniest area so it is most attractive for beach tourism whilst, with irrigation, it is also the best area for banana plantations.

Nonetheless, there are some wonderful areas on the coast. Since the terrain is more level here, the birdlife is different. Great Grey Shrike, Hoopoe, Berthelot's Pipit and Spectacled Warbler are common species here. The best areas are found near the resort of Palm-Mar (route 12 and site A on page 178). The young lava fields sport a very special flora which can be enjoyed on route 12 and the Malpaís de Güimar (site D on page 180). The Montaña Roja next to the airport (site B on page 178) is another hotspot for both birds and wildflowers and has the only (small) area of dunes on the island.

Further inland there are various barrancos (like the famous Barranco del Infierno, site E on page 180), which in scenery and flora do not fall short of the rich gorges in Teno or Anaga. Finally, a visit to La Gomera is easy from here as the boat departs from Los Cristianos.

Route 12: Punta la Rasca

3-4 HOURS
EASY

!

Bring drinking water
and sun protection

Succulent scrub of young lava.
The best places in Tenerife for desert birds.

Don't leave any
valuables in your car

Habitats: Coastal rocks, succuluent scrub
Selected species: Canary Spurge, Balsam Spurge, Brown Ceropegia,
Verode, Great Grey Shrike, Spectacled Warbler, Cory's Shearwater, Barbary
Falcon, Turnstone, Whimbrel, Tenerife Lizard, Bath White

Of interest
Year-round

The southernmost tip of Tenerife consists of lava fields and old craters that were never very attractive for agriculture, nor for tourism. Hence, squeezed between the tourist high rise of Los Cristianos in the north and the banana cultivations in the east, lies a wonderful area of original coastal vegetation and succulent scub. The southern part is the *Reserva Natural del Malpaís de la Rasca*, a level area of young lava. It is the driest part of Tenerife, receiving less than 100 mm of rain annually. It has a rugged appearance and a special flora and fauna.

There is a beautiful walk that can be enjoyed from the tourist resort of Palm-Mar through a flat lava field to the Punta de la Rasca lighthouse (Tenerife's southernmost point). The lighthouse is one of the best sites for seawatching on the island.

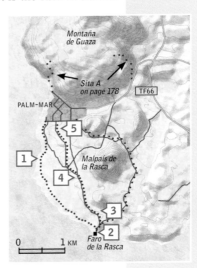

Starting point Pal Mar GPS: 28.021280, -16.705451
Follow the main road in the village and turn left at the roundabout. Follow the road all the way down to the coast where there's a squat tower at the southern end of the village. Park here and follow the track along the coast.

1 This walk starts in a flat lava field with the typical vegetation of the sun-drenched coastline. This pretty rock garden hosts Canary

Spurge, Balsam Spurge, Plocama, Canary Sea Fennel, Sea-heath and Zygophyllum. The most frequent butterfly on this walk is the Bath White. Berthelot's Pipit is common, but look out too for Great Grey Shrike, Kestrel, Spectacled Warbler and Barbary Falcon, which frequently comes down here to hunt. There are plenty of tidal pools where, in winter and during migration, waders can be found. From March to October, there are plenty of Cory's Shearwaters out at sea.

2 The Faro de la Rasca offers excellent seawatching from March to October, although a telescope and some patience are required. Cory's Shearwater is the most common bird and sometimes passes at close range. Barolo Shearwater and Bulwer`s Petrel are seen during the summer months but tend to keep their distance from the coast. Year round there are family groups of Short-finned Pilot Whale around which usually stay close to the shore and may be seen. On days on which the sea is calm, Common and Bottlenose Dolphins are occasionally spotted from the lighthouse.

In winter, this warm spot is one of the few places on the island to see large numbers of Tenerife Lizards, which are elsewhere less active in the cold season.

Take the main track from the lighthouse and turn

Cory's Shearwaters are abundant at the Punta de la Rasca (March - October; left). The interior part of this route is a good place to track down Great Grey Shrike.

View over the Atlantic ocean from the Malpaís de la Rasca.

left at the first side track. Alternatively, if you fancy a longer walk, continue and follow the track around the main hill (see map).

Great Grey Shrikes often use the Canary Spurges as a perch.

3 Around the junction, there are plenty of Brown Ceropegias – a curious plant that consists of grey, skeleton-like, jointed sticks. In spring they sport dark-red flowers (see page 72). It is about half a metre high and often grows underneath (and through) Balsam Spurge bushes.

Continue through the lava fields. Once the El Palm-Mar resort comes in view again, there are various trails. Follow the one in the direction of the resort.

4 Beyond a derelict small building, the trail leads through an area of abandoned fields. In places, the ground is covered in Common and Small-leaved* Iceplants, the latter being the small one with the red leaves. Keep an eye out for birds here, as this is the kind of area where Hoopoe and Lesser Short-toed Lark (very rare on Tenerife) may turn up.

5 The last short section back to El Palm-Mar leads through an intact succulent scrub again, with many Brown Ceropegias.

Additional remarks
Punta de la Rasca is easily combined with a visit to Montaña de Guaza (see map and site A on page 174).

178

Additional sites in south Tenerife

A – Montaña de la Guaza

Of interest
Year-round

GPS: 28.033546, -16.691008. The Montaña de Guaza, a natural park, is the mountain that lies between Los Cristianos and the TF 1 motorway in the north, and the Palm-Mar resort in the south. The mountain's slopes are clad in succulent scrub, while the rather level upland consists of small, fields, now abandoned. Whilst not the prettiest landscape to walk around, it has an attractive birdlife. Berthelot's Pipit, Plain Swift and Great Grey Shrike are common and Spectacled Warbler is frequent. The prize bird is Trumpeter Finch, Tenerife's last population of which is reputed to occur here. Keep in mind that this bird is more frequently missed than seen here (perhaps it has even disappeared altogether), and that there is a much better site for it on La Gomera (site M on page 209).

The trail to the Montaña Roja runs through the only area on Tenerife where fine sand is found making this a small, but precious, site with a flora and fauna that reminds one of Lanzarote and Fuerteventura.

The Montaña de Guaza can be reached from the southernmost outskirt of Los Cristianos and from the resort of Palm-Mar, but the easiest access is just south of the El Rancho bar, about a kilometre before Palm-Mar (GPS: 28.029958, -16.686277). Here, a trail leads up the slope and brings you right in the middle of the abandoned plots.

B – Montaña Roja and El Medano

GPS: 28.037751, -16.548112. The nature reserve of Montaña Roja (Red Mountain) is a conspicuous hill just south of the airport near El Medano. It has a peculiar rounded shape, as it is the result of a suboceanic eruption. The water kept the lava contained so it solidified on the spot. The young lava has an interesting flora, which includes the rare, endemic succulent Brown Ceropegia (see page 72). On the El Medano side of the Moñtana Roja lies Tenerife's only area of (partially fossilised) dunes, which

holds a number of interesting plants, including Zygophyllum and Traganum. On Tenerife, this landscape and several of these species can only be found here at Montaña Roja. It offers a taste of the desert nature as it is found on the East Canary Islands of Lanzarote and Fuerteventura.

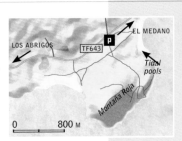

179

Berthelot's Pipit is the most common bird, but Yellow-legged Gull, Spectacled Warbler, Great Grey Shrike and Hoopoe may be present. Barbary Falcon comes down here to hunt, while out on sea, a steady stream of Cory's Shearwaters passes by. At the base of the Montaña Roja on the El Medano side lie a lagoon and various tidal pools, which are the only breeding site of Kentish Plover on the island. In winter and during migration, Little Egret and various waders make the Montaña Roja an attractive site worth spending a morning or two. If you plan a visit, make sure to be early. The area has become very busy with kite surfers, joggers and 'health tourists' in general.

Of interest
Year-round

To arrive at Montaña Roja, take the El Medano exit from the TF 1, and before entering El Medano, turn right, direction *Los Abrigos*. There are two car parks for the Montaña Roja – the first one (closest to El Medano) leads into the best part. From here, walk the trails of your choice, shown on the map.

Below: The Canary Silk-vine has rather inconspicuous flowers but massive fruits. It is a common plant of the warm, south-facing slopes.

C – Punta de Abona

GPS: 28.149481, -16.427309. The low lava outcrops of Punta de Abona form an excellent place for sea watching. From April to October, you'll see plenty of Cory's Shearwaters from this small cape, and with a little luck, you may also find Barolo Shearwater. The nearby tidal pools may hold Little Egret, Grey Plover and Whimbrel.

Of interest
Year-round

Arriving at Punta de Abona is simple – from the motorway, take exit 39 to Poris de Abona and cross the village in southern direction all the way to the lighthouse of Punta de Abona. From there, it is a mere minute's walk to the shore.

Of interest
Year-round

D – Malpaís de Güímar

GPS: 28.298331, -16.371210. The lava fields of Güímar are another wild, unscathed area of young lava, comparable to the Malpaís de la Rasca (route 12). The rocky lava is dotted with Balsam and Canary Spurge, Shrubby Launaea and Canary Sea Fennel, Canary Boxthorn and, locally, Brown Ceropegia. Red-veined Darter, Bath White and Berthelot's Pipit are the most common representatives of a naturally poor fauna.

The trail starts at the northern end of the coastal road of Puertito de Güímar. It is a circular trail taking about 3 hours to complete.

E – Barranco del Infierno

Of interest
Year-round

GPS: 28.126276, -16.723759. The walk through the Baranco del Infierno (Hell's gorge) is one of Tenerife's most famous walks. The gorge, like many of Tenerife's barrancos, is spectacular, but the difference with other gorges is that the trail is easy and fairly level. As you proceed into the seclusion of an increasingly narrow gorge, the atmosphere becomes cooler and moister, as if you were climbing up to higher altitudes.

The Barranco del Infierno (top) is superb for wildflowers, such as Sea Rosemary (bottom)

The fact that this is an easy walk, together with the close proximity to the main tourist centre of Los Cristianos, makes it a popular outing. For naturalists (botanists in particular) the Barranco del Infierno is also a wonderful destination, particularly for the rich flora and the dragonfly fauna (e.g. Yellow Ceropegia and Red-winged Dropwing). Note that access to the Barrance del Infierno is limited and that you need to book a ticket (well!) in advance. See **www.barrancodelinfierno.es**

Routes on La Gomera

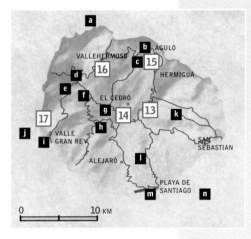

Most people visit the island of La Gomera as a day trip from Tenerife. This is easily done, as it takes only an hour and 15 minutes by boat to cross the 35 km from Los Cristianos to San Sebastian, La Gomera's main town. There are many reasons to endure the 'hassle' of taking the ferry to explore La Gomera, the first one being that the crossing itself is a true delight, usually being enlivened by great views of shearwaters (in season) and cetaceans. La Gomera itself is pretty and very laid-back, almost sleepy. It is spared the mass tourism and accompanying infrastructure of Los Cristianos.

In terms of nature, La Gomera lacks the high altitude habitats of Tenerife, but has, in compensation, much larger areas of intact succulent vegetation and thermophilous scrub. Yet the biggest draw is the Garajonay National Park, which harbours the archipelago's largest area of intact laurel cloud forest. The island's central ridge is precisely the right height to catch the moisture from the tradewinds, while the U-shape of the ridge is like a cup that concentrates the fog in the central valley of El Cedro, the most amazing part of the forest (route 14).

Those interested in wildflowers will be surprised that even though Tenerife is just 35 kms away, many wildflowers on La Gomera are of a

Sunset over La Gomera, seen from the Teide.

The name Garajonay

The name of Garajonay comes from a beautiful, dramatic myth. *Gara* was a Guanche princess on La Gomera and *Jonay* the son of a Guanche king from Tenerife. On a visit to La Gomera they met and fell in love. They announced their engagement, but before they could get married, the Teide erupted. This was interpreted as a bad omen and the young lovers' parents broke off their engagement and Jonay was brought back to Tenerife. Heart-broken, he escaped and swam the channel between the two islands to rejoin his beloved. Together, they fled to the mountains. The fathers organised a search for their children. The unfortunate couple fled further up the mountain until they were trapped on the highest slope. They had no way to escape, except in death. So that is what they did. In a final, deadly embrace they drove a sharpened stake in their hearts. They were found, connected by the very thing that drove them away from this world: the stake through their hearts. Hence the name *Garajonay* – the fusion of Gara and Jonay.

different species. La Gomera has its own, endemic species of sow-thistles, houseleeks, spurges and viper's-buglosses. For birdwatchers a visit to La Gomera used to be all about the seabirds (from the ferry) and finding the endemic pigeons, in particular the Laurel Pigeon, which was hard to find on Tenerife. The Laurel pigeons can still be found on La Gomera, but there are now many more known sites on Tenerife as well. However, the new avian attraction of La Gomera is the presence of the Trumpeter Finch, a desert bird that has nearly disappeared from Tenerife, but can be seen on La Gomera (site M on page 209).

Canary Palm groves are a common sight on the south-facing slopes of La Gomera.

Route 12 connects some of La Gomera's highlights in a single-day visit from Tenerife. However, we recommend you stay a bit longer, for some splendid laurel forest walks (route 14; sites D, E, F and G on pages 204-206). The woods and scrublands on the north slopes have a wonderful flora (routes 15 and 16), whilst the barrancos in the dry south have their own rugged attractions, with palm groves, beautiful succulent vegetation and the perpetual view over the bright blue ocean (route 17 and sites I, L and M on pages207-209).

Route 13: La Gomera by car

**FULL DAY
EASY**

*Splendid daytrip over an unspoilt island.
Sea bird and Dolphin watching from the Ferry.
Unspoilt laurel forest with a splendid flora and birdlife.*

Habitats: Succulent Scrub, laurel forest, cliffs, thermophile forest
Selected species: Gomera Blue Viper's-bugloss, Rough-leaved Viper's-bugloss*, Spoon-leaved Houseleek*, Perfoliate Pericallis*, Gomera Sow-thistle, Pale Monanthes, Canary Palm, Bottlenose Dolphin, Short-finned Pilot Whale, Cory's Shearwater, Little Shearwater, Bulwer's Petrel, Bolle's Pigeon, Laurel Pigeon, Canary Chaffinch, Plain Swift, Canary Red Admiral

A single day visit to La Gomera means compressing some of the best landscapes, most beautiful laurel forests and their flora and fauna in one day. Be warned, though, you'll want to come back!
To get the most out of the day, you need to take the first boat over and the last boat back. You can take your car on the ferry (advised), or rent one in San Sebastian. There are two ferry services, the slow Naviera Armas and the fast Fred Olson. We advise to take the first which offers a much better chance of seabirds and cetaceans.

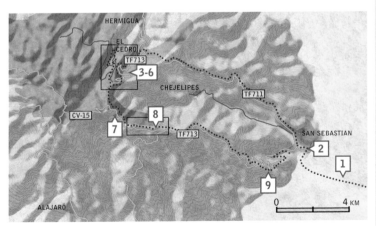

184

Naviera Armas leaves earlier and arrives just after Fred Olsen, so you have about the same time on La Gomera. Book, best in advance, on **www.navieraarmas.com**.

The great attraction of La Gomera is the laurel cloud forest of Garajonay, which is why this route focuses on that part of the island. However, the trip wouldn't be complete without enjoying the sharp contrast afforded by the island's dry, palm-clad south slope. Accordingly, some stops are advised here as well. In comparison to Tenerife, La Gomera's dry habitats are more intact, while the beautiful palm groves in the valleys add an exotic component. Finally, the impressive monolith rocks – a characteristic feature of La Gomera – are also part of the route.

The weather is very changeable in La Gomera's laurel forests, so pick the best possible day for your visit (see **www.tiempo.com**).

1 The ferry crossing can be excellent for seabirds and dolphins from March to October. Note the 'can be' – sometimes it is an absolute heaven for rare Macaronesian seabirds, dolphins and pilot whales, whereas other crossings only yield groups of Cory's Shearwaters. The late afternoon boats offer the best sightings.

Common Dolphins, photographed from the ferry to La Gomera.

Yellow-legged Gulls (year-round) and the Cory´s Shearwater (March – October) are the most common birds. Barolo Shearwaters and Bulwers Petrel (mostly late spring, summer, autumn), Manx Shearwater (spring and autumn) and Gannet (winter) are seen fairly frequently. Less often recorded are Madeiran Storm-petrel, Great Shearwater and Red-billed Tropicbird.

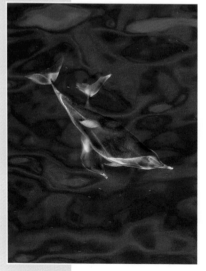

Family groups of Short-finned Pilot Whales are quite common, especially in the first kilometres out of the harbour of Tenerife. When the sea is calm, groups of Common and Bottlenose Dolphins navigate the straits and frequently follow the boat.

2 As you disembark at San Sebastian, note the many Plain Swifts that breed on the cliffs above the petrol station by the harbour. San Sebastian is a pretty town, with some lovely bars in the square overlooking the harbour (there are many Spanish Sparrows in the tall trees) and Monarch is recorded in the

Torre del Conde Park. We advise you not too linger here in the morning, since the weather in the laurel forests often deteriorates in the course of the afternoon.

From San Sebastian, take the TF 711 towards Hermigua and Vallehermoso. It leads up the beautiful Barranco Seco, covered in a splendid succulent scrub. You could schedule a brief stop at km 7.

After about 10 km you pass through the *Tunel de la Cumbre* (tunnel of the ridge). On the other side you enter the green world of the laurel forest.

Take the next turn left onto the very scenic TF 713, towards El Cedro and Parque Nacional Garajonay. After 2 km park at the small car park with information boards on the right (GPS: 28.128434, -17.207922). Walk the trail down to the *hermita* (chapel). At the chapel, take the flight of stairs down to the river (see map).

3 This short and simple walk is a lovely introduction to the laurel forest. Clearly, this part is not entirely natural – there are some small farms in the valley and the trail was one of the routes over the island to Hermigua.

There are many attractive wildflowers along this small stretch. In winter, the impressive Gomera Blue Viper's-bugloss (endemic to the island) grows alongside the trail, together with Canary Bellflower. Canary Crane's-bill, Perfoliate Pericallis* *(Pericallis steetzi)* and Hansen's Pericallis* *(P. hansenii)* are also present. Both pericallises are Gomera endemics – the first very common and the latter very rare. The marguerite here is Broussonet's Marguerite, which is confined to La Gomera and Tenerife and is the typical species of the laurel forest. The picturesque forest stream is lined with Canary Willow and with the local subspecies of Elder – another very rare plant of streamsides on the islands.

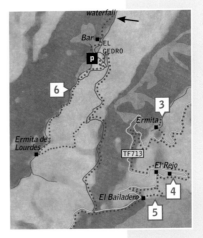

Return to the car and proceed further into the Garajonay National Park. After a sharp hairpin to the right, 2 km ahead, park at the small car park of *Mirador el Rejo* (GPS: 28.125174, -17.206958). If there is no space free, continue to the next (also El Rejo), a few hundred metres ahead. The Miradors del Rejo and the next *Mirador El Bailadero* (point 5) are very close to one another and can be covered on foot (see map).

4 These two viewpoints and the stretch of road between them form an excellent spot for seeing Bolle's and Laurel Pigeons. The latter appears to be the most common here. Just sit down, enjoy the splendid scenery and wait until the pigeons break cover and fly from one tree to the next. Continue a hundred metres or so on foot along the road. The moist cliff on the other side of the road boasts a wonderful flora, which includes the large Spoon-leaved Houseleek* *(Aeonium subplanum)*, endemic to la Gomera, and the Golden Greenovia. Both flower in summer.

Either on foot or by car, move to the next viewpoint, El Bailadero, and walk the short trail over the rim (see map).

5 You are now on the rim, where strong winds and shallow soils do not permit a dense forest to gain a foothold. Instead, there is only a cover of Tree Heath. You have some great views to the south. Here too, both pigeons are possible, as well as Sparrowhawk, Robin, Tenerife Goldcrest, Chiffchaff and Chaffinch. Along the trail there are some specimens of Gomera Blue Viper's-bugloss* *(Echium acanthocarpum)*, as well as the Large-flowered White Broom* *(Chamaecytisus proliferus)*. The last stretch to Mirador Hermiguera leads over a small track through a mossy tree heath forest with many houseleeks growing as epiphytes on branches of the Tree Heaths.

The very rare, tall Hansen's Pericallis* (top; up to 3 m high) grows along the trail to the Ermita. The Perfoliate Pericallis, in contrast, is very common (bottom).

Continue by car for another 500 metres and turn right to El Cedro. You now pass over a narrow through a beautiful, mossy stretch of laurel forest. Ahead, follow the signs *bar-restaurant* and stop at the car park next to the stream GPS: 28.135856, -17.214637.

6 Walk back 150 metres, turn right and follow the signs *Ermita de Lourdes*. At the Ermita (GPS: 28.126953, -17.220802), follow the signs to the *aula de naturaleza*, which brings you back to the road where you turn left to complete the loop. This will take about one hour and is an easy walk, but be aware of slippery patches.

The walk along the El Cedro stream to the Ermita de Lourdes leads through some of the tallest and most beautiful laurel cloud forests. Note the big, antler-like fungi *Laurobasidium lauri* on the Canary Laurel trees. This fungus grows exclusively on this tree species and some trunks are covered almost entirely in them.
The interior forest is very green. There are few wildflowers, but plenty of ferns. Particularly tall and beautiful are the Canary Male-ferns and Woodwardias. Long rags of mosses hang down from the branches and collect the droplets from the fog – the engine behind this ecosystem (see page 43).
In the forest, look for African Blue Tit, Tenerife Goldcrest and Chaffinch. The latter is particularly tame at the ermita, offering a good opportunity for photographers. Both pigeons occur as well, but are hard to get good views of.
In the forest clearing of El Cedro, the same birds can be found, but keep an eye out for Barbary Partridge as well. Among the butterflies, Canary Speckled Wood, Canary Red Admiral and Lang's Short-tailed Blue may be seen. Should you take some refreshments at the bar at El Cedro, keep an eye out for the Gomera Gecko, which is sometimes around on warm days.

The giant, antler-shaped mushroom *Laurobasidium lauri* grows exclusively on old Canary Laurels. It is a rare species, but around de Ermita de Lourdes, there are many of these odd fungi.

Return to the main road and turn right. After about 1.5 km you reach the TF 713 where you turn left towards San Sebastian and after 500 metres, park at the *Mirador de los Roques* (GPS: 28.109050, -17.214685).

7   The mirador on both sides of the road overlooks a total of four *roques*, large, freestanding monoliths of which there are several on La Gomera. These rocks are typical of this island on which there has not been any volcanic activity for a very long time. The *roques* are

solidified, very hard magma that remained in the central vent of an ancient volcano. The volcano itself consisted of softer material and has eroded, leaving only the central columns intact in the form of the *roques*.

Continue and park at the car park on the left side of the road just beyond the turn to Playa de Santiago. On foot, return to the fork in the road and then take the flight of steps on your right, which leads to the trail to the *Ermita de las Nieves*.

8 This trail runs over a ridge and offers spectacular views into dry barrancos on either side. Note how spectacularly steep these barrancos are in comparison to those of central Tenerife – reflecting the much longer period during which erosion could eat away this old bedrock. Also typical of La Gomera: the beautiful palm groves in the valleys. They are now partially abandoned, but were until recently an important crop.

This trail offers a spectacular flora, including Loose-flowered Houseleek* *(Aeonium decorum)*, Dicheranthus, the tiny Pale Monanthes, Willow-leaved Carline-thistle, Rough-leaved Viper's-bugloss* *(Echium aculeatum)*, Golden Greenovia and the non-stinging Small-leaved Nettles* *(Forsskaolea angustifolia)*.

9 Continue towards San Sebastian to complete the trip. Enjoy, during clear skies, the great views of Tenerife as you wind down the road.

The impressive monoliths in central La Gomera are ancient lava plugs that once filled a cladera that has eroded away.

Route 14: Laurel forests of Garajonay

4 HOURS
MODERATE-STRENUOUS

Of interest
Year-round

Best walk to explore the laurel forest in all its diversity.

Habitats: tree heath forest, hillside laurel forest, stream-side laurel forest
Selected species: Canary Laurel, Gomera Sow-thistle, Woodwardia, Laurel Pigeon, Tenerife Goldcrest

Of the many options that you have for hiking in the Garajonay cloud forest, this route is perhaps the most beautiful. It leads down from the ridge into the basin of the El Cedro stream, passing on the way various types of laurel forest.

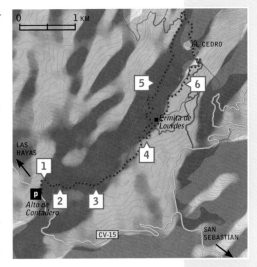

The strength of this route lies in the subtle changes in the landscape and in the ambience, sounds and smells of the forest. Some of the tallest trees of La Gomera are found here, densely covered in mosses. This route offers some of the very best laurel forests in the entire Canaries.

The route is described from the upper part of the forest down to the village of El Cedro. If you are able to arrange transport by car back to your starting point, this is a fairly easy walk. If not, consider walking it the other way round, so the tough climb is at the start, not the end. The trail is in a good state, with flights of steps up the steep bits. Nevertheless, be careful as the wet forest floor may be slippery in places.

Note that this is a fairly popular walk. Be early to beat the crowd and find a parking spot at *Alto de Contadero*.

Starting point Alto de Contadero car park GPS: 28.115676, -17.243150

Getting there The car park is situated on the TF 713 / CV 15 in the centre of the island, 1.3 km from the turn to Alajaró and roughly 7 km to the junction to Las Hayas.

1 The first stretch of the trail is fairly level and runs through a *fay-al-brezal* – a the type of forest that is, because of the wind and infrequent cloud cover, dominated by Tree Heath (*Brezo* in Spanish) and Canary Gale (*Faya*). These two species are a little more drought-resistant than the trees in the true laurel forest. The vegetation is dense and not very high. The tall Gomera Sow-thistle* (*Sonchus gomerensis*), lines the trail in places.

Winter in the Garajonay National Park, when the fog is thickest and the forest most fairytale-like.

2 As you start decending, the shade becomes deeper. Canary Laurel and Canary Laur-ustinus appear as you are walking down into the actual laurel forest. The vegetation is of the type the Spanish call the *lauriselva de la ladera* – the slope cloud forest. This is the most common type of laurel forest. You will start to see very long mosses hanging from the branches. They are able to survive because of the high humidity, soaking up water from the fog and bringing it to the ground – this is the phenomenon of the horizontal rain (*llúvia horizontal* – see page 43).

3 After a pretty steep descent, you arrive at a damp and very mossy canyon (beyond the 6 of the numbered posts along the route). From here on it continues more gently downhill through a long stretch of slope forest, which becomes increasingly impressive and mossy as you get nearer to the most frequently fog-covered part of the slope. The forest is interspersed with patches of Tree Heath, which here are a secondary vegetation and signal sites of former human habitation.

4 After point 6 you arrive at a fork (GPS: 28.12113 -17.22597). Go right and down to the brook. You now enter the rare riparian laurel forest (*Lauriselva de Valle*; see also page 43 and 55). The trees here are massive green giants, some of which grow to over 30 metres tall. The tallest trees are Indian Laurel* *(Persea indica)*, also member of the laurel family and the most moisture dependant of them all. Along the El Cedro brook, the very rare Honey Spurge grows, the only spurge to grow over 10 metres tall.

5 At the T-junction (GPS: 28.12429 -17.22341), go left onto a track, which gently climbs up again. This brings you back into the slope forest, again of the wonderfully mossy variant. Of interest here – apart from the fact that it lies away from the marked trails and therefore sees fewer visitors – is the presence of some small rocky areas, mostly formed when the track was levelled. These artificially made clearings in the forest provide a rich habitat for plants, including Spoon-leaved Houseleek* *(Aeonium subplanum)*, Perfoliate Pericallis* *(Pericallis steetzi)* and Woodwardia. Look out for Laurel Pigeons along this stretch.

The El Cedro stream

At the lefthand bend, follow the trail to the right, signposted for El Cedro (GPS: 28.14203 -17.21707). Note that the next short stretch is fairly steep and slippery so take care. A little further on, there is a branch that turns sharply right (poorly signposted; GPS: 28.14306 -17.21681) – follow this one down to El Cedro. In the hamlet, follow the the road up to the the junction, signposted Ermita de Lourdes 1.6 km.

6 In the forest clearing of El Cedro, look for birds like Tenerife Goldcrest and Barbary Partridge.

At the Ermita, go straight to return to the junction of point 5.

Route 15: Woods and lunar landscape of Agulo

Best season
Feb-July
Of interest
Year-round

FULL DAY
MODERATE

Thermophilous woodland and lunar landscape.
Great flora and butterfly fauna.

Habitats: Thermophilous Juniper woodland, cliffs, 'lunar' tuff fields
Selected species: Gomera Grayling, Gomera Skink, Canary Juniper, Castello-paiva's Houseleek

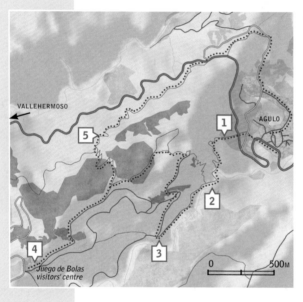

This walk in the very north of La Gomera leads you to three contrasting land-scapes: the Juniper domi-nated barrancos, thermo-phile woodlands and an impressive lunar landscape of reddish mobile, volcanic ash and the typical bar-ranco vegetation. There are many endemic plants to be discovered on the route, plus a number of birds, lizards and a good range of butterflies.

The walk starts with a strenuous but short climb but is otherwise not very demanding. Along the way you visit the Centro de Visitantes of the National Park, which has a botanical garden that is worth visiting.

Starting point Main street of Agulo

Agulo is a scenic, compact village with a rich architectonic history. Walk down the main street along Post office and Farmacia. At Casa Aixa fol-low the yellow-white track up to the Mirador de Abrante.

1 You pass terraces and small gardens where avocados, papayas, bananas and mangos are grown – all fruits from the Spanish overseas territories in South America that were brought back from the colonies and grown here (see page 61). The climb is steep but relatively short. On the way up the whole palette of characteristic plants species pass by, most of which endemic to the Canaries: Lamarck's and Balsam Spurges, Verode, Canary Lavender, Tree Bindweed, Shrubby Sea-lavender* (*Limonium fruticans*), Gomera Sticky Houseleek (*Aeonium lindleyi viscatum*), Gomera Ironwort (*Sideritis gomerae*) and many more. The latter two occur exclusively on La Gomera. Look out on the rocks for the tiny Leafy Monanthes, one of the smallest succulents of the archipel.

Cross the road and continue uphill. At a fork in the road go left direction 'la Palmita'. On your left the weir of the reservoir is in sight.

2 The trail leads along abandoned terraces now covered by Wormwood (*Artemisia thuscula*). Look for butterflies. The best places are yet to come, but Canary Speckled Wood, Canary Blue and Canary Red Admiral should already be present, in season of course. Along the path next to the reservoir (Embalse Agulo) you can find more Canary endemics: Poleo de Monte (*Bystropogon canariense*), the aforementioned Gomera Ironwort and the soil-covering Tree Plantain (*Plantago arborescens*). Look out for Sardinian Warbler and Barbary Falcon too. Both are observed frequently here.

The lunar landscape consists of reddish volcanic ash with deep gullies, which forms a harsh environment for plants.

194

The trail follows some spectacular cliffs (top), where the rare and endemic cabbage-leaved sea-lavender grows (bottom).

At the houses of Casas del Chorro, now used as holiday residences, the path ends and turns to the main road to Juego de Bolas. In the hairpin take this road up.

3 The landscape changes radically. The scrub and woodland make way for heavily eroded, reddish volcanic ash with deep gullies through which the rainwater runs off. Because of the bare soil, this is often called a 'lunar (moon-like) landscape'. The soil is very acidic, somewhat saline and above all very compacted, but with a topsoil that easily washes away – conditions that make it very hard for plants to root and stabilise the soil. The reddish colours reflect the high iron oxide content of these soils.

The current situation isn't entirely natural. Due to excessive exploitation in the past the protective vegetation disappeared. In order to restore the original situation and to prevent the soil from running off through the gullies, a replantation programme has started here, until now with mixed success. When you reach the Mirador de Abrante, you can visit the impressive skywalk with views over the ocean and Tenerife in the background.

Continue your way up through the 'lunar' badlands, following the signs Juego de Bolas visitors' centre.

4 The Vistitors centre, provides information about the unique laurel forest in the Garajonay park including the dramatic forest fire that took place in 2012 which destroyed about 20% of the total forest area. Special attention is given to the recovery programme, funded by the EU LIFE programme. Next door is the Bar Tamor (closed) and the botanical garden which hosts a vast amount of native plants, with convenient name tags that enable you to name some of the plants you may recognise from the walk.

Return the same way, so along Bar Tamor and after 50 m turn left on a concrete track. Here you follow the GR 132.

5 This last, wonderful stretch descends through open forest and barranco woodland. There is a rich birdlife (Canary Chiffchaff, Sardinian Warbler and Barbary Falcon, amongs others) and many butterflies. In late spring and summer, this is a good place to find the Gomera Grayling, the only butterfly that is endemic to La Gomera. More widespread species include Clouded Yellow, Canary Blue and Canary Red Admiral. Look for reptiles too. Besides the widespread Boettger's Lizards, there are Gomera Skinks and Gomera Gecko.

The Gomera Grayling is only found on this island, and is quite common along the route in the summer months. In this case it even rested on our backpack.

6 After 2 km the GR132 follows an old trading route down to Agulo on. Enjoy the shiny greenish Gomera houseleek on the dark slope with in the background the opaque, dark tones of Pine and Juniper. In the deep barrancos some more endemic wildflowers can be found: Canary Sage (*Salvia canariensis*), Cabbage-leaved Sea-lavender* (*Limonium brassicifolium*), and a large variety of houseleeks.

You arrive at the GM 1 road. Follow it to the right in the direction of the tunnel, cross the street after 25 m and walk down the village of Agulo following the signs 'Camino Natural'.

Route 16: The thermophile woodlands of Vallehermoso

FULL DAY
EASY-MODERATE

Best season
Feb-July
Of interest
Year-round

Lovely hike through the thermophilous woodland.
Views of the impressive Roque Caño.

Habitats: Thermophilous Juniper woodland, cliffs
Selected species: Broad-leaved Viper's Bugloss, Leafless Spurge, Castello-paiva's Houseleek, Gomera Lugoa, Canary Islands Chiffchaff

From Vallehermoso you can make an interesting hike through several different landscape types around the monolith Roque Caño. Along the way you pass through remnants of laurel forest, thermophile woodland and barrancos, but the great selling point of this walk are the *sabinares*, an open woodland dominated by Canary Juniper (*sabina* in Spanish) which is a habitat not found on Tenerife. Endemic plants are found all along the trail, but predominantly in the barrancos.

Starting point Centre of Vallehermoso
(GPS: 28.17890, -17.26603)

Walk to the roundabout in the centre of the village and then over the GM 1 along the Centro de Salud. Past the petrol station turn right in the direction of Las Rosas and Garabato, following the Camino Natural indicators.

At the next bifurcation take the tarmac road to El Teón along a number of allotment gardens.

1 Along this road you can already find a good number of Canary endemic wildflowers. Look for Willow-leaved Globularia, Spiny Buckthorn (*Rhamnus crenulata*), Canary Silk Vine, Tree Bindweed and the Gomera endemic Castello-paiva's Houseleek. The Canary Junipers grow on the steep hills around you. They are typical for the north of La Gomera.
Ignore the first exit to the left direction El Teón. After 2,5 km the tarmac road turns into a dirt track; after another 500 m take the path sharp right to El Teón (indicator).

Facing page: The Gomera Skink can be found in the barrancos.
Below: the impressive monotlith Roque Caño is surrounded by scrub and open woodland.

2 The path follows the crest of a hill that is cloaked in a lovely mix of thermophile forest species like Canary Juniper, Canary St. John's-wort, Holly and Tree Heath and *Osyris lanceolata*, another shrub that is typical of the thermophile scrubland grows, together with Dicheranthus in the undergrowth. Be aware of Laurel Pigeon, which regularly flies in the barranco. Other birds present are Canary Islands Chiffchaff, Kestrel and Blackcap. You can take a break at El Teón, which has a picnic bench and viewpoint.

After El Teón, take the path to the left; be careful because this track is a little bit difficult as it is overgrown by brambles and steep on the left side. Fortunately it is only 100 m until you reach a tarmac road which is the border of the Garajonay park. You pass a well and at the next fork you go right.

3 Gradually, the vegetation shifts from thermophile forest to laurel forest, with, amongst others, Tree heath, Canary gale, Leafy Broom and Broad-leaved Viper's-bugloss. Look

PRACTICAL PART

The rugged slopes around Vallehermoso are covered with Canary Juniper (top). The curious, greyish-blue Dicheranthus is a typical plant in this open scrubland (bottom).

here and further on for butterflies. Canary Blue, Canary Cleopatra and Canary Speckled Wood are among the options here.

4 At a three-forked road, keep left. Shortly you arrive at the viewpoint Mirador de Roque Blanco, from where you have a splendid overview over the barranco and afar Roque Caño.

After 500 m take the track to the left, the Camino naturales to Vallehermoso (GR route).

5 By now you have entered a closed forest with Canary Holly and some Laurel trees. As you descent the forest becomes more open and shifts again to a Juniper wood, especially in the last part close to the Roque Caño. Along the way some beautiful old Juniper trees but there are more endemic plants to be enjoyed: Canary Island Sage, Gomera Lugoa and Canary Houseleek show up. Underneath Roque Caño, at Mirador de la Pilarica you have an excellent view over Vallehermoso and the ocean.

Descent over the GR (red/white)/Camino Natural indicated route down to the village of Vallehermoso.

Route 17: The plateau and the cliffs of Valle Gran Rey

4 HOURS
EASY-MODERATE

!
No shade

Spectacular cliff landscape with dry scrubland.
and desolated farmland.
Drought resistant plants and an interesting birdlife.

Best season
Oct-June

Habitats: succulent scrub, cliffs, former cultivated farmland
Selected species: Barbary falcon, Bertelots Pipit, Canary, Willow-leaved
Carline Thistle, Cardoon, Shrubby launaea, Gomera Ceropegia, Barbary
Spurge Hawk-moth

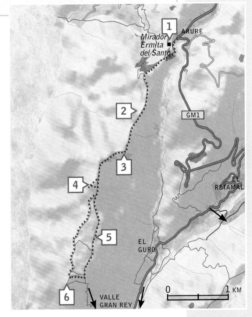

This pleasant walk along cliffs is with its spectacular ocean views very much the counterpart of the routes through laurel forest. Dry to very dry scrublands and desolated farmlands make up the scenery. Reflecting these dry circumstances, drought resistant plants prevail showing their different strategies towards the harsh climate. Among them the rare Gomera Ceropegia* (*Ceropegia dichotoma*). Birds and insects belonging to dry scrublands can be observed easily. During the hike you have spectacular views on the deep cliffs and the village of Valle Gran Rey. It was on these cliffs that in 1999 the Gomera Giant Lizard was rediscovered (see page 103).

Despite the precipitous cliffs and steep slopes around you, this is a fairly easy and level walk. You consider an extension that involves a steep, 900 m drop down into Valle Gran Rey, from where you can consider taking the bus back to the starting point (check bus time tables (e.g. via the the moovit app; see page 212).

Starting point Arure (GPS: 28.1355401, -17.3180710)

Getting there Coming from the north following the GM 1 park your car in the centre of the hamlet of Arure. Walk further down the street until the first hairpin. In the hairpin you take the track to the right, indicated Mirador del Santo.

1 Take a look at Mirador Ermita del Santo. Here you overlook the spectacular valley of Tagaluche. Humans settled here centuries ago, attracted to the benign conditions in the valley as it is one of the places where several springs emerge.

Go back and continue over the road. After ca 1 km keep left on the small footpath indicated Camino Natural. The Camino Natural coincides with the GR 132 you have to follow.

2 First you come along a number of small houses and some local goat farms. Typical plants here are thistles, like Wild Artichoke, Willow-leaved Carline Thistle and various other Mediterranean species. They are all adapted to the dry conditions by minimising the evaporation by reducing the total leaf area and a thick cuticula ('plant skin') that prevents high rates of water loss. Some further you'll find solitary pines, pioneer trees thriving under these harsh conditions. Look for insects as well – the sunny, exposed habitat attracts dragonflies, grasshoppers and butterflies.

The endemic Barbary spurge hawk-moth (top) and its caterpillar (bottom) are found frequently on this route.

3 Look out for the characteristic birds of these open scrublands and cliffs: Kestrel, Berthelot's Pipit, Corn Bunting, Rock Dove, Raven, Canary, Canary Islands Chiffchaff and Barbary Falcon. The views along the cliffs are spectacular. Here the 'drought champions' prevail: Shrubby Launaea, Verode and Lamarck's Spurge also do well under these harsh circumstances. Rather than tolerating the drought, they avoid the driest periods through a so called state of 'early dormancy'. They grow and flower early in the year, when there is plenty of water, and store the sugars in their succulent stems. Look out for the curious Gomera Ceropegia, another succulent, that that only grows on La Gomera.

At a fork in the dirt track take the right path to the Mirador La Merica, which lies another 500 metres ahead.

4 From the mirador, you have a splendid overview of the route, plus great views into the barranco and the ocean beyond. Keep an eye out for birds. Plain Swifts are common in season and you may see Barbary falcon as well.

Continue over the indicated GR route. Just after la Merica you'll pass some ruins, and a water reservoir, now abandoned.

The breath-taking desolate landscape on the plateau.

This solitary Juniper is a striking landmark on the edge of the La Mérica plateau.

5 Some further you come along a solitary house and to the left of it a stone circle that functioned as a threshing floor. This plateau once was farmland. Now it lies fallow and Lamarck's Spurge and various plants of dry grasslands have taken over. Canaries and Plain Swifts are common. It is also one of the few places where Corn Bunting breeds on the island. Look among the spurge plants for hawk-moths. Both Common and Barbary Spurge Hawk-moth may be found here. There is an interesting story behind these species. There is a theory that states that Barbary Spurge Hawk-moth once had a much larger range in Europe than today, but has been pushed further south after a cool period ca 3600 years ago, its place being taken over by Common Hawk-moth which is more resistant to the cold. The scattered isolated populations of the Barbary Spurge Hawk-moth that exist today have developed into distinct subspecies; a speciation process that continues up to this day.

Walk on until you reach the end of the plain. Here the Camino Natural/ GR 132 turns left, down to Valle Gran Rey. This is the extension of the route; in Valle Gran Rey you can take the bus back to Arure. This description turns right and heads for Risco de Merica

6 From afar you see the solitary Juniper which stands on Risco de Merica. From here you've got an excellent view on the surroundings including Valle Gran Rey below. On the cliffs below the rare and endangered Giant la Gomera lizard was rediscovered in 1999, and hereafter bred in capture at the Legartario in Valle Gran Rey. Chances of actually seeing this lizard are rather slim, but a good botanical substitute is *Neochamaelea pulverulenta*, a lavender-like plant that grows on the Risco and is endemic to the Canary Islands.

Next page: Broad-winged Sea-lavender (left; *Limonium redivivum*) and Golden Greenovia (right) grow on the roadside cliffs near Agulo.

Return and follow a track indicated with blue spots on the stones. It follows the cliff edge (be careful!) and re-joins the main track in the vicinity of the viewpoint La Merica. Return via the same way.

Additional sites and routes on La Gomera

A – Los Organos

 GPS: 28.12113 -17.22597. The cliff of *Los Organos* (the organ) is a bizarre and impressive formation of columns of basaltic rock – hence the name. Los Organos can only be admired from the sea. There are excursions from Valle Gran Rey; see **www.excursiones-tina.com**. Especially in the summertime, this excursion may prove to be interesting for watching sea birds and dolphins as well.

Of interest
Year-round

B – Cliff flora along the Las Rosas – Agulo road

 GPS: 28.189275, -17.205359. It's easy pickings for botanists along the stretch of the GM 1 from Las Rosas to Agulo. There are various lay-bys where you can pull over and admire the flora on the cliffs next to the road. La Gomera endemics Spoon-leaved Houseleek* *(Aeonium subplanum)*, Gomera Sticky Houseleek* *(A. viscatum)*, Golden Greenovia and Broad-winged Sea-lavender* *(Limonium redivivum)* are all there, and there is more. From late May onwards, the endemic butterfly the Gomera Grayling may be seen here too.

Of interest
Late winter
to summer

C – Juego de Bolas visitors' centre

Of interest
Year-round

  GPS: 28.177943, -17.214107. The Garajonay visitors' centre (also visited on route 18) is – strangely – situated quite far from the National Park and in a place that is not a logical starting point for an excursion into the park. Nevertheless, it is worth visiting. It has a small but interesting exhibition on the nature

of Garajonay, information on walking routes in the park and a small botanical garden with the most typical plants of the island, complete with names and current distribution maps. The garden is also a good place to photograph some of the more common birds of the island, like Chaffinch and Canary Islands Chiffchaff. Behind the visitors' centre you will find a walking trail through a somewhat degenerated, but still interesting, scrubland.

The road up into Garajonay from the visitors' centre is beautiful, although sometimes difficult to drive when tour buses come from the opposite direction. Orchid aficionados will want to check the road-

Canary Islands
Chiffchaff

sides, some 800 metres north of the visitors' centre on the road towards Garajonay, where, on a cliff next to the road, the endemic Three-fingered Orchid flowers in December and January.

D – Chorros de Epina viewpoint

Of interest
Year-round

  GPS: 28.163755, -17.297506. Where the GM 1 road leaves the Garajonay National Park, just west of the junction to Epina and Alojera, lies the well of *Chorros de Epina*. This seven-pipe water source played an important role in local folklore. Moreover, it is an excellent viewpoint for the endemic pigeons – Laurel Pigeon and Bolle's Pigeon. From the small terrace of the bar *Chorros de Epina* (between the junction and the car park of the *Chorros*), you have excellent views over the forest canopy, from which the pigeons regularly break cover and fly over the trees.

The short loop to the actual fountain has an interesting flora, which includes Golden Greenovia, Castello-paiva's* and Red-lined* Houseleeks (*Aeonium castello-paivae* and *A rubrolineatum*; both Gomera endemics) and the rare Canary Elder.

E - Los Barranquillos

GPS: 28.152505, -17.305180. The short *Los Barranquillos* walk is an easy and quick loop when coming from or going to Valle Gran Rey. It is advertised by the National Park as a good example of more degraded Canary Gale-Heath woodland, but in our opinion, this doesn't do it justice. For a large part, the loop leads through a very old Tree Heath woodland, in which the Tree Heath (in the Mediterranean usually in size somewhere between a tall bush and a small tree) grow to a formidable size. In January to March, the massive bloom of thousands of the small orchid Two-leaved Gennaria is a feast for the eye.

Best season
January-April

F - Las Creces

GPS: 28.142983, -17.285271. The Las Creces walk leads through a superb laurel forest. Trees are heavily draped with mosses and large ferns and masses of Canary Crane's-bill cover the forest floor, making this a true green jungle. At the picnic site of Las Creces, there are some very tame Chaffinches, which are easy to photograph (use your wide-angle lens!). As this walk mostly runs through the interior of the cloud forest, it is not the best route to find a diversity of species, be it birds, wildflowers or otherwise.

Of interest
Year-round

The walk is easy, with little altitude differences and runs over well-maintained forest tracks and trails. It is about 5 km long, which can be extended with another 4 km or so. It leaves from the car park on the GM 2 just 300 metres west of the turn to las Hayas and first leads to the picnic site in the forest where the loop starts.

The forest in Las Creces

G – La Laguna Grande

Best season
February-April

GPS: 28.126454, -17.257648. La Laguna Grande is a large open area and popular picnic spot along the GM 2 road over the ridge in central Gomera. From Laguna Grande, various easy walks through an old Heath-Canary Gale forest (with a sublime undergrowth of Canary Crane's-bill in February – April) and further into the laurel forest.

La Laguna Grande is signposted on the GM 2 and lies just west of the junction with the minor road to Las Rosas and the Juego de Bolas visitors' centre.

H – La Fortaleza

Best season
March-July

GPS: 28.103981, -17.275083. The rock formation of *La Fortaleza* (the fortress) near Chipude was one of the major places of worship for the Guanches. One can easily image why, as the views from this conspicuous table mountain are spectacular, at least when its head is not in the clouds.

La Fortaleza is of similar origin as La Gomera's *roques*: it is the very hard, solidified magma inside the tube of a volcano that itself eroded away over time.

The area used to be a hotspot for wildflowers and its steep slopes may still very well be. Unfortunately, a fire badly affected the main plateau in the summer of 2013 and some of the species have disappeared.

The walk to La Fortaleza and back takes just about two hours and is easy except for a short, strenuous climb

The broad and easy trail through the laurel forests near La Laguna Grande (bottom). A common bird here is the familiar Robin, which' local subspecies have a much lighter belly and brighter red throat than the European birds (top).

207

along vertical cliffs without any safety measures. This makes a visit only suitable for the more experienced hikers. Don't go up in mist (slippery rocks!) or in strong winds.
To get there, take the road down from Chipude in the direction of La Dama. Before the last house of the hamlet in Pavón (just south of Chipude) park next to the cobbled road that leads up the mountain. Walk up the road and follow the signs *La Fortaleza*.

The barrancos of Guarimiar (site L, next page) offer spectacular views and walks. Due to the precipitous landscape, the hikes here are challenging.

I – Valle Gran Rey

   GPS: 28.091815, -17.340158. The Valle Gran Rey (Valley of the Great King) is, after Garajonay, the biggest attraction for hikers and visitors of La Gomera. Scenically, it is an impressive, palm-clad valley (canyon is a better word for it), and it has a superb flora and fauna. The highlight of Valle Gran Rey is the presence of the La Gomera Giant Lizard, which was rediscovered as late as 1999 on the large west-facing cliff on the northern side of the valley – the cliff behind the football course (see page 103). There is a Giant Lizard breeding program to increase the numbers of this extremely rare animal (also behind the soccer field), but sadly it is not open to the public.

Of interest
year round

208

The trouble with Gran Rey is that the good sites are simply inaccessible: it all happens on the sheer cliffs and whilst there are trails running up them, a mere glance on the massive rock walls would deter all but the most sportive of naturalists of starting a walk. The Valle Gran Rey resort is a laid-back and peaceful place where you can go snorkelling or take a boat excursion to Los Organos (site A) or to watch dolphins (see below).

Plain Tiger

J – Dolphin watching trips

Of interest
Year-round

The same company that offers boat trips to Los Organos, also provides 3-hour dolphin-watching trips, leaving from Valle Gran Rey. See **www.excursiones-tina.com**.

K – Chejelipes reservoir

Of interest
Year-round

GPS: 28.116468, -17.167779. The Chejelipes reservoir is an excellent place to kill an hour before taking the boat to Los Cristianos. It is one of the few sites on La Gomera where Moorhen and Coot breed, but many other birds turn up (there was an Osprey when we were last here). A couple of Yellow-legged Gull breed here too. You can view the reservoir from the dam, while the stream below the dam is a good place for searching marsh and scrubland birds and dragonflies. The latter includes the rare Ringed Cascader. There is a population of Monarch butterflies as well.
From San Sebastian take the CV 1 to Hermigua and take the turn to Chejelipes. The reservoir dam is next to the road.

L – Barrancos of Guarimiar

Of interest
Year-round

GPS: 28.059453, -17.213357. The narrow but well-maintained road to the hamlet of Guarimiar brings you to some of the most attractive hiking areas of the south of La Gomera. It is spectacular like (and ecologically similar to) the Valle Gran Rey, but with fewer visitors. You can opt for brief stops along the road or strenuous, day-filling walks and everything in between.
From Playa de Santiago, take the turn to Guarimiar. At the fork, go left, signposted for Taco. This brings you further into the valley. Par at the next junction and continue on foot throughthe barranco.

209

The area between the airstrip and Playa de Santiago is the driest and sunniest part of La Gomera.

M – Cemetery Las Trincheras

 GPS: 28.027467, -17.206820. This small area just west of Playa Santiago is very close to the airport. A walk along the promenade offers good views of the nearby sea-cliffs. Exploring the wastelands, it is surprising how many birds you can see: Barbary Partridge, Spectacled Warbler, Berthelot's Pipit, Linnet, Corn Bunting, Canary, Chiffchaff, Spanish Sparrow, Kestrel, Raven, Hoopoe and even groups of Trumpeter Finches and Rock Sparrows can be about.
To get there, take the exit signposted *Cementerio* between Playa de Santiago and the airport.
Park near the entrance of the cemetery and explore the surrounding fields. From here you can enter the fields and walk the path along the steep sea-cliffs. Another good site for these birds is in the barranco towards Playa de Santiago. Park next to the petrol station and explore the barranco to the north of the road.

The dry fields and barranco valleys harbour many birds, including the rare Trumpeter Finch.

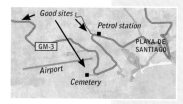

N – Ferry to El Hierro

  If you are based on La Gomera consider a trip on the slow ferry (Trasmediterranea, from San Sebastian) to El Hierro. It sails once a week returning on the same day (six hours). This is a good opportunity to see seabirds.

GUACHINCHE
CASA CHIQUI

* GUESO BLANCO
* CROQUETAS DE CABALLA
* HUEVOS AL ESTAMPIDO
  CARNES A LA BRASA.
* POLLO
* CHULETA DE COCHINO NEGRO.

TOURIST INFORMATION & OBSERVATION TIPS

Travel and accommodation

Travelling to Tenerife and La Gomera

Most visitors arrive on Tenerife by air, as this is the fastest and cheapest way. Depending on where you fly from in Europe, a flight takes about 3 to 5 hours. Prices are variable but reasonable. Many airlines, particularly the low cost ones, fly to Tenerife.

Most international flights arrive at Tenerife Sur (Aeropuerto Reina Sofía) on the south coast. From Tenerife Norte airport (Los Rodeos) there are flights to all other Canary Islands and to many destinations in mainland Spain.

From Cádiz and Huelva in southern Spain, you can also take the ferry to Tenerife. The journey takes 60 hours and sails once a week to Santa Cruz (**www.trasmediterranea.es**). The company Fred Olsen **www.fredolsen.es** sails from Huelva to Gran Canaria. Both are good services if you want to take a camper van.

The easiest way to get to La Gomera is to book a flight to Tenerife Sur, take a taxi or bus (20 minutes) to the port of Los Cristianos and embark on one of the regular ferries to San Sebastian de la Gomera. There are two companies navigating the strait between Los Cristianos and San Sebastian, each with several departures per day. Naviera Armas has the slow boat, which takes about 1.15 hours (**www.navieraarmas. com**), while Fred Olson crosses in about 45 minutes (**www.fredolsen.es**). We don't recommend flying to La Gomera. Besides the environmental concerns, it takes longer and you miss out on the experience of crossing the water between the islands.

Travelling on Tenerife and La Gomera

A hire care is by far the easiest way to travel around. The roads are in very good condition and you can also take the car on the ferry. You can rent a car at one of the airports and in all the main cities, including San Sebastian de la Gomera. All the main car rental companies have offices on the islands. Both car hire and petrol are inexpensive. Just to be certain, we recommend to hire your car in advance via your travel agent or the internet, although usually it is possible to arrange it on the spot.

The alternative to the hire care is the public bus service. Buses in Canarian dialect are called guaguas (pronounced *wah-wah*). Though not very fast, the guaguas are without doubt the most economical way to travel. There are more than 600 services on Tenerife (see **www.titsa.com**) connecting even the most remote villages and the main sites in the Cañadas del Teide. The bus service on La Gomera is equally extensive (**https://guaguagomera.com**).

The bus is also a very handy way of travelling when you are walking long linear routes. The bus can bring you back to your starting point. Be aware though that although the bus service is extensive, it is not very frequent. If travelling by bus, make sure you know the time table, in particular the time of the last bus. You don't want to get stuck in Taganana overnight, no matter how lovely the village is! One way to avoid this is, where possible, to park at your destination and take the bus back to the proposed starting point, thus avoiding a long wait or worrying about missing the last bus. An excellent tool to check the bus tables is the free app Moovit (**https://moovitapp.com**) which has route bus maps and time tables for both islands.

Taxis can take you all over the islands and are cheaper than in most other European countries. Public taxis have a SP license plate *(servicio público)*. Consult for Tenerife **www.officialtaxitenerife.com**. There are only few taxis on La Gomera, ask in your hotel or check **www.gomeralive.com/taxis.**

Accommodation

Choosing your place to stay is not straightforward, as there is not a single best place from which to explore the islands. Travelling around and staying a couple of days in various places (as you would in Europe) is possible, but needs to be arranged and booked beforehand.

The first choice you need to make is whether to stay on La Gomera or on Tenerife. La Gomera is much quieter and more authentic, but also more expensive and, with no direct flights, more hassle to arrange. This, plus the greater diversity of wildlife on Tenerife, means staying on that island, perhaps with one or two overnight stays on La Gomera, is the better option.

When choosing your accommodation on Tenerife, you have two choices: go for a package deal that includes flight and hotel, or choose your hotel independent from the flight.

Package deal: as a sun and beach destination, package deals of flight and hotel are almost the rule if booking through a travel agency. This most likely takes you in one of the less inspiring hotel blocks in Los Cristianos or another resort on the west coast. If carefully selected, this can be a cheap option, and the west coast is not a bad place to be based. From here you have easy access to the sites in the south and to the pine forest and caldera sites on the centre of the island. The motorway even makes a visit to Santa Cruz quite easy (Los Cristianos to Santa Cruz takes 50 minutes), whilst the Teno mountains are within reach via the winding road to Santiago del Teide. In addition, as ferries leave from here, you can visit the laurel forests on La Gomera quite easily (the price ofor a round trip is about € 130 for a single person plus car, and about half that price without car).

Choosing your own hotel: There are wonderful, traditionl guest houses (*casa rural*), in particular on the north side of Tenerife. They are quite a bit more expensive than an

apartment in a holiday resort on the coast, but have the advantage of being beautifully
situated between the green allotments. What's better than to start the day after sleeping
in a proper house, with your own coffee on the terrace, together with a Tenerife Lizard
on the wall next to you and Canary picking out the seeds of an endemic sow-thistle?
Another point is – arguably – that by staying in a casa rural you are supporting a more
local and less wasteful economy.

To start your search, simply look for casa rural tenerife, and you'll find a wealth of websites to choose from. Many *casas rurales* are situated between Santiago del Teide and
La Oratava, which provide perfect access to all of Tenerife's sites except those in the far
south and the ferries for La Gomera (Los Cristianos to Icod takes 1 ¼ hours). Keep in
mind that the weather in places like Erjos, Santiago and the Oratava valley can be cold
and rainy in winter. Further down in Icod or Garachico it is usually fine.

Camping: Camping isn't very popular on the islands, nor is it easy to do. There are several commercial camp sites (most of them not very attractive) in the south of the island.
For a list, see **www.todotenerife.es** and look for camp sites under the entry 'what to do'.
There are quite a few designated camp sites in natural areas, but due to bureaucratic
hurdles it is difficult to get a permit for them (permits can only be obtained from the
Cabildo (government) of Tenerife, which need to be applied for at the cabildo office in
person at least seven days in advance). On La Gomera there is a camp site in El Cedro
www.camping-lavista.jimdofree.com.

Shops – opening hours

Shops are usually open between 9:00 and 13:00 and again from 15:00 pm to 20:00.
Large supermarkets don't close for a lunch-break and stay open until later. Banks and
Post-offices open only in the morning, mostly from 9 am to 2 pm. Some pharmacies
stay open for 24 hours.

Bars open early, sometimes at 7 am and some stay open until 1 am the next morning. Between 1 and 3 pm restaurants serve lunch. The *menu del día* is an inexpensive
choice, with three courses, wine, bread and water.

Safety issues

Dangerous animals

No dangerous or poisonous animals occur on Tenerife and La Gomera except honey
bees and Canarian Banded Centipedes.

Preparations for walking

Although walking on Tenerife and La Gomera is usually very pleasant, you need
to come prepared. The islands have a subtropical climate, but wind, fog and rain

can make it quite cold on the north slopes in winter. In particular in the Anaga mountains on Tenerife and in the Garajonay on La Gomera, be prepared for rain and cold, even when the weather is warm and sunny on the south side.

The Cañadas del Teide can also be cold in winter, with heavy winds and (less often) snow storms. Throughout the year, but particularly in summer, you need to be aware that there is very little to no shade in the Cañadas, nor on the south slopes of Tenerife and La Gomera. Even though the breeze makes the weather comfortable, the sun remains very strong, even in winter. Take precautions against sunburn.

Finally, make sure you have proper footware and perhaps even walking poles. The younger lavas are rough and sharp. In certain sections there are loose rocks while in the laurel forests, trails can be very slippery. The combination of steep trails and, in some places, deep canyons is potentially dangerous, so take care in choosing your trails.

Responsible tourism

There is no such thing as an environmentally friendly trip to the Canary Islands, but there are ways to minimise your impact on the environment. The food you choose to buy is one way to take responsibility. A lot of food is imported from the mainland – either by boat or, if it is fresh, by plane. As far as possible choose foods produced on the islands, in particular the fresh goods like vegetables, fish and meat. This cuts back the pollution that comes with transport. Tap water is safe all over the islands, although not always very palatable because it is usually desalinated sea water. At least when making your own tea and coffee, consider using tap water to minimise waste.

Coastal lagoons and freshwater ponds are important resting spots for migrant birds. When you go out birding, keep in mind that as these sites are small, birds are easily disturbed. Especially at the coast, where it is busy with tourists anyway, disturbance is a problem. So don't get too close, but enjoy the birds from a distance instead.

Food

Both on Tenerife and on La Gomera, there is a lot of good, tasty, local food available. The *papas arrugadas* (wrinkled steamed potatoes), *gofio* (baked flour from which a variety of products is made), *mojo verde* and *mojo picante* (green and spicey sauces typical of the Canaries) are sold everywhere, but there is much more to Canarian cuisine than this. You need to search for it, though. Cheap tourist dishes frequently sold as *Comida Canaria*, are found everywhere, but it takes luck and skill to find the better places. As a rule of thumb, in tourist resorts the good food is found in the more fancy restaurants. There are good restaurants in the cities as well, but the original Canarian food is mostly found in the local bars, stalls, restaurants and *guachinches* (see further on) in the villages – usually at very reasonable prices.

The best food you'll find, in our opinion, on the north slopes of the islands, such as in the valley of Orotava in Tenerife, where the climate is more favourable for growing vegetables, fruit and for keeping a variety of animals. There are plenty of small restaurants that sell a wide variety of local dishes. Try the *potajes de verdura* (vegetable stews) or the *conejo en salmorejo* (savoury rabbit stew). *El puchero canario* is a traditional dish consisting of various types of meat and home-grown vegetables.

Fresh fish *(pescado)* either cooked or fried, is available in some restaurants at the north coast and in the larger towns. Typical is the *sancocho canario* – a dish of cooked fish.

Guachinche

You shouldn't leave Tenerife without trying a Guachinche – a home dinner at a local farm house. Anywhere in northern Tenerife (but mostly from the Orotava valley to La Laguna and further north to Tejina) improvised signs direct you to a Guachinche. Here you sit down in a shed, garage or living room and eat the most wonderful roasts, cheeses, sausages and drink home-made wines for next to nothing.

Guachinches originated in an attempt to cut out the middle man. At the local markets farmers sold their wines and food to buyers and the first tourists without a shopkeeper or distributor to claim his share. Later, the Guachinches were held at home, but at some point, the local restaurants began to complain about this unregulated form of competition. At present, a new system is being set up to regulate the Guachinches without destroying this wonderful tradition. A word of warning: the Guachinche is not the place for vegetarians or abstainers.

A final tip before you set out to enjoy the local gastronomy: try to learn some Spanish. In the less touristy areas (where the food is often at its best) doors will open and people will do their best if you show you are trying to speak the language. *Que aproveche!*

Planning your trip

When to go

Tenerife and La Gomera have a climate that favours insects and wildflowers throughout the year. The majority of the birds are residents – present and active from January to December. Hence, every season is attractive, whether your interest lies with the birds, wildflowers, landscape or just the joy of going for long walks. Nevertheless there are differences between the seasons.

The winter season (December to February) is the coolest season – away from the (south) coast, it can by chilly. Various wildflowers (in particular orchids and Canary Bellflower) are in bloom at this time of year. The fog cover is at its thickest, turning the laurel forest into a mysterious green jungle. Insects and reptiles are active at warm cloud-free parts of the islands (south coast and the south-facing parts of Tenerife's west and east coasts). Nearly all birds are present and active (except for sea birds and Plain Swifts which are rare at this time of year).

In February to April, many plants in the succulent scrub and thermophile scrub start to bloom. This is an excellent time for many of the viper's-buglosses and sow-thistles, while the Canary Crane's-bill forms a pink carpet in the laurel forests. In March, Plain Swifts and Turtle Doves flock in from Africa and butterflies become increasingly common. Cory's Shearwaters arrive off the coast and the wintering waders are joined by migrants. This is a superb time to be on the islands.

From late March, nature on the Teide starts to awaken, but it isn't until May that the wildflowers are at their peak. Late May to early July is the most beautiful season on the Teide. There are butterflies everywhere and the amazing Teide Viper's-buglosses are in flower. The winter flowers of the laurel forests have disappeared, but a series of new species is in bloom, including various houseleeks, pericallises and Canary Foxglove. The dragonflies emerge and will stay active well into the winter. In the lowlands, the succulent bushes and thermophile scrubs are past their prime.

Later in summer, more houseleeks start to flower and the Teide has put on its summer cloak of wildflowers. Summer is a good time for insects (e.g. Praying Mantises) but above all, for seabirds. This is the time in which you are most likely to see Barolo Shearwater and Bulwer's Petrel – chances increase towards the end of August.

In October, Plain Swifts disappear as do most seabirds (Cory's Shearwaters stay until November). The autumn migration brings a new influx of waders to the shores of Tenerife and La Gomera. Most wildflowers are disappearing, but a few individuals of most species continue to flower. A more modest show of autumn flowers appear, like the inflorescences of the Verodes in the succulent scrub and the beautiful white flowers of the Canary Sea Daffodil.

Nearby destinations worth visiting

Tenerife and La Gomera have more than enough to offer for a two-week holiday. However, it is also interesting to compare the nature of these two islands with that of the other Canary Islands. Of great appeal are the two easternmost islands of Lanzarote and Fuerteventura (see Crossbill Guide about these islands), as they offer the greatest contrast with La Gomera and Tenerife. The desert-like environments and large areas of relatively flat terrain offer a harsh but very beautiful landscape which is home to a limited flora and fauna, which contains some special species. Birdwatchers, in particular, will be pleased to be here, since it is only here that you can find the (local races of) Houbara Bustard, Cream-coloured Courser, Egyptian Vulture and Lesser Short-toed Lark and the endemic Fuerteventura Stonechat. In addition birds that are quite rare on Tenerife and La Gomera, such as Trumpeter Finch, Hoopoe, Canarian Grey Shrike and Osprey, are more easily seen here.

Travelling to El Hierro or La Palma offers roughly similar landscapes and wildlife as Tenerife and La Gomera, but with other endemic plants and reptiles, a quiet and unspoilt atmosphere that is of course subtly different from La Gomera and Tenerife.

El Hierro is quite exceptional, as only very few visitors make it to this island, while La Palma is very green and a paradise for hikers. Gran Canaria is perhaps the least interesting choice – it is a bit like Tenerife, but rather touristy and without the high altitude areas and with only very small pockets of laurel forests. However, it has a good number of endemic wildflowers and the Gran Canaria Giant Lizard which, at nearly a metre, is the largest of the Canary lizards.

Inter-Island travel

Tenerife is connected with all other Canary islands by plane and to all the western islands by a direct ferry. Ferries from La Gomera are few and irregular, except the one to Tenerife of course.

Several companies maintain regular ferry services to other islands. This means of transport has the advantage of being less environmentally unfriendly, of offering good opportunities to spot sea birds and dolphins from the boat, and of enabling you to bring along your hire car.

On Tenerife, there are two ports. Los Cristianos in the south connects with La Palma, El Hierro and La Gomera, while Santa Cruz in the northeast connects with La Palma and with the ports of Ageate and Las Palmas on Gran Canaria. Three companies connect the islands by ferry: Naviera Armas (**www.navieraarmas.com**), Fred Olsen (**www.fredolsen.com**) and Trasmediterranea (**www.trasmediterranea.es**). A good website to look for a ferry connection is **www.directferries.co.uk** and search the destination guide.

The downside of taking the ferry is of course that it is slow. The eastern islands of Lanzarote and Fuerteventura are further away and taking the ferry requires changing ferries on Gran Canaria, which means another delay. In this case, a flight is worth considering.

Ferry Crossings

Tenerife (Santa Cruz) – Gran Canaria (Ageate):	2 hours
Tenerife (Santa Cruz) – Gran Canaria (Las Palmas):	3 1/2 hours
Tenerife (Santa Cruz) – La Palma (Santa Cruz):	8 hours
Tenerife (Los Cristianos) – La Gomera (San Sebastian):	1 1/4 hours
Tenerife (Los Cristianos) – El Hierro (Puerto):	4 1/2 hours
La Gomera (San Sebastian) – El Hierro (Puerto):	3 hours
La Gomera (San Sebastian) –La Palma (Santa Cruz):	4 hours

Island-hopping by plane: All Canary Islands are interconnected by air, either directly or via Tenerife Norte. Most of these flights are daily, or even several times a day and are run by Binter Canarias. For more information, check **www.bintercanarias.com**. The flights depart from Tenerife Norte (next to La Laguna). There is also a flight to La Gomera, which lands at the airport at Playa de Santiago. Unless you have a specific destination in the south or south-west of La Gomera in mind, taking the ferry instead of the plane to La Gomera is faster, cheaper and more enjoyable.

Additional information

Recommended reading

Many, but not all, field guides that cover Europe also include the Canary Islands. Besides these general guidebooks, we recommend the following books and websites:

Flora It is remarkable that, given the superb flora of the Canary Islands and the large numbers of tourists, there are no good field guides to the flora of the Canary Islands in english. Hence we also recommend, even to English readers, the German *Kosmos Kanarenflora* (Schönfelder and Schönfelder, ISBN 9783440126073), which has excellent photographs and information on distribution per island. *Die Farn- und Blütenpflanzen der Kanarischen Inseln* (the ferns and flowering plants of the Canary Islands) by Thomas Muet, Herbert Sauerbier and Francisco Cabrera Calixto (Margraf Publishers; ISBN 978-3-8236) is a lot heavier and more academic than the Kosmos guide, but it also has colour photographs and many more species listed, making it superior to the Kosmos guide.

Joël Lodé (2010): *Succulent Plants of the Canary Islands* (ISBN 9788492648368) is an excellent book with all texts in Spanish, English, German and French. As it only deals with succulent plants, it covers a small portion of the entire flora. Haroun Tabraue, Gil-Rodriguez, Wildpret de la Torre and Prud'Homme van Reine: *Marine Plants of the Canary Islands* (ISBN 9788461246816) is a guide to the sea weeds and sea grasses of the islands.

On the web, **www.floradecanarias.com** has photographs, short descriptions (in Spanish) and distribution information of nearly all wildflowers of the Canary Islands.

Birds and bird finding guides Three field guides go into detail on identification and distribution of Canary Islands birds: *Field Guide to the Birds of Macaronesia* by Eduardo García del Rey (2011), *Field Guide to the Birds of the Atlantic Islands* by Tony Clark, Chris Orgill and Tony Disley (2006) and Birds of the Canary Islands by Eduardo Garcia del Rey (2018). Also published in 2018 is the photographic field guide Wildlife of Madeira nd the Canary Islands, by WildGuides. This book covers not just birds but all wildlife groups. Published in 2013 is *Rare Birds of the Canary Islands* by Eduardo García del Rey and Francisco Javier García Vargas (available from **www.nhbs.com** or **www.lynxeds.com**).

The most recent where-to-watch birds information is in the book that you are currently holding in your hands. Besides the Crossbill Guide, you can use *Finding Birds in the Canary Islands* by Dave Gosney, dating from 2013.

A number of interesting websites on Canarian birds have been launched by local birdwatchers, some show many excellent photos and others lots of information. Consult **http://blog.birdingcanarias.com/** and for rarities, **www.rarebirdspain.net** and **www.avescanarias.blogspot.com.es**.

Hiking guides Both for Tenerife and La Gomera, there are a score of simple walking guides to choose from. They are perfect for finding your way, but hopeless when it comes to choosing the most interesting route and will tell you nothing about what you can find along the way. Hence we warmly recommend the one exception to this: *Tenerife Nature Walks* by Sally Lamdin-Whymark (ISBN 9780957548602), available at **www.nhbs.com**. It is the only walking guide that tells about the flora that can be found along the way (wildflower walks would actually fit the content better than nature walks). It is an excellent guide that helps you to choose your favourite walk. It is in approach not unlike our guide, but there is very little overlap, as Lamdin-Whymark's book is strictly for walking and focusses on wildflower species alone. Sally Lamdin-Whymark (a Tenerife resident) also has a blog with other routes: **www.tenerifenaturewalks.wordpress.com**

If you are interested in walking without all the biology baggage, there are several simple guides of the go-left-here-and-right-there type. Look at Rother *Walking Guide to Tenerife* (Klaus and Annette Wolfsperger), available in English, Dutch and German, in which it was written originally. There is also one on La Gomera by the same authors. The *Cicerone Guides* have a title covering La Gomera and El Hierro together and another on Tenerife, both by Paddy Dillon. Another option are the Discovery Walking Guides: *Walk! Tenerife* by David and Ros Brawn and *Walk! La Gomera* by Charles Davis.

Biology and Evolution If you want to understand more about evolution, island ecology and extinctions on islands (including but not exclusively the Canaries), we can recommend two books which read like a novel: David Quammen *The Song of the Dodo* and *Demons in Eden* by Jonathan Silvertown. In the Song of the Dodo the author travels all over the world to understand the role of biological isolation and its consequences for nature conservation. Likewise, in Demons in Eden the author travels the globe to understand how it is possible that an evolutionary struggle for the best adaptation leads to a high instead of a low species diversity. In both cases, volcanic islands like the Canaries play a crucial role in understanding these processes.

History The web **mdc.ulpgc.es** with hundreds of photos shows a digital memory of former times (mdc stands for *memoria digital de canarias*).

Apps The apps of **observation.org, naturgucker.de** and **eBird** (birds only) are great for posting your sightings and look for what others have found.

Observation tips

Walking on Tenerife and La Gomera

Both Tenerife and La Gomera are dream destinations for anyone who loves to walk. The combination of stunning scenery, a great diversity of landscapes, beautiful weather, impressive flora and wildlife, just makes it perfect. Moreover, both islands have a very good network of trails that can keep you pacing for weeks if you want. The routes described in this guidebook are primarily designed for naturalists and only scratch the surface when it comes to the hikes. Basically, all you need for your walks is a good map (widely available) and good gear. There are some hiking guides available as well, should you want additional suggestions (see page 203).

For the rambling naturalists, here are some suggestions and tips to explore the islands on foot.

Tenerife

The hiking areas on Tenerife are clearly centred around specific spots.

Main hiking centres

The Teide and Cañadas: most hikes start from the visitors' centres *El Portillo* in the north and *Caldera Blanca* in the centre. These visitors' centres are also connected by trails that lead to and over the crater. These are excellent hikes, although they are linear and quite long. In the Cañadas there are easy and strenuous walks of various lengths.

The Canary pine zone: The two main hiking centres here are the village of Vilaflor in the south and *La Caldera* in the north (see also route 4). Both used to offer stunning hikes, but sadly, the entire forest aronud La Caldera burnt down in 2023. The great attraction of Vilaflor is the (lengthy) hike to the Lunar Landscape (see site D on page 135).

Anaga mountains: This is a hiker's paradise! Rugged, quiet, and with a great diversity of landscapes, including laurel cloud forest, intact succulent scrub, beautiful barrancos, coastal cliffs, partially abandoned traditional villages and terraced fields and remnants of the thermophilous scrubwoods.

Several trails depart from *Cruz del Carmen* (see route 11). Furthermore, there are trails that connect the various villages. The rugged terrain makes many hikes in

Anaga fairly strenuous. Note that in winter, it can be quite cold and wet on the north slopes, and that some trail sections in the cloud forest are slippery.

Teno mountains: Teno mountain walks are almost invariably barranco walks, which makes them usually linear, steep and strenuous. You are rewarded with beautiful scenery and a very rich flora. The most popular walk used to be the Barranco de Masca walk, which is one of the botanically most diverse areas of Tenerife. Unfortunately, access has become very difficult (see site A on page 150). Other walking routes connect the villages in the mountains (Masca, Teno Alto, Santiago del Teide) with those at the coast (Los Silos, Buenavista del Norte).

La Gomera

Hiking on La Gomera is a delight everywhere on the island and consequently, there are less clear centres for walkers to start. Nevertheless we give some hints, based on the different vegetation zones you can explore.

Walks in the succulent scrubs and palm groves: The south-facing succulent scrub on La Gomera is somewhat underrated. There are some spectacular walks here. Several depart from Valle Gran Rey (spectacular but strenuous). There are others near Parajaró and the hamlet of Guarimiar (site L on page 208). A wild and little visited hiking area is the *Parque Natural Barranco del Cabrito* – the big, roadless wedge of mountains between San Sebastian and Playa de Santiago.

Walks in the laurel cloud forest: The hamlet of El Cedro (see routes 12 and 13) is the main centre for walks in the laurel cloud forest. Other short and long walks depart from the roads CV 14 and CV 15, which lead through the forest.

Walks in the fields and thermophilous scrub: The most beautiful sections are found near Vallehermoso in the northwest of the island. There are beautiful walks from here over to Epina, Las Rosas and the deserted land towards the west and north of the village.

Tips for exploring the laurel forest

The laurel forest is one of the exceptional habitats of Tenerife and La Gomera and a highlight that cannot disappoint. There are various things to be found here, and each of them requires a different strategy and location.

The laurel forest is at its most special when there is fog. The mystique that comes with the limited sight and the deep green mosses that hang in long rags from the branches – all of this comes out best on foggy days. These are most frequent in winter, which is also when the cloak is thickest. In summer, you need to choose your moment more carefully. If this sensation is what you are after, note that not all laurel forests are heavily cloaked in mosses. On Tenerife, the Anaga mountains are the best for this phenomenon, but central La Gomera (routes 13, 14 and sites E, F and G on pages 205-206) are even more spectacular. Note that trails can be slippery on wet days. If this is a problem for you, choose some of the simple short walks that depart from the TF 12 over the Anaga ridge (and bring hiking poles). On La Gomera, there are plenty of short and simple trails departing from the CV 14/CV 15.

To see the endemic Bolle's and Laurel Pigeons, fog is precisely what you don't want. The best strategy for finding them is to stand and wait at specific vantage points. The right timing maximises your chance of seeing them. Late afternoons and evenings are best.

The special flora of the laurel forest is most frequently seen along broad tracks, rocky outcrops and forest clearings rather than in the interior forest. Route 8, 9, 13 and14 are best for this.

Tips for seabird watching

Seabirds are hard to spot. The best way of finding them is by taking a specialised boat trip out to the waters where they frequently feed. Unfortunately, these trips are not in any standard tourist package. The best alternative is the ferry crossing, either to La Gomera or to one of the other islands.

There are a couple of good sites for seabird watching from land. The best are Punta Teno and Punta de la Rasca on Tenerife (route 5 and 10). The most interesting sea birds (Barolo Shearwater and Bulwer's Petrel) can be seen from here, but are usually far out at sea, so bring a telescope. The best period to see them is July to early October. The first and last couple of hours of daylight are the best; migration (if any) takes place at this time of day as do movements to and from nest sites and feeding areas.

Ocean exploring

One of the great ecological treasures of the Canaries is the exuberant, colourful submarine world. Unfortunately, it is difficult to explore. Only a trained and skilled scuba diver can fully appreciate this habitat. If you are serious about discovering the submarine life, you can go to a diving school. There are more than ten in the south of Tenerife. They will teach you the basics of diving and bring you to the best places not far from the coast of southern Tenerife. On La Gomera, you can find diving schools in Valle Gran Rey and in San Sebastian. Two other rewarding, if suboptimal, alternatives are snorkelling and going out on a glass-bottom boat.

Snorkelling in sheltered bays and *Piscinas Naturales*: You can snorkel in many places, especially on the east coasts. Look for sheltered bays with a sandy or gravelly beach (for easy access) and some rocky capes (this is where most of the fish are). Be aware though, that in some seemingly good bays, the current is too strong to swim. Such areas have warning signs or red flags.

Snorkelling can also be good in the *piscinas naturales* – places where one or a series of troughs, filled by sea water, are created in the tidal pool. Depending on the tide, they can be gentle or rough. The more elaborate *piscinas naturales* are calm even during high tides – excellent for snorkelling.

The best one is at Garachico (site C on page 151). The tidal pools of Hidalgo are also interesting (site E on page 172). The bay at Punta Teno (route 5) is good for snorkelling, as is on La Gomera, the bay of Valle Gran Rey and Hermigua.

Glass bottom boats and submarines Book a seat on a glass-bottomed boat or submarine and watch the marine life swim by in front of you. In ports of the South-west of Tenerife you can find several companies offering excursions on glass-bottomed boats. There are also submarines that go down some 30 metres. Obviously, such trips are perfect for families (albeit rather costly) and not the sort of activity the keener naturalist might choose. However, they do give you a way to get to know an otherwise hidden submarine world if you cannot scuba dive. Have a look at **www. tenerifedolphin.com** and **www.submarinesafaris.com** or ask around in Los Cristianos, Las Américas or Los Gigantes.

Birdlist Tenerife and La Gomera

The following bird list includes all breeding and wintering birds and regular passage migrants. Numbers between the brackets (...) refer to the routes from page 113 onwards.

Grebes Black-necked Grebe is scarce and localised on reservoirs during migration and even a rarer visitor during winter.

Shearwaters and petrels Cory´s Shearwater is common and easily seen (March-October) from the coast of Tenerife in particular (best 5, 12, 13 and sites G on page 154, E on page 172 and B and C on page 178-179 and J and N on pages 208-209). Manx Shearwater is rarely seen from ferries, as it stays out far at sea. Bulwer's Petrel and Barolo (Little) Shearwaters can be seen in small numbers from the Gomera ferry (12), especially during summer and autumn, and are sometimes discovered with a telescope from Punta de la Rasca (12) and Punta Teno (5). White-faced, European and Madeiran Storm-petrels stay well out at sea and are only very occasionally seen from ferries in summer, In winter and during passage, Manx, Great and Sooty Shearwaters and Wilson´s and Leach's Storm-petrel are very occasionally seen.

Gannets, cormorants and tropicbirds Northern Gannet is scarcely seen near the coastand from ferries in winter (5, 12, 13, N on page 209). Great Cormorant is scarce during passage. The rare Red-billed Tropicbird is seen in increasing numbers in the Canarian waters, especially on ferry crossings between the islands.

Herons and egrets, Spoonbill and storks Low numbers of both Little Egret and Blue Heron are present in winter all along the coast (8, 12 and E on page 172, B and C on page 178-179). The other birds of this group visit mainly freshwater bodies (8 on Tenerife and site K on page 208 on La Gomera). Little Bittern is scarce in summer and during passage. Night and Squacco Heron are scarce during migration periods and Cattle Egret is scarce during pasage as well as in winter. Spoonbill and both Black and White Storks are rare migrants.

Ducks Ducks are very few on the islands. None breed but occasionally Gadwall, Teal,Mallard or some of the other European species turn up at reservoirs in winter (8). Teal is the most regular visitor.

Birds of Prey Common Kestrel is the most abundant breeding raptor on both islands, present in all open areas. Barbary Falcon has increased over the years, now regularly found all over Tenerife, in particular in barrancos and near cliffs (1, 5, 7, 17, site F on page 180, and sites A, B and D on page 147-149), but also in coastal lowlands, where they hunt (12, site A and B on page 178). Buzzard is a sparse breeding bird, except in open, grassy areas, particularly at Teno and northern Gomera (5, 6, 7 and 8 on Tenerife and 13, 15, 16 and 17, plus sites I, K L and M on La Gomera). Sparrowhawk is a rare breeding bird of the laurel forest (8 and 9 on Tenerife and 13 and 14 on La Gomera). Osprey is a rare breeding bird of the coastal cliffs of Teno (5). Lone birds on migration may be seen on reservoirs.

Many of the migrating European raptor species have been seen on Tenerife during passage.

Partridges, rails, crakes and coots Barbary Partridge is a resident bird on both islands, widespread and generally scarce but increasing. It occurs in all open areas and seems to be more easily seen on 1, 2, 5, 8, site A on page 178 and F on page 180. On La Gomera, Barbary Partridge is widespread; we've seen it on verious routes and sites. Common Quail is a rare breeder of agricultural fields in the North of both islands, e.g. route 5 and near the Airport *Tenerife Norte*. Moorhen is uncommon but resident at 8 and 9 on Tenerife. Common Coot is more numerous on Tenerife on the same sites.

Waders Kentish and Little Ringed Plovers breed on Tenerife only at Montaña Roja where they are rare (site B on page 178). Unknown numbers of resident Woodcock breed in all the laurel forests. Their nocturnal habits make them very difficult to find (except when giving their flight displays). A small population of Stone Curlews remains on Tenerife (12 and site A and B on page 178, but very hard to find).

During passage and in winter, a large variety of waders is found at tidal pools at the coast and at inland lakes. The best coastal sites for waders are at route 12 and site E on page 172, and B on page 178. About 50 species of waders have been recorded here, the majority as vagrants on migration or in winter. The more frequent are Turnstone (common), Ringed Plover (frequent), Whimbrel (frequent),

Dunlin (rare), Bar-tailed Godwit (regular), Grey Plover (regular), Lapwing (rare), Common Snipe (frequent), Redshank (regular) and Greenshank (regular). Inland wetlands (8) regularly see wintering Redshank, Greenshank, Common and Green Sandpipers. The sandy coasts (best site B on page 178) often have a few Sanderling and Dunlin during the winter.

Gulls, terns, skuas Yellow-legged Gull is the only breeding gull, and a common resident at the coast. Black-headed Gull and Lesser Black-backed Gull are rather common winter visitors, but numbers fluctuate (best 5, 12 and 13 – the ferry). Great Black-backed Gull and Kittiwake are rare winter visitors. Sandwich Tern and Common Tern are fairly common winter visitors (5, 12, 13 (the ferry) and site G on page 154). Other terns and skuas are occasionally seen from ferries at sea in winter, with an occasional South Polar Skua in summer.

Doves and pigeons Rock Dove / Feral Pigeon is widely distributed on both islands. Fairly pure birds are common on cliffs (5, 7, 13, 17). Collared Dove is an abundant resident in built-up areas while Turtle Dove is a fairly common summer visitor (April onwards) in the allotment zone on the north slopes (8, 9, site D and F on page 152-153, site A and E on page 169 and 172, and on La Gomera, sites C, D, F and I on pages 204-207). There are small populations of the introduced Barbary Dove in Puerto de la Cruz, Los Cristianos and in San Sebastian de la Gomera. Laughing Dove is local and rare (e.g. I on page 207).

The endemic Bolle's Pigeon is quite common in laurel forests but hard to spot (1, 6, 8, 9 and site E on page 136 and D on page 171 on Tenerife). On La Gomera, route 13 and site D (page 204) are the places. The endemic Laurel Pigeon is less common in laurel forests but in contrast to Bolle's, also frequents remnants of thermophile scrub in barrancos. On Tenerife, route 7 and 8 may produce this species, but much better are sites A, B and D on pages 169-171 and on La Gomera, route 12 and site E on page 204. The pigeons are mostly seen in flight over the canopy or along a barranco from a good vantage point and are most active at the beginning of the evening.

Parakeets Introduced Monk Parakeets occur in Santa Cruz, Los Cristianos and Puerto de la Cruz on Tenerife and San Sebastian on La Gomera. The introduced Ring-necked Parakeet is rather rare on Tenerife (e.g. La Laguna).

Owls and cuckoos Barn Owl and Long-eared Owl are both widespread. The latter in particular can be seen at dusk in the allotment zone of northern Tenerife. Great Spotted and Common Cuckoo are rare on passage.

Swifts The Plain Swift is common on both islands and is mostly seen flying over barrancos and roads in forested areas (looking almost like a very fast bat). They are common from March to October and a few stay during the winter. Pallid Swift is a rare breeding bird, with the only important colonies in cliffs near Las Eras and Punta Prieta la Caleta, on the east coast of Tenerife. Common and Alpine

Swift are regular during passage, in small numbers. It takes a fair amount of skill to tell the swift species apart.

Hoopoe The Hoopoe is a rare breeding bird of the south of both islands (12 and site A on page 178 on Tenerife and site M on page 209 on La Gomera).

Woodpeckers Great Spotted Woodpecker is frequent in the pine forests of Tenerife (1, 4 and F on page 153).

Larks Lesser Short-toed Lark is a rare breeding bird of the very south of Tenerife (12 and site A on page 178, also reported on route 5). Skylark is a rare winter visitor (5).

Martins and swallows No martins or swallows breed, but Barn Swallow and House Martin are fairly common on passage and rare in winter; other species are rare.

Pipits and wagtails Berthelot's Pipit is common and widely distributed in open, dry habitats on both islands, especially in level terrain (e.g. 1, 2, 5, 12, sites B, C, D on pages 134-136, site E on page 172 and sites A, B and C on pages 178-179). On La Gomera, it is only common in the far south (17, L and M on page 208-209). Grey Wagtail is a fairly common bird of wet barrancos and artificial freshwater ponds (e.g 7, 8, 9 on Tenerife and 13 and sites K and L on La Gomera).

Red-throated Pipit is reported from the golf courses in southern Tenerife, where White and various forms of Yellow Wagtails are seen on passage.

Thrushes and Robin Blackbird and Robin are common breeding birds in the laurel forest and in the allotment zone of the northern part of the islands. In the south, they are restricted to gardens and parks. Song Thrush and Redwing are sometimes seen in winter. Northern Wheatear passes through in fairly large numbers.

Warblers Spectacled Warbler is a localised resident bird of dry low scrub (1, 5, 12 and site A on page 178). Sardinian Warbler is a widespread and fairly numerous breeding bird of gardens, allotments and bushy vegetation (7, 8, 9, 10, 11, 13). On La Gomera, route 13 15, 16 and 17 and most of the mentioned sites are good for this species. Both Canary Islands Chiffchaff and Blackcap are common birds of gardens and bushy areas. The Tenerife Goldcrest seems to be strongly tied to areas with tall heaths, either in the laurel forest or the pine forests. They are common at 1, 6, 7, 8, 9 and sites E on page 136, F on page 153 on Tenerife, and routes 13, 14 and sites D, E, F and G on La Gomera. Many other European warblers pass through during migration, mostly in small numbers.

Tits African Blue Tit (sometimes called Tenerife Blue Tit) is a common bird of the laurel forest, thermophilous forest and allotment zone on the north of both islands. It also occurs in gardens throughout and is in lesser numbers present in succulent scrub and pine forests.

Shrikes Great Grey Shrike occurs in a small strip along the coast of Tenerife, often on roadside wires. It is fairly common on 12 and site A on page 178 and scarce on sites B an C on pages 178-179. It is also a scarce breeding bird of the Cañadas (1).

Crows and starlings Raven, belonging to a distinctive local race, is the only member of the crow family. It is rare, except at Teno (5 and sites A and B on pages 150) and 17 on La Gomera. The Common Myna, native to southern Asia, is an introduced species and scarce in southern Tenerife. The Common Starling holds a small breeding population in the North of Tenerife. During winter it visits both islands in variable numbers.

Sparrows The Spanish Sparrow is the only common sparrow, occurring in villages and towns. Rock Sparrow occurs on both islands and is most easily seen at 5, 9 (Chamorga) and Punta Teno (site B on page 150). On La Gomera, the fields above Playa de Santiago (site L and M on page 208-209) sometimes have Rock Sparrows.

Finches The Canarian race of Chaffinch is common in Tenerife's laurel forests, allotments and the pine forest zone, especially in clearings. It occurs all over La Gomera, except in the driest areas. Blue Chaffinch is exclusive to the Canary Pine forests. Route 1 has all the sites where this species is easily seen, but site D on page 136 may also turn up this species. Route 4 used be good as well, before the wildfire of 2023. The Canary is in many places very common, particularly in forest clearings, allotments, fields, parks and gardens on the north side of Tenerife. It occurs throughout La Gomera, except in the dense laurel forests. Greenfinch and Goldfinch occur in similar terrain as Canary but are both quite rare (best 5 and the allotment zone of northern Tenerife, and the El Cedro clearing on La Gomera (13, 14). Serin is a scarce breeding resident in the north of Tenerife while Linnet is a common breeding bird of open areas, mostly seen in small groups. The Trumpeter Finch shows an alarming decline and the last birds on Tenerife, from where it eventually may disappear, have been seen near Montaña de Guaza (site A on page 178). On La Gomera it is – surprisingly – easier to find (Site M on page 209).

Buntings Corn Bunting is the only resident bunting on the islands. It is rare and occurs only near fields. Teno Alto (6) is its site on Tenerife. On La Gomera, try 17 and the dry fields above Playa Santiago (site M on page 209).

PICTURE AND ILLUSTRATION CREDITS

In the references that follow, the numbers refer to the pages and the letters to the position on the page (t=top, c=centre, b=bottom, with l and r indication left and right).

Appelmelk, Nel: 172 (b)
Aragon Birding / Boyer, David: cover, 19, 90
Aragon Natuurreizen / Woutersen, Kees: 64 (t), 68, 106 (t), 147
Baptist, Henk: 4 (b)
Boskma, Meindert: 92
Crossbill Guides / Hilbers, Dirk: cover, 4 (1st, 2nd and 3rd from top), 5 (3rd from top), 10, 14, 20 (t+b), 21, 22, 25, 26 (t+b), 28 (t+b), 29, 33 (t+b), 34 (t), 35, 36, 37 (t+c+b), 39, 40 (t+b), 41, 42 (t+b), 43, 45 (t+b), 46, 47, 48 (t+b), 49, 50, 51, 52 (t+b), 53, 54, 56, 60, 64 (b), 67, 70, 72 (t+b), 74, 75, 76, 77, 78 (t+b), 80, 81, 83, 84 (t+b), 85 (l+r), 86, 87, 88, 95, 96, 100, 103 (l), 105, 107, 108, 110, 114, 116, 117, 119 (t+b), 121, 123, 124 (t+b), 126, 127, 130 (t+b), 133 (b), 134, 135 (b), 140 (t+b), 142 (b), 145 (t+b), 146 (t+b), 148 (t+b), 150, 151 (t+b), 152, 153, 154, 157 (t+b), 158, 159, 160, 161, 163, 164 (b), 166 (b), 169 (t), 170, 171 (t), 172 (t), 176 (t+b), 177, 178, 179, 180 (t+b), 181, 182, 186 (t+b), 187 (t+b), 188, 190, 191, 203 (l+r), 204, 205, 209 (t+b), 210
Crossbill Guides / Laan, Peter: 139, 142 (t), 143 (l), 166 (t), 167 (t+b), 168, 193, 194 (t+b), 195, 196, 198 (t+b), 200 (b), 201, 202
Crossbill Guides / Swinkels, Constant: 5 (top), 104, 143 (r), 173, 200 (t), 208
Grunsven, Roy van: 5 (b), 23, 40 (c), 82, 129
Fikkert, Cor: 44, 98, 169 (b)
Frijns, Rob: 101 (l)
Janssen, Michiel: 93, 133 (t)
Peels, Fons: 164 (t)
Pether, Jim: 103 (r)
Messemaker, Ronald: cover
Vliegenthart, Albert: 109
Verdurmen, Edwin: 5 (2nd from top), 184
Verstrael, Theo: cover, 34 (b), 97, 106 (b), 135 (t)
Visser, Gerard: 101 (r)
Wijn, Peter: 171 (b)

All illustrations by Crossbill Guides / Horst Wolter

SPECIES LIST & TRANSLATION

The following list comprises all species mentioned in this guidebook and gives their scientific, German and Dutch names. It is not a complete checklist of the species of Lanzarote and Fuerteventura. Some names have an asterisk (*) behind them, indicating an unofficial name. See page 7 for more details.

Plants

English	Scientific	German	Dutch
Aichryson, Crenulated	Aichryson punctatum	Punktiertes Aichryson	Zwartpuntsteenlook*
Aichryson, Hairy	Aichryson laxum	Lockerblättriges Aichryson	Behaard steenlook*
Aizoon, Canary	Aizoon canariense	Kanaren-Eiskraut	Canarisch ijsplantje*
Allagopappus	Allagopappus canariensis	Gabelästiger Allagopappus	Allagopappus
Artichoke, Wild	Cynara cardunculus	Artischocke, Kardone	Wilde artisjok, Kardoen
Arum, Canary Dragon	Dracunculus canariensis	Kanaren-Schlangenwurz	Canarische drakenwortel*
Asparagus, Pastor's	Asparagus pastorianus	Pastors Spargel	Pastors asperge*
Balm, Canary	Cedronella canariensis	Kanaren-Zitronenstrauch	Cedronella
Bellflower, Canary	Canarina canariensis	Kanaren-Glockenblume	Canarisch klokje
Bindweed, Tree	Convolvulus floridus	Blütenreiche Winde	Boomwinde*
Bluebell, Brown	Dipcadi serotinum	Schweifblatt	Bruine hyacint*
Boxthorn, Canary	Lycium intricatum	Sparriger Bocksdorn	Mediterrane boksdoorn
Broom, Large-flowered White*	Chamaecytisus proliferus	Sprossender Zwergginster	Grootbloemige brem*
Broom, Leafy*	Adenocarpus foliolosus	Blättchenreiche Drüsenfrucht	Dichtbladige brem*
Broom, Sticky	Adenocarpus viscosus	Klebrige Drüsenfrucht	Kleverige brem*
Broom, Teide	Spartocytisus supranubius	Echter Teideginster	Teidebrem*
Bush, Justice*	Justicia hyssopifolia	Ysopblättrige Justicie	Justice struik*
Bush-burnet	Bencomia caudata	Geschwänzte Bencomia	Struikpimpernel*
Bush-madder, Noble*	Phyllis nobla	Edle Phyllis	Struikmeekrap*
Butcher's-broom, Climbing	Semele androgyna	Zwittrige Semele	Klimmende muizendoorn*
Buttercup, Canary	Ranunculus cortusifolius	Kanaren-Hahnenfuss	Canarische boterbloem
Catmint, Teide	Nepeta teydea	Teide-Katzenminze	Teide-kattenkruid*
Ceballosia	Ceballosia fruticosa	Strauchige Ceballosie	Ceballosia
Ceropegia, Brown	Ceropegia fusca	Rotbraune Leuchterblume	Roodbruine lantaarnplant*
Ceropegia, Yellow	Ceropegia dichotoma	Gabelige Leuchterblume	Gele lantaarnplant*
Chestnut, Sweet	Castanea sativa	Ess-Kastanie	Tamme kastanje
Cistus, Canary	Cistus symphytifolius	Beinwellblättrige Zistrose	Canarische cistusroos*
Cistus, Narrow-leaved	Cistus monspeliensis	Montpellier-Zistrose	Montpellier cistusroos*

Cistus, Teide*	Cistus osbekiifolius	Osbeckienblättrige Zistrose	Teide cistusroos*
Crane's-bill, Canary	Geranium reuteri	Kanaren-Storchschnabel	Canarische ooievaarsbek
Dicheranthus	Dicheranthus plocamoides	Hahnensporn	Dicheranthus
Diplazium	Diplazium caudatum	Schattenfrauenfarn	Diplazium
Elder, Canary	Sambucus (nigra) palmensis	Kanaren-Holunder	Canarische vlier*
Eucalyptus	Eucalyptus sp.	Eukalyptus	Eucalyptus
Fennel, Canary Sea	Astydamia latifolia	Nymphendolde	Canarische zeevenkel
Fennel, Link's	Ferula linkii	Links Rutenkraut	Links reuzenvenkel*
Fern, Canary Male	Dryopteris oligodonta	Kanaren-Wurmfarn	Canarische mannetjesvaren*
Fern, Disc-leaved*	Adiantum reniforme	Talerfarn	Schijfvaren*
Fern, Golden Rustyback*	Asplenium aureum	Gold-Milzfarn	Gouden schubvaren*
Fern, Guanche Buckler*	Dryopteris guanchica	Guanchen-Wurmfarn	Guanche stekelvaren*
Fern, Hare's-foot	Davallia canariensis	Kanaren-Davallia	Davallia*
Fern, Lady	Athyrium filix-femina	Wald-Frauenfarn	Wijfjesvaren
Figwort, Glabrous	Scrophularia glabrata	Verkahlte Braunwurz	Kaal helmkruid
Figwort, Smith's	Scrophularia smithii	Smith-Braunwurz	Smith's helmkruid*
Flixweed, Teide	Descurainia bourgeauana	Teide-Rauke	Teide-raket*
Foxglove, Canary	Isoplexis canariensis	Tenerife-Kanarenfingerhut	Canarisch vingerhoedskruid
Gale, Canary*	Myrica faya	Makaronesischer Gagelbaum	Canarische gagel*
Gennaria, Two-leaved	Gennaria diphylla	Zweiblättriger Grünstendel	Tweehartenorchis
Gentian, Laurel Forest*	Ixanthus viscosus	Kanarenenzian	Canarische gentiaan*
Globularia, Willow-leaved*	Globularia salicina	Weidenartige Kugelblume	Wilgbladige kogelbloem*
Greenovia, Golden	Greenovia aurea	Gold-Greenovia	Gouden greenovia*
Heath, Besom	Erica scoparia	Besen-Heide	Bezemdophei
Heath, Tree	Erica arborea	Baum-Heide	Boomhei
Heberdenia	Heberdenia excelsa	Heberdenie	Heberdenia*
Houseleek, Canary	Aeonium canariense	Kanaren-Aeonium	Canarisch huislook*
Houseleek, Castello-paiva's	Aeonium castello-paivae	Castello-Paiva Aeonium*	Castello-paiva huislook*
Houseleek, Gomera Sticky*	Aeonium (lindleyi ssp.) viscatum	Gomera Klebriges* Aeonium	Gomera kleverig huislook*
Houseleek, Haworth's	Aeonium haworthii	Haworth-Aeonium	Haworth's huislook*
Houseleek, La Palma	Aeonium palmense	La Palma-Aeonium*	La Palma huislook*
Houseleek, Lindley's	Aeonium lindleyi	Lindley-Aeonium	Lindley's huislook*
Houseleek, Loose-flowered*	Aeonium decorum	Zierliches Aeonium	Sierlijk huislook*
Houseleek, Pyramidal*	Aeonium cuneatum	Keilblättriges Aeonium	Pyramide-huislook*
Houseleek, Red-lined	Aeonium rubrolineatum	Gomera Baum-Aeonium*	Gomera boomhuislook*
Houseleek, Rooftop*	Aeonium urbicum	Stadt-Aeonium	Dakhuislook*
Houseleek, Saucer-leaved	Aeonium tabulaeforme	Tellerförmiges Aeonium	Schotelvormig huislook*

Houseleek, Smith's	*Aeonium smithii*	Smith-Aeonium	Smith's huislook*
Houseleek, Spade-leaved*	*Aeonium spathulatum*	Spateliges Aeonium	Spaltelhuislook*
Houseleek, Spoon-leaved*	*Aeonium subplanum*	Breitblättriges Kanaren-Aeonium*	Lepelbladig huislook*
Houseleek, Stonecrop-leaved	*Aeonium sedifolium*	Mauerpfefferblättriges Aeonium	Vetkruidbladig huislook*
Houseleek, Tree*	*Aeonium arboreum (ssp. holochrysum)*	Baum-Aeonium	Boomhuislook*
Hypopcist, Pink	*Cytinus ruber*	Zistrosenwürger	Rode hypocist
Iceplant, Common	*Mesembryanthemum crystallinum*	Kristall-Mittagsblume	IJsplantje
Iceplant, Small-leaved*	*Mesembryanthemum nodiflorum*	Knotenblütige-Mittagsblume	Smalbladig ijsplantje*
Ironwort, Canary	*Sideritis canariensis*	Kanaren-Gliedkraut	Ccanarisch ijzerkruid*
Ironwort, Southern	*Sidiritis soluta*	Gelöstes Gliedkraut	Opgeblazen ijzerkruid*
Ironwort, Tenerife	*Sideritis oroteneriffae*	Tenerife-Gliedkraut	Tenerife-ijzerkruid*
Ivy, Canary	*Hedera canariensis*	Kanarischer Efeu	Canarische klimop
Jasmine, Wild	*Jasminum odoratissimum*	Wohlriechender Jasmin	Welriekende jasmijn
Juniper, Canary	*Juniperus turbinata ssp. canariensis*	Kanaren-Wacholder	Canarische jeneverbes*
Launaea, Shrubby	*Launaea arborescens*	Strauch-Dornlattich	Struikdoornsla*
Laurel, Barbusano*	*Apollonias barbujana*	Barbusano	Barbusano laurier*
Laurel, Bosea*	*Bosea yervamora*	Yerbamora	Bosea laurier*
Laurel, Canary	*Laurus novocanariensis*	Kanaren-Lorbeer	Canarische laurier
Laurel, Indian*	*Persea indica*	Indische Persea	Indische laurier*
Laurel, Portuguese	*Prunus lusitanica*	Portugiesischer Kirschlorbeer	Portugese laurierkers
Laurel, Stink	*Ocotea foetens*	Stinklorbeer	Stinklaurier*
Laurustinus, Canary	*Viburnum rigidum*	Kanaren-Schneeball	Canarische sneeuwbal*
Lavender, Canary	*Lavandula canariensis*	Kanaren-Lavendel	Canarische lavendel*
Lavender, Tenerife	*Lavandula buchii*	Buch-Lavendel	Tenerife-lavendel*
Lugoa	*Gonospermum revolutum*	Umgerollte Lugoa	Lugoa*
Mallow, Red Rock*	*Lavatera phoenicea*	Phönizische Strauchpappel	Phoenisisch struikkaasjeskruid*
Marguerite, Broussonet's	*Argyranthemum broussonetii*	Broussonet-Kanarenmargerite	Broussonet's margriet*
Marguerite, Graceful*	*Argyranthemum gracile*	Zierliche Kanarenmargerite	Sierlijke margriet*
Marguerite, Pinewood*	*Argyranthemum adauctum*	Kiefernwald-Kanarenmargerite	Dennenbos-margriet*
Marguerite, Shrubby	*Argyranthemum frutescens*	Strauchmargerite	Struikmargriet
Marguerite, Teide	*Argyranthemum tenerifae*	Canadas-Kanarenmargerite	Teide-margriet*
Marguerite, Vincent's	*Argyranthemum vincentii*	Vincents-Kanarenmargerite*	Vincent's margriet*

Mignonette, Besom	Reseda scoparia	Besen-Resede	Bezemreseda*
Mint, Teide*	Micromeria lachnophylla	Canadas-Bergminze	Teide-bonenkruid*
Monanthes, Leafy*	Monanthes polyphylla	Vielblättriges Monanthes	Veelbladig vetkruid*
Monanthes, Loose-flowered	Monanthes laxiflora	Lockerblütiges Monanthes	Losbloemig vetkruid*
Monanthes, Pale	Monanthes pallens	Bleiches Monanthes	Bleek vetkruid*
Monanthes, Red-leaved	Monanthes brachycaulos	Kurzstängeliges Monanthos	Kortstengelig vetkruid*
Nettle, Small-leaved*	Forsskaolea angustifolia	Schmallblättrige Forsskaolea	Smalbladige netel*
Orchid, Bumblebee	Ophrys bombyliflora	Drohnen-Ragwurz	Weidehommelorchis
Orchid, Canary	Orchis canariensis	Kanaren-Knabenkraut	Canarische orchis
Orchid, Dense-flowered	Neotinea maculata	Gefleckte Waldwurz	Nonnetjesorchis
Orchid, Small-flowered Tongue	Serapias parviflora	Kleinblütiger Zungenstendel	Kleine tongorchis
Orchid, Tenerife Giant*	Himantoglossum metlesicsiana	Metlesics-Mastorchis	Tenerife-reuzenorchis*
Orchid, Three-fingered	Habenaria tridactylites	Kanarenstendel	Canarische nachtorchis*
Palm, Canary	Phoenix canariensis	Kanarische Dattelpalme	Canarische dadelpalm
Palm, Date	Phoenix dactylifera	Echte Dattelpalme	Dadelpalm
Pansy, Teide	Viola cheiranthifolia	Teide-Veilchen	Teide-viooltje*
Pear, Prickly	Opuntia sp.	Feigenkaktus	Vijgcactus
Pellitory, Bush*	Gesnouinia arborea	Strauchglaskraut	Struikglaskruid*
Pericallis, Bloody*	Pericallis cruenta	Blutrote Cinerarie	Bloedrode pericallis*
Pericallis, Colt's-foot*	Pericallis tussilaginis	Huflattichartige Cinerarie	Hoefbladpericallis*
Pericallis, Hansen's*	Pericallis hansenii	Hansen-Cinerarie	Hansen's pericallis*
Pericallis, Hedgehog*	Pericallis echinata	Igelhüllkelch-Cinerarie	Egelpericallis*
Pericallis, Perfoliate*	Pericallis steetzi	Steetz-Cinerarie	Stengelomvattende pericallis
Pericallis, Woolly*	Pericallis lanata	Wollige Cinerarie	Wollige pericallis*
Pine, Canary	Pinus canariensis	Kanaren-Kiefer	Canarische den
Plantain, Tree	Plantago arborescens	Bäumchen-Wegerich	Boomweegbree*
Pleiomeris	Pleiomeris canariensis	Pleiomeris	Pleiomeris
Plocama	Plocama pendula	Plocama	Plocama
Polypody, Macaronesian	Polypodium macaronesicum	Makaronesischer Tüpfelfarn	Eilandeikvaren*
Reed, Giant	Arundo donax	Pfahlrohr	Spaans riet
Reichardia, Crystal	Reichardia crystallina	Kristall-Reichardie	Kristal-reichardia*
Rockrose, Julia's	Helianthemum juliae	Julia-Sonnenröschen	Julia's zonneroosje*
Rosemary, Sea	Campylanthus salsoloides	Kanaren-Krummblüte	Canarische krombloem*
Sage, Canary	Salvia canariensis	Kanaren-Salbei	Canarische salie*
Schizogyne	Schizogyne sericea	Seidenhaarige Schizogyne	Schizogyne
Scrub-knapweed, Teide*	Cheirolophus teydis	Teide-Strauchflockenblume	Teide-struikcentaurie*
Scrub-knapweed, Teno*	Cheirolophus canariensis	Kanaren-Strauchflockenblume	Teno-struikcentaurie*

Scrub-scabious, Teide*	*Pterocephalus lasiospermus*	Behaarter Federkopf	Teide-struikduifkruid*
Sea-daffodil, Canary	*Pancratium canariense*	Kanaren-Trichternarzisse	Canarische zeenarcis*
Sea-heath	*Frankenia sp.*	Frankenie	Zeehei*
Sea-kale, Gomera	*Crambe gomerae*	Gomera-Meerkohl	Gomera bolletjeskool*
Sea-kale, Laurel*	*Crambe strigosa*	Schmächtiger Meerkohl	Laurierbos-bolletjeskool*
Sea-lavender, Broad-winged*	*Limonium redivivum*	Breit Geflügelter Strandflieder*	Breedgevleugeld lamsoor*
Sea-lavender, Bush*	*Limonium arborescens*	Hoher Strandflieder*	Hoog lamsoor*
Sea-lavender, Cabbage-leaved*	*Limonium brassicifolium*	Kohlblättriger Strandflieder	Koolbladige lamsoor*
Sea-lavender, Large-leaved*	*Limonium macrophyllum*	Grossblättriger Strandflieder	Grootbladig lamsoor*
Sea-lavender, Perez's	*Limonium perezi*	Perez Strandflieder*	Perez lamsoor*
Sea-lavender, Shrubby*	*Limonium fruticans*	Strauchiger Strandflieder	Struiklamsoor*
Sea-lavender, Small-leaved*	*Limonium pectinatum*	Kammförmiger Strandflieder	Kleinbladig lamsoor*
Sea-lavender, Tree*	*Limonium dendroides*	Baumartiger Strandflieder	Boomlamsoor*
Silk-vine, Canary	*Periploca laevigata*	Glatte Baumschlinge	Canarische melkwingerd*
Smilax, Canary	*Smilax canariensis*	Kanaren-Stechwinde	Canarische steekwinde
Sorrel, Cape	*Oxalis pes-caprae*	Nickender Sauerklee	Knikkende klaverzuring
Sow-thistle, Canary Tree	*Sonchus canariensis*	Kanaren-Gänsedistel	Canarische melkdistel*
Sow-thistle, Cliff*	*Sonchus radicatus*	Bewurzelte Gänsedistel	Klifmelkdistel*
Sow-thistle, Gomera*	*Sonchus gomerensis*	Gomera-Gänsedistel*	Gomera-melkdistel*
Sow-thistle, Hair-leaved*	*Sonchus capillaris*	Haarfeine Gänsedistel	Fijnbladige melkdistel*
Sow-thistle, Hierro*	*Sonchus hierrensis*	Hierro-Gänsedistel	Hierro-melkdistel*
Sow-thistle, Laurel Forest*	*Sonchus congestus*	Baum-Gänsedistel	Lauriermelkdistel*
Sow-thistle, Small-headed*	*Sonchus leptocephalus*	Dünnköpfige Gänsedistel	Kleinbloemige melkdistel*
Sow-thistle, Stemless	*Sonchus acaulis*	Stängellose Gänsedistel	Stengelloze melkdistel
Spleenwort, Black	*Asplenium adiantum-nigrum*	Schwarzstieliger Streifenfarn	Zwartsteel
Spleenwort, Ivy-leaved*	*Asplenium hemionitis*	Efeufarn	Klimopvaren*
Spurge, Balsam	*Euphorbia balsamifera*	Balsam-Wolfsmilch	Balsam-wolfsmelk*
Spurge, Blunt-leaved	*Euphorbia obtusifolia*	Stumpfblättrige Wolfsmilch	Stompladige wolfsmelk*
Spurge, Canary	*Euphorbia canariensis*	Kanaren-Wolfsmilch	Canarische wolfsmelk*
Spurge, Dark-red	*Euphorbia atropurpurea*	Dunkelpurpurrote Wolfsmilch	Donkerrode wolfsmelk*
Spurge, Honey	*Euphorbia mellifera*	Honiggebende Wolfsmilch	Honingwolfsmelk*
Spurge, Honey*	*Euphorbia mellifera*	Honiggebende Wolfsmilch	Honingwolfsmelk*
Spurge, King Juba's	*Euphorbia regis-jubae*	König-Juba-Wolfsmilch	Koning Juba wolfsmelk

English	Scientific	German	Dutch
Spurge, Lamarck's	*Euphorbia lamarckii*	Lamarck-Wolfsmilch	Lamarck's wolfsmelk*
Spurge, Leafless	*Euphorbia aphylla*	Blattlose Wolfsmilch	Naakte wolfsmelk*
Squill, Broad-leaved	*Scilla latifolia*	Breitblättriger Blaustern	Brede sterhyacint*
Squill, Canary	*Scilla haemorrhoidalis*	Rotschäftiger Blaustern	Rode sterhyacint*
St. John's-wort, Canary	*Hypericum canariense*	Kanaren-Johanniskraut	Canarisch hertshooi*
St. John's-wort, Cross-leaved*	*Hypericum reflexum*	Kreuzblättriges Johanniskraut	Kruisbladig hertshooi*
St. John's-wort, Glandular	*Hypericum glandulosum*	Drüsiges Johanniskraut	Beklierd hertshooi*
St. John's-wort, Large-leaved	*Hypericum grandifolium*	Grossblättriges Johanniskraut	Grootbladig hertshooi*
Stemmacantha	*Stemmacantha cynaroides*	Artischocken-Akanthuskrone	Schijnartisjok*
Thistle, Teide Carline*	*Carlina xeranthemoides*	Strohblumen-Eberwurz	Teide-driedistel*
Thistle, Willow-leaved Carline	*Carlina salicifolia*	Weidenblättrige Eberwurz	Wilgbladige driedistel*
Traganum	*Traganum moquinii*	Moquin-Traganum	Traganum
Tree, Canary Strawberry	*Arbutus canariensis*	Kanarischer Erdbeerbaum	Canarische aarbeiboom
Tree, Dragon	*Dracaena draco*	Drachenbaum	Drakenbloedboom
Verode	*Kleinia neriifolia*	Oleanderblättrige Kleinie	Kleinia*
Viera	*Vieraea laevigata*	Viera	Viera
Violet, Anaga	*Viola anagae*	Anaga-Veilchen	Anaga-viooltje
Viper's-bugloss, Anaga*	*Echium leucophaeum*	Anaga-Natternkopf*	Anaga-slangenkruid*
Viper's-bugloss, Auber's*	*Echium auberianum*	Aubers Natternkopf	Aubers slangenkruid*
Viper's-bugloss, Bonnet's	*Echium bonnetii*	Bonnetts Natternkopf	Bonnets slangenkruid*
Viper's-bugloss, Broad-leaved*	*Echium strictum*	Steifer Natternkopf	Breedbladig langenkruid*
Viper's-bugloss, Giant	*Echium giganteum*	Riesengrosser Natternkopf	Reuzenslangenkruid*
Viper's-bugloss, Gomera Blue*	*Echium acanthocarpum*	Stachelfrüchtiger Natternkopf	Gomera slangenkruid*
Viper's-bugloss, Greenish*	*Echium virescens*	Grünlicher Natternkopf	Groenig slangenkruid*
Viper's-bugloss, Purple	*Echium plantagineum*	Wegerichblättriger Natternkopf	Weegbreeslangenkruid
Viper's-bugloss, Rocket*	*Echium simplex*	Einfacher Natternkopf	Raketslangenkruid
Viper's-bugloss, Rough-leaved*	*Echium aculeatum*	Stachliger Natternkopf	Stekelig slangenkruid*
Viper's-bugloss, Teide	*Echium wildpretii*	Wildprets Natternkopf	Teide slangenkruid*
Wallflower, Teide	*Erisymum scoparium*	Besen-Schöterich	Teide muurbloem*
Willow, Canary	*Salix canariensis*	Kanaren-Weide	Canarische wilg
Woodwardia	*Woodwardia radicans*	Wurzelnder Kettenfarn	Woodwardia
Zygophyllum	*Zygophyllum fontanesii*	Desfontaines-Jochblatt	Zygophyllum*

Mammals

English	Scientific	German	Dutch
Barbastelle	*Barbastella barbastellus*	Mopsfledermaus	Mopsvleermuis

English	Scientific	German	Dutch
Bat, European Free-tailed	*Tadarida teniotis*	Bulldoggfledermaus	Bulvleermuis
Bat, Tenerife Long-eared	*Plecotus teneriffae*	Teneriffa-Langohr	Canarische grootoorvleermuis
Dolphin, Bottlenose	*Tursiops truncatus*	Grosser Tümmler	Tuimelaar
Dolphin, Common	*Delphinus delphis*	Gemeiner Delfin	Gewone dolfijn
Hedgehog, Algerian	*Erinaceus algirus*	Wanderigel	Trekegel
Mouse, House	*Mus musculus*	Hausmaus	Huismuis
Mouflon	*Ovis (ammon) musimon*	Mufflon	Moeflon
Noctule, Lesser	*Nyctalus leisleri*	Kleinabendsegler	Bosvleermuis
Pipistrelle, Kuhl's	*Pipistrellus kuhlii*	Weissrandfledermaus	Kuhl's dwergvleermuis
Pipistrelle, Madeira	*Pipistrellus maderensis*	Madeira-Zwergfledermaus	Madeira dwergvleermuis
Pipistrelle, Savi's	*Hypsugo savii*	Alpenfledermaus	Savi's dwergvleermuis
Rabbit	*Oryctolagus cuniculus*	Wildkaninchen	Konijn
Rat, Black	*Rattus rattus*	Hausratte	Zwarte rat
Rat, Brown	*Rattus norvegicus*	Wanderratte	Bruine rat
Rat, Tenerife Giant	*Canariomys bravoi*	Tenerife-Riesenratte*	Tenerife reuzenrat*
Shrew, Etruscan Pygmy	*Suncus etruscus*	Etruskerspitzmaus	Wimperspitsmuis
Whale, Short-finned Pilot	*Globicephala macrorhynchus*	Kurzflossen-Grindwal	Indische griend

Birds

English	Scientific	German	Dutch
Bittern, Little	*Ixobrychus minutus*	Zwergdommel	Woudaapje
Blackbird	*Turdus merula*	Amsel	Merel
Blackcap	*Sylvia atricapilla*	Mönchsgrasmücke	Zwartkop
Bunting, Corn	*Miliaria calandra*	Grauammer	Grauwe gors
Bustard, Houbara	*Chlamydotis undulata*	Kragentrappe	Westelijke kraagtrap
Buzzard	*Buteo buteo*	Mäusebussard	Buizerd
Canary	*Serinus canaria*	Kanarengirlitz	Kanarie
Chaffinch (Canary)	*Fringilla coelebs*	Buchfink	Vink
Chaffinch, Blue	*Fringilla teydea*	Teydefink	Blauwe vink
Chiffchaff	*Phylloscopus collybita*	Zilpzalp	Tjiftjaf
Chiffchaff, Canary Islands	*Phylloscopus canariensis*	Kanarenzilpzalp	Canarische tjiftjaf
Coot	*Fulica atra*	Blässhuhn	Meerkoet
Cormorant, Great	*Phalacrocorax carbo*	Kormoran	Aalscholver
Courser, Cream-coloured	*Cursorius cursor*	Rennvogel	Renvogel
Cuckoo, Common	*Cuculus canorus*	Kuckuck	Koekoek
Cuckoo, Great Spotted	*Clamator glandarius*	Häherkuckuck	Kuifkoekoek
Curlew, Stone	*Burhinus oedicnemus*	Triel	Griel
Dove, Barbary	*Streptopelia roseogrisea*	Lachtaube	Izabeltortel
Dove, Collared	*Streptopelia decaocto*	Türkentaube	Turkse tortel
Dove, Rock	*Columba livia*	Felsentaube	Rotsduif
Dove, Turtle	*Streptopelia turtur*	Turteltaube	Tortelduif
Dunlin	*Calidris alpina*	Alpenstrandläufer	Bonte strandloper
Egret, Cattle	*Bubulcus ibis*	Kuhreiher	Koereiger

Egret, Little	Egretta garzetta	Seidenreiher	Kleine zilverreiger
Falcon, Barbary	Falco pelegrinoides	Wüstenfalke	Barbarijse valk
Finch, Trumpeter	Bucanetes githagineus	Wüstengimpel	Woestijnvink
Gadwall	Anas strepera	Schnatterente	Krakeend
Gannet, (Northern)	Morus bassanus	Basstölpel	Jan van Gent
Godwit, Bar-tailed	Limosa lapponica	Pfuhlschnepfe	Rosse grutto
Goldcrest, Tenerife	Regulus teneriffae	Kanarengoldhähnchen	Tenerifegoudhaan
Goldfinch	Carduelis carduelis	Distelfink	Putter
Grebe, Black-necked	Podiceps nigricollis	Schwarzhalstaucher	Geoorde fuut
Greenfinch	Carduelis chloris	Grünling	Groenling
Greenshank	Tringa nebularia	Grünschenkel	Groenpootruiter
Gull, (Atlantic) Yellow-legged	Larus michahellis	Weisskopfmöwe	Geelpootmeeuw
Gull, Black-headed	Chroicocephalus ridibundus	Lachmöwe	Kokmeeuw
Gull, Great Black-backed	Larus marinus	Mantelmöwe	Grote mantelmeeuw
Gull, Lesser Black-backed	Larus fuscus	Heringsmöwe	Kleine mantelmeeuw
Heron, Grey	Ardea cinerea	Graureiher	Blauwe reiger
Heron, Night	Nycticorax nycticorax	Nachtreiher	Kwak
Heron, Squacco	Ardeola ralloides	Rallenreiher	Ralreiger
Hoopoe	Upupa epops	Wiedehopf	Hop
Kestrel	Falco tinnunculus	Turmfalke	Torenvalk
Kittiwake	Rissa tridactyla	Dreizehenmöwe	Drieteenmeeuw
Lapwing	Vanellus vanellus	Kiebitz	Kievit
Lark, Lesser Short-toed	Calandrella rufescens	Stummellerche	Kleine kortteenleeuwerik
Linnet	Carduelis cannabina	Bluthänfling	Kneu
Mallard	Anas platyrhynchos	Stockente	Wilde eend
Martin, House	Delichon urbicum	Mehlschwalbe	Huiszwaluw
Moorhen	Gallinula chloropus	Teichhuhn	Waterhoen
Myna, Common	Acridotheres tristis	Hirtenmaina	Treurmaina
Osprey	Pandion haliaetus	Fischadler	Visarend
Owl, Barn	Tyto alba	Schleiereule	Kerkuil
Owl, Long-eared	Asio otus	Waldohreule	Ransuil
Parakeet, Monk	Myiopsitta monachus	Mönchsittich	Monniksparkiet
Parakeet, Ring-necked	Psittacula krameri	Halsbandsittich	Halsbandparkiet
Partridge, Barbary	Alectoris barbara	Felsenhuhn	Barbarijse patrijs
Petrel, Bulwer's	Bulweria bulwerii	Bulwersturmvogel	Bulwers stormvogel
Pigeon, Bolle's	Columba bollii	Bolles Lorbeertaube	Bolles laurierduif
Pigeon, Feral	Columba livia f. domestica	Stadttaube	Stadsduif
Pigeon, Laurel	Columba junoniae	Lorbeertaube	Laurierduif
Pipit, Berthelot's	Anthus berthelotii	Kanarenpieper	Berthelots pieper
Pipit, Red-throated	Anthus cervinus	Rotkehlpieper	Roodkeelpieper
Plover, Grey	Pluvialis squatarola	Kiebitzregenpfeifer	Zilverplevier
Plover, Kentish	Charadrius alexandrinus	Seeregenpfeifer	Strandplevier
Plover, Little Ringed	Charadrius dubius	Flussregenpfeifer	Kleine plevier

English	Scientific	German	Dutch
Plover, Ringed	*Charadrius hiaticula*	Sandregenpfeifer	Bontbekplevier
Quail, (Common)	*Coturnix coturnix*	Wachtel	Kwartel
Raven	*Corvus corax*	Kolkrabe	Raaf
Redshank	*Tringa totanus*	Rotschenkel	Tureluur
Redwing	*Turdus iliacus*	Rotdrossel	Koperwiek
Robin	*Erithacus rubecula*	Rotkehlchen	Roodborst
Sanderling	*Calidris alba*	Sanderling	Drieteenstrandloper
Sandpiper, Common	*Actitis hypoleucos*	Flussuferläufer	Oeverloper
Sandpiper, Green	*Tringa ochropus*	Waldwasserläufer	Witgat
Serin	*Serinus serinus*	Girlitz	Europese kanarie
Shearwater, Cory's	*Calonectris borealis*	Gelbschnabelsturmtaucher	Kuhls pijlstormvogel
Shearwater, Great	*Puffinus gravis*	Grosser Sturmtaucher	Grote pijlstormvogel
Shearwater, Little	See Barolo Shearwater		
Shearwater, Barolo	*Puffinus baroli*	Makaronesischer Sturmtaucher	Kleine pijlstormvogel
Shearwater, Manx	*Puffinus puffinus*	Schwarzschnabel-Sturmtaucher	Noordse pijlstormvogel
Shearwater, Sooty	*Puffinus griseus*	Dunkler Sturmtaucher	Grauwe pijlstormvogel
Shrike, Great Grey	*Lanius excubitor*	Raubwürger	Klapekster
Skua, South Polar	*Stercorarius maccormicki*	Antarktikskua	Zuidpooljager
Skylark	*Alauda arvensis*	Feldlerche	Veldleeuwerik
Snipe, Common	*Gallinago gallinago*	Bekassine	Watersnip
Sparrow, Rock	*Petronia petronia*	Steinsperling	Rotsmus
Sparrow, Spanish	*Passer hispaniolensis*	Weidensperling	Spaanse mus
Sparrowhawk	*Accipiter nisus*	Sperber	Sperwer
Spoonbill	*Platalea leucorodia*	Löffler	Lepelaar
Starling, Common	*Sturnus vulgaris*	Star	Spreeuw
Stonechat, Fuerteventura	*Saxicola dacotiae*	Kanarenschmätzer	Canarische roodborsttapuit
Stork, Black	*Ciconia nigra*	Schwarzstorch	Zwarte ooievaar
Stork, White	*Ciconia ciconia*	Weissstorch	Ooievaar
Storm-petrel, European	*Hydrobates pelagicus*	Sturmschwalbe	Stormvogeltje
Storm-petrel, Leach	*Oceanodroma leucorhoa*	Wellenläufer	Vaal stormvogeltje
Storm-petrel, Madeiran	*Oceanodroma castro*	Madeirawellenläufer	Madeirastormvogeltje
Storm-petrel, White-faced	*Pelagodroma marina*	Weissgesicht-Sturmschwalbe	Bont stormvogeltje
Storm-petrel, Wilson's	*Oceanites oceanicus*	Buntfuss-Sturmschwalbe	Wilsons stormvogeltje
Swallow, Barn	*Hirundo rustica*	Rauchschwalbe	Boerenzwaluw
Swift, Alpine	*Tachymarptis melba*	Alpensegler	Alpengierzwaluw
Swift, Common	*Apus apus*	Mauersegler	Gierzwaluw
Swift, Pallid	*Apus pallidus*	Fahlsegler	Vale gierzwaluw
Swift, Plain	*Apus unicolor*	Einfarbsegler	Madeiragierzwaluw
Teal	*Anas crecca*	Krickente	Wintertaling
Tern, Common	*Sterna hirundo*	Flussseeschwalbe	Visdief
Tern, Sandwich	*Sterna sandvicensis*	Brandseeschwalbe	Grote stern

238

English	Scientific	German	Dutch
Thrush, Song	Turdus philomelos	Singdrossel	Zanglijster
Tit, African Blue	Cyanistes teneriffae	Kanarenmeise	Tenerifepimpelmees
Tropicbird, Red-billed	Phaethon aethereus	Rotschnabel-Tropikvogel	Roodsnavelkeerkringvogel
Turnstone	Arenaria interpres	Steinwälzer	Steenloper
Vulture, Egyptian	Neophron percnopterus	Schmutzgeier	Aasgier
Wagtail, Grey	Motacilla cinerea	Gebirgsstelze	Grote gele kwikstaart
Wagtail, White	Motacilla alba	Bachstelze	Witte kwikstaart
Wagtail, Yellow	Motacilla flava	Schafstelze	Gele kwikstaart
Warbler, Sardinian	Sylvia melanocephala	Samtkopf-Grasmücke	Kleine zwartkop
Warbler, Spectacled	Sylvia conspicillata	Brillengrasmücke	Brilgrasmus
Wheatear, Northern	Oenanthe oenanthe	Steinschmätzer	Tapuit
Whimbrel	Numenius phaeopus	Regenbrachvogel	Regenwulp
Woodcock	Scolopax rusticola	Waldschnepfe	Houtsnip
Woodpecker, Great Spotted	Dendrocopos major	Buntspecht	Grote bonte specht

Reptiles and Amphibians

English	Scientific	German	Dutch
Frog, Iberian Water	Pelophylax perezi	Iberischer Wasserfrosch	Iberische meerkikker
Frog, Stripeless Tree	Hyla meridionalis	Mittelmeer-Laubfrosch	Mediterrane boomkikker
Gecko, Gomera	Tarentola gomerensis	Gomera-Gecko	Gomeragekko
Gecko, Tenerife	Tarentola delalandii	Kanarengecko	Delalandes gekko
Lizard, (Tenerife) Giant	Gallotia goliath	Grosse Rieseneidechse*	Grote reuzenhagedis*
Lizard, Boettger's	Gallotia caesaris	Kleine Kanareneidechse	Boettgers hagedis
Lizard, Gomera Giant	Gallotia bravoana	La-Gomera-Rieseneidechse	Gomerareuzenhagedis
Lizard, Gran Canaria Giant	Gallotia stehlini	Gran-Canaria-Rieseneidechse	Gran-Canaria reuzenhagedis
Lizard, Tenerife	Gallotia galloti	Kanareneidechse	Canarische Hagedis
Lizard, Tenerife Speckled	Gallotia intermedia	Gesprenkelte Kanareneidechse	Tenerifereuzenhagedis
Skink, Gomera	Chalcides coeruleopunctatus	Südlicher Kanarenskink	Gomeraskink
Skink, West Canary	Chalcides viridanus	Nördlicher Kanarenskink	West-Canarische skink

Fish

English	Scientific	German	Dutch
Eel	Anguilla anguilla	Europäische Aal	Paling

Invertebrates

English	Scientific	German	Dutch
Admiral, Canary Red	Vanessa vulcanica	Kanarischer Admiral	Canarische atalanta
Admiral, Red	Vanessa atalanta	Admiral	Atalanta
Argus, Spanish Brown	Aricia cramera	Südlicher Sonnenröschen-Bläuling	Moors bruin blauwtje
Blue, African Grass	Zizeeria knysna	Amethist- Bläuling*	Amethistblauwtje

English	Scientific	German	Dutch
Blue, Canary	*Cyclyrius webbianus*	Kanarischer Bläuling	Canarisch blauwtje
Blue, Common	*Polyommatus icarus*	Hauhechel-Bläuling	Icarusblauwtje
Blue, Lange's Short-tailed	*Leptotes pirithous*	Kleiner Wander-Bläuling	Klein tijgerblauwtje
Bluetail, Sahara	*Ischnura saharensis*	Sahara-Pechlibelle	Saharalantaarntje
Bluetail, Ubiquitous	*Ischnura senegalensis*	Senegal-Pechlibelle	Senegalees lantaarntje
Brown, Meadow	*Maniola jurtina*	Grosses Ochsenauge	Bruin zandoogje
Cardinal	*Argynnis pandora*	Kardinal	Kardinaalsmantel
Cascader, Ringed	*Zygonyx torridus*	Wasserfall-Kreuzer	Watervallibel
Centipede, Canarian	*Scolopendra valida*	Kanarische Riesenläufer*	Canarische reuzenduizendpoot*
Cleopatra, Canary	*Gonepteryx cleobule*	Teneriffa-Zitronenfalter	Canarische cleopatra
Copper, Small	*Lycaena phlaeas*	Kleiner Feuerfalter	Kleine vuurvlinder
Crab, Marbled	*Pachygrapsus marmoratus*	Rennkrabbe	Renkrab
Darter, Island	*Sympetrum nigrifemur*	Madeira-Heidelibelle	Eilandheidelibel
Darter, Red-veined	*Sympetrum fonscolombii*	Frühe Heidelibelle	Zwervende heidelibel
Dropwing, Red-veined	*Trithemis arteriosa*	Rotader-Sonnenzeiger	Rode zonnewijzer
Dropwing, Violet	*Trithemis annulata*	Violetter Sonnenzeiger	Purperlibel
Emperor, Blue	*Anax imperator*	Grosse Königslibelle	Grote keizerlibel
Emperor, Lesser	*Anax parthenope*	Kleine Königslibelle	Zuidelijke keizerlibel
Emperor, Vagrant	*Anax ephippiger*	Schabrackenlibelle	Zadellibel
Grasshopper, Tenerife Sand	*Sphingonotus picteti*	Teneriffa-Sandschrecke*	Tenerife-kiezelsprinkhaan*
Grayling, Gomera	*Hipparchia gomera*	Gomera-Samtfalter*	Gomeraheivlinder
Grayling, Tenerife	*Hipparchia wyssi*	Teneriffa-Samfalter*	Tenerifeheivlinder
Hawk-moth, Barbary Spurge	*Hyles tithymali*	Mittelmeer-Wolfsmilchschwärmer*	Mediterrane Wolfsmelkpijlstaart*
Hawk-moth, Spurge	*Hyles euphorbiae*	Wolfsmilchschwärmer	Wolfsmelkpijlstaart*
Man-o-War, Portuguese	*Physalia physalis*	Portugiesische Galeere	Portugees oorlogsschip
Mantis, Praying	*Mantidae*	Gottesanbeterin	Bidsprinkhanen
Migrant, African	*Catopsilia florella*	Afrikanischer Einwanderer	Gele trekvlinder
Monarch	*Danaus plexippus*	Monarchfalter	Monarchvlinder
Scarlet, Broad	*Crocothemis erythraea*	Feuerlibelle	Vuurlibel
Skimmer, Epaulet	*Orthetrum chrysostigma*	Rahmstreif-Blaupfeil	Epauletoeverlibel
Skipper, Canary	*Thymelicus christi*	Kanarischer Braun-Dickkopffalter	Canarisch dwergdikkopje
Tiger, Plain	*Danaus chrysippus*	Afrikanischer Monarch	Kleine monarchvlinder
White, Bath	*Pontia daplidice*	Reseda Falter	Resedawitje
White, Canary Islands Large	*Pieris cheiranthi*	Kanaren-Weissling	Canarisch koolwitje
White, Large	*Pieris brassicae*	Grosser Kohl-Weissling	Groot koolwitje
White, Small	*Pieris rapae*	Kleiner Kohlweissling	Klein koolwitje
White, Tenerife Green-striped	*Euchloe eversi*	Teneriffa Grüngestreifter Weissling	Tenerife marmerwitje*
Wood, Canary Speckled	*Pararge xiphioides*	Kanaren-Waldbrettspiel	Canarisch bont zandoogje
Yellow, Clouded	*Colias crocea*	Postillion	Oranje luzernevlinder

CROSSBILL GUIDES

IF YOU WANT TO SEE MORE

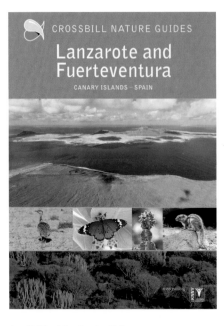

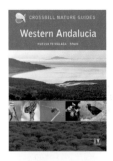

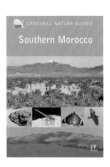

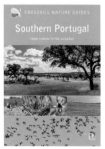

Available titles in English
Bulgaria   Rhodope Mountains
Finland   Finnish Lapland
France   Cévennes
            and grands causses
            Dordogne
            Provence and Camargue
Greece   Lesbos
Iceland   Iceland
Ireland / UK Ireland
Italy   Tuscany
Morocco   Southern Morocco
Polen   North-east Poland
            Biebrza, Bialowieza,
            Narew and Wigry
Portugal   Madeira
            Southern Portugal
            From Lisbon to the Algarve

Spain   Eastern Andalucía
            From Córdoba to Cabo de
            Gata
            Extremadura
            Lanzarote and Fuerteventura
            Spanish Pyrenees
            and the steppes of Huesca
            Tenerife and La Gomera
            Western Andalucía
            From Huelva to Málaga

Available titles in Dutch
Netherlands Achterhoek en Liemers
            Veluwe
            Wadden
            Weerribben-Wieden

Available titles in German
Germany   Eifel
Iceland   Island
Ireland / UK Irland
Spain   Extremadura

More titles are in preparation. Check our website for further details and updates.
WWW.CROSSBILLGUIDES.ORG